Political Protest in Contemporary Africa

D0705790

From spray-painted slogans in Senegal to student uprisings in South Africa, twenty-first century Africa has seen an explosion of protests and social movements. But why? Protests flourish amidst an emerging middle class whose members desire political influence and possess the money, education, and political autonomy to effectively launch movements for democratic renewal. In contrast with pro-democracy protest leaders, rank-and-file protesters live at a subsistence level and are motivated by material concerns over any grievance against a ruling regime. Through extensive field research, Lisa Mueller shows that middle-class political grievances help explain the timing of protests, while lower-class material grievances explain the participation. By adapting a class-based analysis to African cases where class is often assumed to be irrelevant, Lisa Mueller provides a rigorous yet accessible explanation for why sub-Saharan Africa erupted in unrest at a time of apparent economic prosperity.

LISA MUELLER is Assistant Professor of Political Science at Macalester College, Minnesota. She has published her research in several journals, including *Electoral Studies*, *African Affairs*, and the *African Studies Review*, as well as in the *Washington Post*. She is also a regular consultant and principal investigator for USAID and other American Government agencies, having recently been selected as the U.S.-based country expert on an extensive USAID assessment of Niger.

Political Protest in Contemporary Africa

LISA MUELLER
Macalester College

CAMBRIDGE
UNIVERSITY PRESS

CAMBRIDGE
UNIVERSITY PRESS

University Printing House, Cambridge CB2 8BS, United Kingdom

One Liberty Plaza, 20th Floor, New York, NY 10006, USA

477 Williamstown Road, Port Melbourne, VIC 3207, Australia

314–321, 3rd Floor, Plot 3, Splendor Forum, Jasola District Centre,
New Delhi – 110025, India

79 Anson Road, #06–04/06, Singapore 079906

Cambridge University Press is part of the University of Cambridge.

It furthers the University's mission by disseminating knowledge in the pursuit of
education, learning, and research at the highest international levels of excellence.

www.cambridge.org
Information on this title: www.cambridge.org/9781108423670
DOI: 10.1017/9781108529143

© Lisa Mueller 2018

First published 2018

Printed and bound in Great Britain by Clays Ltd, Elcograf S.p.A.

A catalogue record for this publication is available from the British Library.

ISBN 978-1-108-42367-0 Hardback
ISBN 978-1-108-43825-4 Paperback

Contents

Figures

Tables

Tables

Preface and Acknowledgments

"The president is long dead," I often overheard while I was in Conakry, Guinea. I traveled there in 2008 to find a research question for my doctoral dissertation. By then, rumors about President Lansana Conté's death were almost cliché. In power for twenty-four years, Conté suffered from chronic diabetes and heart disease. His authoritarian regime was deeply unpopular; to some Guineans, the gossip may have been wishful thinking. Yet, unfounded text messages and whispers had swirled for so long that they became like crying wolf. The president occasionally appeared on television to prove he was still alive, and I expected him to reappear any day.

But in the early morning of December 23, 2008, I gathered with my Guinean friends around the radio to hear the head of the National Assembly confirm that Conté had finally succumbed to his illnesses. Within hours, Captain Moussa Dadis Camara announced a military takeover of the government and suspension of the constitution. The coup d'état was, he claimed, the only way to undo rampant poverty and corruption of the Conté era. At the time, not even the capital city had reliable electricity – students studied at the airport because it was the only building with light at night. Some Guineans initially welcomed the junta's visions of change. Dadis pledged to restore democracy and vowed not to run for president. He ultimately reneged on both promises.

I evacuated the country amid a threat of civil war, but I continued following every news update from Guinea. On September 28, 2009, opposition leaders defied a ban on public assembly by rallying 50,000 citizens to demand a return to civilian rule. The demonstration took place at the Stade 28 Septembre in Conakry, on the fifty-first anniversary of a referendum in which Guineans voted for complete independence from France. Government troops opened fire on the crowd, killing at least 157 people, injuring innumerable others, and raping women in broad daylight. Eyewitnesses reported seeing soldiers drag bodies away to hide the true death count. One of my friends sustained a non-life-threatening wound while standing up for his democratic rights.

What, I wondered, led some Guineans to risk their lives in protest while others chose to stay home? What fears and hopes raced through the minds of people at the stadium that day? Was the demonstration about democracy plain and simple, or about something else, too? These puzzles applied to contexts beside Guinea. In 2011, I went to Niger to try and understand protests surrounding another putsch in which army officers ousted President Mamadou Tandja for trying to change the constitution and remain in office for a third term. That research motivated this book, which eventually expanded to address protest leadership and not just participation.

I am grateful for the countless friends, colleagues, and students who made the project possible. Thierno Mamadou Sow was by my side in those distressing moments of the Guinean coup and has since been a consummate project manager, sounding board, and champion during my fieldwork in several countries. Kim Dionne invited me to collaborate in Malawi, where I had the chance to observe student protests in 2011. I also owe a debt to my Nigerien research team, especially Bachirou Ayouba Tinni, Adam Malla, and Moussa Yayé. The Laboratoire d'Etudes et de Recherches sur les Dynamiques Sociales et le Développement Local was my operating base in Niger; the West African Research Center hosted me in Senegal. I spent many non-working hours in the field with Sue Rosenfeld, who welcomed me into her Niamey home and was always up for a drink at the Grand Hôtel.

I extend my appreciation to the thousands of people in Niger, Senegal, Burkina Faso, Guinea, Mali, and Malawi who answered my survey and interview questions. They were generous with their knowledge, which I hope to disseminate accurately and report back to them in an ongoing conversation. Linda Tuhiwai Smith reminds us that "research is not an innocent or distant academic exercise but an activity that has something at stake and that occurs in a set of political and social conditions," including vestiges of Western imperialism (Smith, 2012, 5). As I penned the last word of this manuscript, the hard work of decolonizing my scholarship and my thoughts was only just beginning.

Chapters 5 and 6 started as parts of a dissertation that I wrote at the University of California–Los Angeles under the guidance of Miriam Golden, Daniel Posner, Edmond Keller, and Pierre Englebert. Pierre was also my undergraduate advisor at Pomona College and is a close friend and mentor to this day. Against his better judgment, he let me into his advanced African Politics seminar during my first semester. His courses laid the foundation for everything I have written, though all the mistakes are my own. Chapter 5 additionally benefited from Afrobarometer surveys, whose creators do a great service to the scholarly community by making their data available.

It was my immense fortune to complete this project at Macalester College, where I received endless support. I knocked on almost every door in the Political Science department at one time or another seeking advice, and each time found inspiration and clarity. In the spring of 2016, I taught a course on "The Politics of Fear and Hope: Africa from Colonial Times to the Cheetah Generation." The entire class participated in my book workshop, which was funded by the G. Theodore Mitau Endowment, and commented on chapters in progress. Two students, Lukas Matthews and Susanna Figueroa, lent diligent research assistance over the summers. Colleagues at and beyond Macalester provided feedback on drafts at various stages. Paul Dosh, Zachariah Mampilly, and Pierre Englebert read the full manuscript. Further input came from members of the Sahel Working Group, the Working Group in African Political Economy, and informal circles: Sebastian Elischer, Martha Wilfahrt, Abhit Bhandari, Alice Kang, Amy Damon, Landry Signé, Emily Beaulieu, Ruth Carlitz, Dan Eizenga, Catherine Kelly, Julia YuJung Lee, Raffaele Asquer, Devesh Tiwari, Eric Kramon, and Amy Porter. Thanks to two anonymous peer reviewers and to Maria Marsh, my commissioning editor at Cambridge University Press, for facilitating the review process.

My loved ones buoyed me throughout the joyful and stressful journey of writing a book. They include my mother, Claudia Ding Mueller, and the scholars of the extended Tang family: Doctors Peggy Tang Strait, David Strait, and Michael Quon. Finally, I lack adequate words to thank my partner, Eric Sammuli, for his love, companionship, patience, and humor – not just while I wrote this book, but in all my professional and personal endeavors. I have cherished our adventures together and look forward to a lifetime's more to come.

1 | Introduction: The Puzzle of Africa's Third Wave of Protests

A cloud of acrid smoke wafted off the burning tire that blocked the road leading to Chancellor College in Zomba, Malawi on August 18, 2011. Student demonstrators, some brandishing mock weapons and wearing armor made from milk cartons, howled insults at the government of President Bingu wa Mutharika, which had closed the campus and frozen staff salaries in April after Professor Blessings Chinsinga delivered a lecture on the Arab Spring, purportedly inciting social unrest. Students described feeling caught in the middle of a standoff between the striking faculty and the authorities.[1] There was a sense that the president was paranoid to expect uprisings in Tunisia, Egypt, or Libya to spark similar events in Malawi. Protesters said they hoped to restore academic freedom so they could return to class, not start a revolution.

It is easy to see why Mutharika hedged his bets. In 2011, as popular movements toppled autocratic regimes in North Africa and the Middle East, the incidence of protests south of the Sahara was on a steep climb. The graph in Figure 1.1 plots the annual frequency of protests and riots[2] in sub-Saharan Africa from 1997 to 2016, the period for which data are available. Estimates are from the Armed Conflict Location and Event Data Project (Raleigh et al., 2010), which is coded using reports from national and local media, humanitarian agencies, and research groups. Roughly 19,816 major protests erupted between 2011 and 2016, spanning the continent. This spike interrupted a flatlining in protest frequency from the late twentieth century through the first decade of the twenty-first. Political scientists declared a third wave of African protests – the first wave having led to decolonization in the 1960s and the second wave having ushered in democratic transitions in

---

[1] Interviews and direct observations of the protest.
[2] The difference between protests and riots is vague. "Riot" sometimes connotes a higher degree of violence or transgression (Murphy, 2011).

1

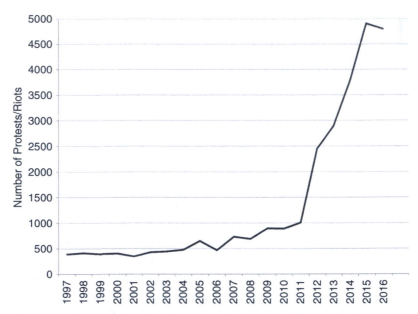

Figure 1.1: Protest/Riot Frequency in Sub-Saharan Africa, 1997–2016
Data are from the Armed Conflict Location and Event Data Project (Raleigh et al., 2010).

the 1990s (Dionne, Banch, and Mampilly, 2015). The intensity of social disturbances was as impressive as their frequency. While there is no comprehensive database of protest participation levels, news reports cited turnout reaching hundreds of thousands in certain cases (*Al Jazeera*, 2012; Allison, 2012). A recent dip in protest frequency (Figure 1.1) suggests that the third wave has peaked, though it is too early to tell. Ghanaian President John Dramani Mahama vented, "I have seen more demonstrations and strikes in my first two years. I don't think it can get worse. It is said that when you kill a goat and you frighten it with a knife, it doesn't fear the knife, because it is dead already. I have dead goat syndrome" (Quist-Arcton, 2015). Protests[3] in sub-Saharan African between 2011 and 2016 received less media attention than the Arab Spring (Antwi-Boateng, 2015, 774), but they were no less varied or dynamic. Youths spray-painted opposition slogans on monuments in Dakar and demonstrators squeezed beneath the

---

[3] By "protests" I mean collective actions aimed at achieving a goal by influencing decisions of a target (Opp, 2009, 38).

gates of the U.S. Embassy in Bujumbura to escape government repression. More than a thousand people were arrested for protesting the narrow re-election of President Ali Bongo in Gabon. In the Democratic Republic of Congo, an untold number of rioters died preempting President Joseph Kabila's refusal to step down when his term limit expired. This was the first era in which protests also played out on the Internet: Activist social media lit up with Facebook posts supporting Occupy Nigeria, YouTube videos promoting political hip-hop from Tanzania, and Twitter campaigns to free activists from Congolese prisons. This boom of discontent sent shockwaves through top tiers of government. Citizens thwarted the autocratic maneuvers of presidents in Burkina Faso, Niger, and Senegal, to name just a few. Existing scholarship teaches us that such turmoil can influence a host of other important phenomena like democracy, development, and human rights (Baudais and Chauzal, 2011; Beaulieu, 2014; Oxford Analytica, 2015).

What explains the third wave of protests in sub-Saharan Africa? Early analyses pointed to the influence of protests outside the region (de Waal and Ibreck, 2013). Scholars and journalists described "an African Spring in the making" (Harsch, 2012; Dibba, 2013; Sowore, 2013). Ugandan intellectual Mahmood Mamdani wrote, "… the memory of Tahrir Square feeds opposition hopes and fuels government fears in many African polities. A spectre is haunting Africa and its rulers – the spectre of Tahrir Square" (Mamdani, 2011). Former Chadian minister of foreign affairs Acheikh Ibn-Oumar postulated, "when demonstrators in Tahrir Square, Habib Bourguiba Avenue, or Al Mahkama Square (Benghazi) shouted their anger against protracted dictatorship … many Africans felt they had been victims to the same evils for ages" (Ibn-Oumar, 2013). North Africans echoed the view that their revolutions emboldened Africans south of the Sahara. "Nothing aids the erosion of one's fear," said one Egyptian journalist, "more than knowing there are others, somewhere else, who share the same desire for liberation – and have started taking action" (el Hamalawy, 2011).

It is possible that some protesters were inspired by the Arab Spring, but north-south contagion is not a satisfying explanation for the latest wave of uprisings in sub-Saharan Africa. This is because economic and political conditions are markedly different across the two regions. Arab Spring protesters were disproportionately – if not uniformly – educated and middle-class (Andersen, 2011; The World Bank, 2015). The middle class in sub-Saharan Africa is growing (Ncube and Lufumpa, 2015) and is more likely than the poor to support democracy (Cheeseman, 2014), but it is still relatively tiny at only about one-third the size of the middle class in North Africa and the Middle East (Kharas, 2011; *The Economist*, 2015). Protests in Blantyre, Lagos, and other cities brought many thousands of people to the streets – more than local populations of salaried professionals and business owners could realistically supply.

Scholars have begun to criticize the narrative of a middle-class revolt for downplaying "the very real participation of poorer and more marginalized classes" (Branch and Mampilly, 2015, 203). A prominent counter-narrative states that people in sub-Saharan Africa are rising up because they are hungry or resent inequality, not because they oppose dictatorship on ideological grounds (Smith, 2013; Berazneva and Lee, 2013; Lofchie, 2015). The main support for this claim is the failure of economic growth to produce significant improvements in well-being. Sub-Saharan Africa's total GDP per capita has improved starting around 1995 (The World Bank, 2017), but aggregate gains mask the persistence of poverty that would not exist if total income were distributed equally. The number of Africans living on less than a dollar a day rose from 140 million in 1975 to over 360 million in 2000, during a period culminating in significant economic expansion (Artadi and Sala-i-Martin, 2003, 7). In 1970, one in ten poor people in the world was African; by 2000, the fraction was close to one in two (Artadi and Sala-i-Martin, 2003, 7).[4]

Poverty and inequality are not the same thing, but inequality "acts as a filter between growth and poverty" (Nissanke and Thorbecke, 2006, 1339). When growth occurs in countries that are very poor at the outset, people at the bottom of an unequal income distribution experience inequality as chronic poverty (Milanovic, 2016b). Noting this macroeconomic situation and the small middle class in sub-Saharan Africa, some analysts argue that protests in the region cannot be likened to the Arab Spring (Antwi-Boateng, 2015; Kigwangalla, 2014). Their arguments find further evidence in a 2013 Gallup poll of

---

[4] These increases partly reflect population growth, which scholars warn could produce a Malthusian dilemma, especially in the Sahel (Potts, Henderson, and Campbell, 2013).

people in twenty-six sub-Saharan African countries, which revealed that seven in ten respondents had not followed recent political developments in the Arab world (Loschky, 2014). In countries where poverty is widespread, the middle class is presumably more likely to be the target of protests than the vanguard of revolution (Lofchie, 2015, 53).

Beyond economic differences, political regimes in sub-Saharan Africa barely resemble political regimes in North Africa and the Middle East. One could say that sub-Saharan Africa already experienced its African Spring more than a decade ago. Between 1990 and 1994, fifty-four founding elections took place in twenty-nine countries across the region (Bratton, 1998). Multi-party competition has become routine since Bratton and van de Walle (1992, 419) prophetically wrote about "the turbulent 'spring' of 1990." Practically all African leaders after 1990 have exited office by means of term limits or elections; very few have left through coups d'état or assassinations (Cheeseman, 2015; Posner and Young, 2007). The strength of democratic institutions varies considerably across countries (Bratton, 1998; Bratton and Mattes, 2009), but "democracy in sub-Saharan Africa is not starting from scratch, unlike in most of the Arab world" (Siegle et al., 2011, 1). Elections, even when not perfectly free and fair, seem to have enhanced African voters' awareness of their rights, spawned civil society organizations, and created new roles for state institutions and the media (Lindberg, 2006; Gandhi and Lust-Okar, 2009). These changes have in turn expanded civil liberties well beyond the levels that most people in North Africa and the Middle East enjoy: Freedom House rates sub-Saharan Africa as 12 percent free and North Africa and the Middle East as only 5 percent free (Freedom House, 2015). Democratic transitions do not, of course, guarantee stronger states. State control over people and territory remains weaker in sub-Saharan Africa than in other parts of the world (Herbst, 2000). States like Nigeria and the Democratic Republic of Congo are notoriously ineffective at providing citizens with public goods such as health care and rule of law, even if they are quite effective at providing "public bads" such as state-sanctioned violence and environmental degradation. The contradictory mixes of freedom with repression and state weakness with state brutality make sub-Saharan Africa politically exceptional (Herbst, 2000; Englebert, 2009; Young, 2012).

For all three reasons – poorer populations, stronger democracies, and weaker states – protests in Ouagadougou or Nairobi might be systematically different from protests in Tripoli or Algiers. Perhaps the former are not "an African Spring in the making" but rather something altogether different. An obvious alternative interpretation is that protests in sub-Saharan Africa are materially motivated revolts of the poor – bread riots, essentially (Smith, 2013; Berazneva and Lee, 2013; Macatory, Oumarou, and Poncelet, 2010; Adam, 2008). This narrative is consistent with what we know about the region's general economic and political conditions, but it is ultimately just as unsatisfying as the narrative of a middle-class revolution. A long line of research suggests that mobilizing collective action is extremely difficult under any circumstances, because coordinating large groups is costly, and risk-averse individuals free-ride on the anticipated participation of others (Olson, 1971; Tarrow, 1998; Weinstein, 2007). Resource scarcity further hinders collective action by limiting access to "mobilization goods" such as selective incentives, transportation, and communication technology (Bates, 1981). In short, political science predicts that poverty should correlate with less protest, not more. Sociologists respond that absolute or relative deprivation can inflame popular grievances that are necessary for protest to occur (Gurr, 1970; Cramer, 2003). However, grievances are latent and ubiquitous; they cannot explain the timing of protests or how aggrieved people overcome collective action problems (Corning and Myers, 2002).

The Argument

Some observers see the third wave of protests in sub-Saharan Africa as a politically motivated revolution of the middle class akin to the Arab Spring, whereas others label it a materially driven revolt of the chronically poor. These interpretations are not mutually exclusive. Members of an emerging middle class desire political influence commensurate with their economic status and possess the money, education, and communication skills that make them effective protest organizers. Meanwhile, most rank-and-file protesters in sub-Saharan Africa are not middle-class but rather live at a subsistence level. This group is motivated foremost by materialist concerns – especially low expectations of upward mobility – and not by grievances against a ruling regime. People abstain from protesting even amid objectively bad conditions because they are optimistic, not necessarily because they are too oppressed or disenfranchised.

Africa's third wave of protests resulted when middle-class people reacted to political shocks by deploying their talents and resources to mobilize poor people who harbored latent materialist grievances. I use Afrobarometer surveys from thirty-one African countries and original data from seven months of field research in Senegal, Niger, Burkina Faso, and Malawi to show that middle-class political grievances help explain the timing of protests, while lower-class materialist grievances help explain protest participation. Analyzing these data in their historical context, I observe some continuity with the past: The middle class and the poor have protested in sub-Saharan Africa since before independence, often against one another. What sets the third wave apart, I assert, is the symbiotic roles that these groups increasingly play: Middle-class people serve as strategic leaders of political opposition movements (what I call "the generals of the revolution") and poorer people serve as strategic joiners ("the foot soldiers of the revolution"). They form protest coalitions, pooling resources while keeping their distinct identities.[5]

Generals and foot soldiers are both integral to a social movement, no matter how hierarchical or horizontal the movement's structure (Hardt and Negri, 2017). A protest with weak, resource-strapped leadership may have trouble getting off the ground in the first place, while one without an enthusiastic mass following is unlikely to grow or last. Protests thus involve "a provisional equalization of relationships" (Mische, 2011, 82) in which actors depend on each other and jointly determine what Shorter and Tilly (1971) call the "shape" of protests – onset, growth, and duration. This idea stems from the field of Relational Sociology, which underscores existing connections among potential allies and "the creative effort people make establishing, maintaining, negotiating, transforming, and terminating interpersonal relations" (Zelizer, 2011). Protests are not merely embedded in the context of class; they are constituted by class conflicts and affinities.

---

[5] Coalitions differ from mergers, which fuse constituent group identities, and networks, which have looser ties and little purposive collective action (McCammon and Moon, 2015).

Class Analysis and the Study of African Politics

A class-centered explanation for Africa's third wave of protests – or any other aspect of African politics – is unconventional. Class analysis, though canonical in political science as a whole, "has not been as popular or successful" in the study of African politics (Englebert and Dunn, 2013, 109). The analytical frameworks of Karl Marx (1846/ 1963), E.P. Thompson (1963), or Barrington Moore (1978) bewilder scholars of African politics because Africa's low levels of industrial capitalism make it difficult to apply categories like "workers" and "owners of the means of production."[6] Manufactured exports comprise only 55 percent of total exports in the typical African country, compared to 76 percent in the typical non-African developing country (Page, 2012, ii96). African leaders in the early post-independence era, eager to shed dependence on former colonial powers, pushed their countries to industrialize by sheltering domestic producers and building factories with public funds. State-led import substitution ultimately proved unsustainable, and African countries de-industrialized in the 1980s and early 1990s (Page, 2012, ii95). Light manufacturing is a point of entry into the formal labor force in emerging economies, especially for women and young people (Ross, 2008). Today, however, African manufacturing sectors are even smaller and less diverse than during the first decade of independence (Page, 2012). The region's youth unemployment rate of 11.9 percent falls below the world average of 13.1 percent but is far higher in certain countries. Almost half of youth in South Africa, for instance, cannot find work (Amare, 2014). "Would that I had an employer to exploit me!" is the cynical sentiment of a few African job-seekers I have encountered. Observing low participation in the formal workforce reinforces scholars' preconception that African societies have no economic classes whatsoever (Stichter, 1975; Grillo, 1974) or that ethnicity at least dominates class as more politically significant (Jackson, 1973).

There are dangers in adhering to orthodox views about a "classless Africa." First, those views may simply be incorrect if one adopts a broader understanding of class as determined not just by relations

---

[6] Studies of India seem to confirm "the difficulties of class organization in the so-called informal sector of labor, where the capitalist and the petty mode of production are intertwined in a mutually reinforcing tangle" (Chatterjee, 2006, 64).

of production, but also by relations of power (Sklar, 1979; Daloz, 2003). Some scholars point out ways in which corrupt African leaders use state institutions to accumulate wealth and oppress the poor (Daloz, 2003; Sklar, 1979; Diamond, 1987; Boone, 1998). They employ the vocabulary of "the state class" and "the political class" alongside the Marxist vocabulary of "capitalists" and "the bourgeoisie" (Keller, 1991a; Boone, 1998; Amin, 1969; Swainson, 1977). Fauré and Médard (1995) introduce the hybrid terms "state-business" and "politicians-entrepreneurs"; Markovitz (1987) adds the "organizational bourgeoisie." Studying "bourgeois" social movements in Nigeria, Olukoshi (1995) writes about "primitive" forms of wealth accumulation via the misappropriation of public funds. Such adapted class frameworks are useful for comprehending the politics of exclusion and state contributions to Africa's extreme inequalities in income, wealth, and consumption.[7] This book explains how those inequalities shape the onset and size of protests through the channels of grievances and resource mobilization.

Another downside of dismissing class frameworks is the risk of assuming that Africans are monolithically poor and that differences in economic standing are politically irrelevant. Africans of disparate means need not form self-conscious classes "in themselves and for themselves," as Marx envisioned, in order for economic disparities to become politicized; nor do Africans need to form labor unions and go on strike, although they sometimes do (Zeilig, 2009). The political importance of class in Africa is subtler: It influences the grievances that make people *want* to protest and the access to mobilization goods that make them *able* to protest. Ignoring class differences has impeded scholars from unearthing satisfying explanations for Africa's third wave of protests, because protests in contemporary Africa contain both middle-class and popular elements. I use class to contextualize actors' motivations, resources, and behavioral choices while acknowledging the limitations of an orthodox class framework in African settings.

I define the African middle class as *the stratum of Africans who meet their basic material needs with income from sources outside the state.*

---

[7] For data and commentary on inequality in Africa, see Cogneau et al. (2006); Christiaensen, Demery, and Stefano (2002); Frankema and Bolt (2006); Okojie and Shimeles (2006).

I do not rely on the classical Marxist understanding of the middle class as the bourgeoisie (roughly, the class between the elite and the proletariat),[8] because the powers of consumption and political participation are often more salient than the power of production in largely un-industrialized African societies. I depart, too, from common income-based metrics (e.g., Ncube, Anyanwu, and Hausken, 2013). Income cut-offs are arbitrary and do not travel well across geographic space (Banerjee and Duflo, 2008). They also ignore the sociological, as opposed to the economic, connotations of class (Ansell and Samuels, 2014, 39). My working definition of the middle class disagrees with some existing definitions. I aim not to advance a universal theory of the middle class, but rather to avoid "conceptual stretching" by adopting a "diminished subtype" of the core concept that refers to a specific set of African cases (Collier and Levitsky, 1997). I follow Darbon (2014) in treating the middle class not as an objective given, but rather as a "code name" that lets us decipher social phenomena like protest.[9]

The middle class emerged in Africa from economic liberalization in the late twentieth century, which generated opportunities to accumulate private wealth but also to spend private incomes on consumer goods and political causes. Before then, the "middle class" was best described as the state class; loyalty to the state was the primary path to upward mobility, creating a conflict of interests for the would-be political opposition. In the 1990s, Western-mediated integration of developing countries into the global capitalist economy sharpened class differences along both political and economic dimensions. "The result has been, on the one hand, greater assertion by organizations of middle-class citizens of their right to unhindered access to public spaces ... On the other hand, government policy has rapidly turned away from the idea of helping the poor to subsist ..." (Chatterjee, 2006, 144). Economic categories are essential for comprehending Africa's third wave of protests because they are inseparable from the political autonomy of the middle class and the material adversity of the poor.

My focus on class is reminiscent of earlier work on class relations and modernization theory by Lipset (1959), Moore (1978), Collier (1999),

---

[8] Marxist theory lacks a single, coherent concept of class (Kivinen, 1989).

[9] For more on the meaning and importance of the African middle class, see Melber (2016), Darbon and Toulabor (2014), Ncube and Lufumpa (2015), and Sumner (2012).

Acemoglu and Robinson (2006), and others. It especially recalls the work of Rueschemeyer, Huber Stephens, and Stephens (1992), who noted that the working classes of twentieth-century Europe and Latin America were too weak on their own to win democratic concessions from autocrats and therefore had to form alliances with the urban bourgeoisie. Democracy then resulted in cases where members of the bourgeoisie did not fear a populist threat to their property rights. I similarly analyze the political significance of a rising middle class and emphasize class position over class consciousness. I agree with these authors, too, that class "is a social category determined, in the extreme, by the observer and analyst." (Rueschemeyer, Huber Stephens, and Stephens, 1992, 53). Research on Latin America by Levine (1992) and Dosh (2009) informs my theory that rank-and-file protesters have materialist agendas whereas middle-class protest leaders have non-materialist or "post-materialist" agendas.[10] Scholars have studied at length how cross-class alliances led to revolutionary success or failure in Mexico, Bolivia, Cuba, and Nicaragua (Wickham-Crowley, 1994). I owe a debt to the Europeanist and Americanist literatures on class politics for providing some of my basic terminology and for situating my analysis in a broader geographical and historical frame of reference. This book adds an Africanist perspective to an existing project of "bringing capitalism back into protest analysis" (della Porta, 2015).

However, my argument is novel in both substance and scope. A key difference between this book and related texts is that the dependent variable is protest, not democracy. Protests do not always lead to democratic reforms. They can instead lead to autocratic retrenchment, violence, and economic decline (Beaulieu, 2014; Aizenman and Marion, 1993; Alesina et al., 1996). It is important to investigate the links between class relations and protest before (or in addition to) investigating the links between class relations and regime type. I highlight variation in the extent to which protesters are motivated first and foremost by grievances about democracy. In cases where they are not, it becomes less surprising when democracy fails to ensue. The macroeconomic context of my study is also different from European and Latin American contexts. Poverty in sub-Saharan Africa is more severe than it was in Europe or Latin America on the

---

[10] On post-materialist values, see Inglehart and Abramson (1999), Johnston, Laraña and Gusfield (2010), and Benson and Rochon (2004).

eve of democratic transition. It is therefore plausible that the immediate concerns of many Africans have more to do with basic material needs than with democracy. It further follows that barriers to collective action will be higher in sub-Saharan Africa than in Europe or Latin America. Most Africans work in the informal sector and lack the structure of labor unions to help them organize around their shared interests. And access to information and social networking technology remains limited despite improvements in recent years (Antwi-Boateng, 2015; Kigwangalla, 2014). The third wave of African protests demands its own set of explanations. This book is a starting point for exploring how ideas about protest in Europe and Latin America, where scholars take the political salience of class differences for granted, translate to Africa, where scholars widely view class as irrelevant.

The Mechanisms

Some historic protests revolve around a single person. Consider, for example, Mahatma Gandhi's twenty-one-day hunger strike in 1933 against a British-colonial electoral system that separated Indians by caste, Thích Quang Đuc's self-immolation in 1963 to raise awareness of the South Vietnamese Government's persecution of Buddhists, or American football player Colin Kaepernick's decision to kneel during the national anthem before games to bring attention to violence against African Americans. At each of these moments, a solo[11] action captured international attention and accelerated reforms for social justice.

Typically, though, protests alter the course of history because they involve many people. Demonstrators are physically and symbolically stronger in numbers, even if their actions are very brief. Huge crowds instantly signal the malign nature of a regime to a country's population and to the world, such that a regime facing mass uprisings can collapse in a matter of hours (Lohmann, 1994). Dispersing across a city, disrupting traffic, and occupying buildings can be effective strategies for countering incumbents' efforts to maintain territorial

---

[11] Individual protesters often have support behind the scenes. For instance, black activist Rosa Parks refused to relinquish her bus seat to a white passenger in segregated Montgomery, Alabama in 1955. The usual telling of this story "misrepresents an organized and carefully planned movement for social change as a spontaneous outburst based upon frustration and anger" (Kohl, 2005, 13).

sovereignty (Jansen, 2001; Cresswell, 1996). In the 1996–1997 Serbian protests against the Milosevic regime, controlling space became "an articulation of power: the dominating power of the regime aimed to keep people, information and goods *in place*, whereas the demonstrators relied on their being *out of place*" (Jansen, 2001, 39). In Kyrgyzstan, protest organizers allegedly hired "professional activists" to pad the numbers in crowds (Druker et al., 2012). Larger gatherings better withstand government repression and signal to intransigent leaders that thwarting the opposition will be impossible or very costly. Unlike peasant revolutions or rebellions in areas with low population densities, urban protests rely "primarily on the disruption generated by massing hundreds of thousands of civilians in central urban spaces in a concentrated period of time so as to generate pressure on an incumbent regime and induce key members of the ruling coalition to defect" (Beissinger, 2013, 1).

A protest consists of two distinct processes that the academic literature often conflates: the start of a protest and the growth of a crowd. Examining only one or the other process yields an incomplete story. Focusing just on protest initiation ignores the significant challenges of recruitment and organization that initiators face, while focusing just on protest participation fails to account for why protests start when they do. In fact, each process involves a different set of actors. The start of a protest involves first movers – protest leaders, or "the generals of the revolution." The growth of a crowd involves secondary movers – protest joiners, or "the foot soldiers of the revolution." Generals and foot soldiers theoretically have different motivations and constraints, which I analyze in an effort to develop a complete story of what happens inside protests. The civil war literature examines onset and intensity separately, but I consider onset and intensity to be inextricable dimensions of protest.[12] Protests become historic because one person takes to the streets *and* because many more follow.

Generals of the Revolution

The protest literature centers almost exclusively on barriers to collective action, but there are also practical and psychological barriers to

---

[12] Intensity refers to battle deaths in the civil war literature and participation rates in the protest literature.

individual action. These are pronounced among the poor, who have little defense against penalties for defiance and may be discouraged from activism by the "shame bred by a culture which blames them for their plight" (Piven and Cloward, 1977, 7). Political authorities can credibly threaten to repress or co-opt ordinary citizens who would become revolutionaries. Even if the poor have political power today, they are uncertain about whether they will have it tomorrow (Acemoglu and Robinson, 2006, 24). That is to say, launching a protest is not an option equally available to everyone. "[O]nly under exceptional conditions are the lower classes afforded the socially determined opportunity to press for their own class interests" (Piven and Cloward, 1977, 7).

The attributes of protest leaders – advanced communication skills, access to resources, and willingness to accept risk – are concentrated among middle-class people (Jenkins, 1983). In general, white-collar professionals and college students are better positioned than subsistence farmers and street vendors to co-opt institutional resources from private foundations, universities, businesses, and governments (Jenkins, 1983, 533). Their relatively good access to education lets them perform intellectual tasks such as debating, writing, speaking to the media, and strategizing (Morris and Staggenborg, 2005, 175). Salaried people have flexible schedules and regular incomes allowing them to spend time on networking and activism.[13]

Capitalists are in an even better position than wage earners to resist the status quo, because they do not risk employers' disapproval. As American women's rights advocate Gloria Steinem observed, "All movements need a few people who can't be fired" (Steinem, 2015). Empirical studies from various parts of the world support the theory that protest leaders are predominantly middle-class (McCarthy and Zald, 1973; Veltmeyer and Petras, 2002; Wang et al., 2013; Beissinger, 2013).

Economic advantages make the middle class better able to lead protests and also more willing to do so for "expressive" reasons such as civic duty and consciousness-raising, versus "instrumental" reasons such as material gain and the achievement of concrete policy reform (Pichardo, 1997; Parkin, 1968). Even if one rejects the dichotomy

---

[13] This was not lost on students at Oberlin College in the United States, who petitioned in 2014 for an $8.20 hourly activism wage (Heller, 2016).

between expressive and instrumental motivations,[14] higher-income people empirically have stronger preferences for democracy than the poor, who in an unequal society might reasonably be skeptical that democracy will benefit them (Ansell and Samuels, 2014). Chants about human rights, rule of law, and other post-materialist issues have historically emanated from "a distinct stratum of intellectuals, often playwrights and actors" (Bagguley, 1995, 281). World Values Survey data indicate that higher social class correlates with greater concern for protecting free speech instead of fighting price inflation (Inglehart and Abramson, 1999). Social movements with middle-class leadership include the British Campaign for Nuclear Disarmament (Parkin, 1968) and the United States women's movement (Katzenstein and Mueller, 1987). Additional examples abound in the literature on "new social movements," which contrasts expressive protests of the 1960s through the present with "classical" protests like peasant uprisings and labor strikes (Olofsson, 2014; Chaudhuri, 2014; Laraña, Johnston, and Gusfield, 1994; Kriesi, 1989; Klandermans, 1986). Middle-class protest leadership can seem contradictory in movements that are supposedly about questioning class hierarchies, but privileged individuals commonly militate for populist agendas. For example, well-to-do black students and church ministers played decisive roles in the U.S. civil rights movement (Barker, Johnson, and Lavalette, 2001, 12). Granted, not all middle-class people are left-leaning activists. "Middle class radicalism" (Parkin, 1968) is weaker among managerial professionals and stronger among "sociocultural" professionals – those who "are supposed to have both a postmaterialist or socially liberal outlook and to support a classic social-democratic position with respect to economic policy and the welfare state" (Kriesi, 1998). The protest leaders that I profile in Chapter 4 embody this heterogeneity.

Middle-class people certainly existed before social movements of the 1960s, even in African countries with weak economies (Sandgren, 2012; West, 2002). However, new social movements targeting incumbent regimes arose only with the emergence of a new middle class that derived its income from private sources and was therefore autonomous from state power (Tripp et al., 2009; Fernandes, 2006; Kriesi, 1989).

---

[14] Middle-class demands for democracy often accompany demands for reforms that materially benefit the middle class: property rights, control of corruption, and lower taxes (Ansell and Samuels, 2014, 41).

Bagguley (1995) calls this group the "freelance middle class," comprised of business owners and salaried professionals who work outside the civil service and came of age in an era of rising per capita incomes, economic liberalization, and gradually shrinking government. Public-sector employment was the surest path to a comfortable living across much of the world into the late twentieth century, but the proportion of the world's population on government payrolls declined from 2.5 percent to 1.5 percent between the early 1980s and the early 1990s (Schiavo-Campo, De Tommaso, and Mukherjee, 1999, 9). Washington policymakers promoted global free-market reforms that created "a more independent, less state-oriented, more entrepreneurial middle class that is less of a special interest and more of a force for accountability" (Bernstein, 2015). Members of this class are "urban, educated haves who are in some ways the principal beneficiaries of the regimes they now reject" (Keller, 2013).[15] Recent uprisings of mostly middle-class crowds in Brazil, India, Turkey, Iran, and the "Arab world" seemed to vindicate modernization theorists in the tradition of Lipset (1959) who predicted that prosperity would beget democracy (*The Economist*, 2013). Watching these events unfold, journalists hailed the "revolt of the rising class" (Friedman, 2013; Keller, 2013; Rohde, 2013; Surowiecki, 2013).

Africa's third wave of protests is both similar to and different from new social movements elsewhere. It is similar in that prominent protest leaders are largely of the new middle class, motivated by expressive interests and well supplied with the skills and resources to mobilize enormous crowds. For example, I profile the founders of Senegal's Y'en a Marre (Fed Up) movement and Burkina Faso's Le Balai Citoyen (The Citizen's Broom) movement – urban rap artists, journalists, and intellectuals who strategically acknowledged bread-and-butter concerns of the poor but used rhetoric suggesting that their primary interests were defending constitutional democracy and nurturing civic culture. They employed their particular talents and entrepreneurial

---

[15] Beissinger (2013) documents this phenomenon in the context of Ukraine's
      Orange Revolution of 2004. In a survey, only 18 percent of Orange
      revolutionaries reported being unable to afford basic food items during the
      previous twelve months, as opposed to 31 percent of revolution opponents and
      30 percent of inactive and apathetic Ukrainians (Beissinger, 2013, 13).
      Beissinger determines that the Orange Revolution was "not a revolution of the
      have-nots, but disproportionately a revolution of the want-mores" (Beissinger,
      2013, 13).

tactics to form civic organizations and stage huge rallies outwardly resembling those of the Arab Spring. A reporter referred to the site of one rally, La Place de l'Obélisque in Dakar, as "Senegal's Tahrir Square" (Tall, 2012). I analyze public statements and interviews to identify protest leaders' motives. Leaders such as Fadel Barro of Y'en a Marre started their organizing work in response to political triggering events: controversial elections, political scandals, and human rights abuses. The high number of such events between 2010 and 2012, including fifty-four major elections, might explain the spike in protest frequency during that period and why it coincided with protests in North Africa and the Middle East.

According to theories of social movement organization, protest leaders have diverse identities and interests but share several traits in common. They are risk-loving people with the communication skills, social connections, and access to resources required to mobilize collective action (Licht and Siegel, 2004; Popkin, 1988; Tilly, 1977). They help citizens obtain public goods such as redistribution or democracy in return for "profits" from voluntary donations and, sometimes, looted goods (Frohlich, Oppenheimer, and Young, 1971, 19). They also seek abstract benefits including prestige (Melucci, 1996, 337) and agency (Jones, 1978, 500). Ordinary people may desire those same things, but protest leaders possess an extraordinary "impulse to fight, to prove oneself superior to others, to succeed for the sake, not of the fruits of success, but of success itself" (Schumpeter, 1934, 93). Besides being competitive, they are tenacious, creative, and willing to accept risk (Christopoulos, 1978). "In short, these actors can respond to exceptional challenges and rise above their peers by means of their strategic forethought and ability to manipulate their environment" (Christopoulos, 1978, 758).

Some protests might be truly unplanned and spontaneous "moments of madness" (Zolberg, 1972), but most involve elaborate planning (Chaudhuri and Fitzgerald, 2015; Kurtulus, 2003). Political elites have historically called protests "spontaneous" as a way to discredit organizers' knowledge and hard work, like during European labor struggles in the 1960s and 1970s (Hardt and Negri, 2017, 21). Gramsci (1971, 196) went so far as to claim that pure spontaneity in social movements does not exist; we only perceive spontaneity where there is no obvious evidence of "conscious leadership." In other words, "belief in spontaneity, in politics as in physics, is based simply on an ignorance of causes" and "ignorance of the existing social organization from which it emerges" (Hardt and Negri, 2017, 21).

Protest leaders use a variety of tactics to facilitate two types of collective action: coordination and cooperation. *Coordination* occurs when actors harmonize their behaviors while being indifferent about where their behaviors harmonize (Snidal, 1985). One example is when friends do not care where they meet for lunch, so long as they dine at the same restaurant. Likewise, most people are indifferent about driving on the left or the right side of the road; their main concern is driving with traffic to avoid accidents. In the context of social movements, coordination happens when people who want to protest manage to show up at the same place and time to express their grievances. To enable coordination, generals of the revolution do the following:

- Disseminate political literature on the Internet, in print, or on radio.
- Provide communication technology.
- Provide transportation to protests.
- Train protesters on how to withstand repression.
- Send signals before or during a protest about fluctuations in the strength of the regime. This helps potential protesters calculate the costs and benefits of participating (Lohmann, 1994).

Cooperation occurs when people act in the collective interest despite their conflicting self-interest. Reluctance distinguishes this from coordination; people generally do not cooperate without some selective benefit, coercion, or psychological predisposition to feel pleasure in agency (Olson, 1971; Wood, 2001). Citizens often pay taxes despite a preference for retaining their own income, lest they incur legal penalties for tax evasion. Some people are reluctant to buy environmentally friendly cars, because hybrid and electric models tend to be more expensive than conventional models; the government of California therefore rewarded drivers of clean vehicles with "green stickers" permitting them to use express lanes. Protesters cooperate when they participate in a demonstration despite the individual costs of travel, foregone income, repression, and so on. Protest leaders enable cooperation in the following ways:

- Generate common knowledge about people's intentions to participate in a protest (Chwe, 2001) and raise the costs of free-riding by sharing the names of shirkers (Popkin, 1988, 21).

- Offer selective incentives such as cash, food, or positions in their organizations in exchange for participation in collective action.
- Maintain morale (Gusfield, 1966) and provide psychic benefits through affirming rhetoric (Morris III and Browne, 2001).
- Monitor defections and punish people who fail to contribute to the collective effort (Popkin, 1988). This role is especially important in ethnically diverse societies, where people may lack the social ties that allow them to sanction one another for shirking (Habyarimana et al., 2007).
- Activate unifying identities, link the like-minded, and represent group interests (Weinstein, 2007). For example, Bosnian Serb leaders brokered connections between Serbs in Bosnia and Serbs in Serbia by sharpening cultural differences vis-à-vis Muslims and Croats and advocating for the establishment of Serbian political institutions (Tilly, 2003, 34). Likewise, leaders of the Hutu Power movement in Rwanda used radio messages to unite Hutus against the Tutsi minority and mobilize a countrywide genocide.
- Break up a large goal into smaller steps in order to increase the marginal importance of individual contributions and make results seem more immediate and attainable (Popkin, 1988, 21). If people believe that their personal cooperation will make a difference, they will be less tempted to free-ride.

In sum, protest leaders initiate protests and then facilitate protest participation by using their ingenuity and ambition to furnish aggrieved people with the resources they need to coordinate and cooperate. Scholars have documented these roles in diverse countries including India (Mitra, 1992), Vietnam (Popkin, 1988), El Salvador (Wood, 2001), and South Africa (Wood, 2001), even in cases where protest leaders claimed to be part of hyper-egalitarian, "leaderless" movements (Barker, Johnson and Lavalette, 2001, 2).

Observers of contentious politics in the developing world place hope in economic growth and social media to level the playing field between protest leaders and ordinary demonstrators – that is, to democratize social movements (Levitsky and Way, 2010; Castells, 2015). In a growing number of countries, near-universal literacy hypothetically allows anyone with a grievance to circulate revolutionary ideas, while Twitter and Facebook put the tools of activism in more hands. However, the turn "from tweets to streets" is easy to overstate (Young, 2016a).

20   *Introduction*

Protesters rely on leaders to help them coordinate in sizable parts of Africa (most rural areas and some cities) where access to communication technology remains limited. By highlighting the privileged position of leaders in a study of African protests, I do not mean to overlook the important roles of poorer foot soldiers. The poor face structural limits on their ability to start protests and can overcome those limits by forging alliances across class lines.[16]

Foot Soldiers of the Revolution

The puzzle of why thousands of people join protests requires a separate explanation from the puzzle of why a few people start them. The third wave of protests in sub-Saharan Africa differs from recent unrest in Egypt or Brazil because middle-class people formed the leadership but not the base of social movements. As I show in Chapter 6, the majority of rank-and-file African protesters are poor and inclined to disagree, sometimes outspokenly, with better-off protest leaders who tout political ideology above material well-being. In Niger, where approximately half of the population lives on less than two dollars per day (The World Bank, 2017), tens of thousands of citizens turned out to protest after President Mamadou Tandja tried to extend his mandate in late 2009. Although international onlookers understandably described this as a democratic revolution (Nossiter, 2009; RFI, 2010), a large portion of the crowd actually supported the incumbent. President Abdoulaye Wade of Senegal followed Tandja in seeking an extra-constitutional third term in 2011. Political opposition leaders called citizens to the streets with the rallying cry, "Don't touch my constitution!" As I detail in Chapter 4, poor people joined the protests but many adopted their own slogan. They chanted, "Don't touch my table!" in response to rowdy demonstrators who burned the wooden tables that informal-sector merchants in Dakar use to sell their wares and earn a living.

Middle-class protest leaders and poor protest joiners form precarious coalitions that sometimes fall apart. In a comparative study of protest leadership in Senegal (Chapter 4), I find that protests are more successful when their leaders actively appeal to popular grievances

---

[16] See Morris and Staggenborg (2005) and Diani (2003) on structure and agency in social movements.

rather than concentrate on their own interests. Despite these variations, the general eagerness of protest leaders to recruit from lower classes distinguishes the third wave of African protests from earlier waves. Protests during the colonial era and the 1990s involved frequent conflicts between contingents of different socioeconomic standing. The indigenous African middle class under colonial rule was an elite cohort of European-educated bureaucrats and wage-earners who drew resentment from the poor majority. For example, striking railway workers in French West Africa received scant sympathy from peasants when they rose up to defend, not defeat, the colonial system that advantaged them (Cooper, 1996). Despite the old stereotype of African societies as classless (Stichter, 1975; Grillo, 1974), class differences continued to hinder broad-based protest coalitions well into post-colonial times. The middle class of the twentieth century was a rentier class, beholden to state patrons (Boone, 1998). The new middle class of the twenty-first century, benefiting from business opportunities in liberalized markets, is less dependent on patronage and hence increasingly eager to challenge incumbents (Arriola, 2013a). Its members are not sufficiently numerous to fill the streets by themselves like in Brazil, Turkey, or Bulgaria in 2013 (Faiola and Moura, 2013), so they use material inducements and emotional appeals to recruit the poor. The current wave of African protests is noteworthy because many activists are disillusioned with party politics as a way of effecting political change. This book spotlights social movements like Y'en a Marre in Senegal and the Ufungamano Initiative in Kenya, which arose expressly to counterbalance political parties that citizens perceived as conservative and corrupt. Nonpartisan alignment makes protest leaders credible allies for the masses (Baldez, 2002, 3).

Still, some poor people are more disposed than others to answer calls to action. Using Afrobarometer surveys (Chapter 5) and original surveys from Niger (Chapter 6), I show that the most salient grievances in protesting crowds are concerns about upward mobility. People who expect their living conditions to be no better in the future are more likely, ceteris paribus, to participate in protests than people who are more optimistic. This result corrects earlier research dismissing economic grievances as unrelated to protest behavior. Scacco (2008), for example, studied riot participation in Nigeria and found income to make no difference. Economic grievances are multifaceted. Low expectations of upward mobility are more salient on average than other perceived

economic problems like poverty and inequality; they are also more
salient than attitudes about the ruling regime. This can help scholars
make sense of authoritarian nostalgia. Surveys reveal Africans to prefer
democracy over autocracy but at rates below world averages (Bratton,
2002; Chang, Chu and Park, 2007). My findings suggest that Africans
become disaffected with democracy when democratic governments fail
to instill confidence that economic opportunities will expand.

Why, then, do protests in Africa appear from the outside to be about
politics more than economics? Why do pundits and scholars assume that
protesters are democratic revolutionaries? I answer that the generals of
the revolution, and not the foot soldiers, serve as spokespeople for
protests. They address the media, meet with politicians, and frame
collective action using the rhetoric of democracy, rule of law, and civic
responsibility. "Elite-articulated master narratives" (Beissinger, 2013, 2)
reflect the privileged agency of protest leaders relative to protest joiners.
Such narratives are often contentious at the local level but deceptively
unequivocal from afar (Benford and Snow, 2000). Observing the
Senegalese uprisings of 2011, international journalists and academics
heard the cries of "Don't touch my constitution!" but not the cries of
"Don't touch my table!"

Interpreting Events, Explaining Behavior

My broad objective is to interpret the third wave of protests in sub-
Saharan Africa. Interpretation involves answering the question, "what
exactly are we looking at when we see crowds of Africans taking to the
streets?" Are we witnessing democratic revolutions, electoral protests,
populist movements, or something else?[17] Social scientists tend to
eschew interpretation in order to tackle the higher-order challenge of
explaining variation in protest frequency (Beaulieu, 2014; Meier, 2007;
Bratton and van de Walle, 1997), protest participation (McClendon,
2014; Beissinger, 2013; Stürmer and Simon, 2009; Scacco, 2008;
Klandermans et al., 2002), or both (Lehman-Wilzig and Ungar, 1985;
Shorter and Tilly, 1971). Their quest to identify causal mechanisms has
inspired innovative longitudinal and experimental research designs
(Klandermans et al., 2002; Stürmer and Simon, 2009; McClendon,
2014).

---

[17] See Schwandt (1994) for a thorough explanation of interpretivist epistemology.

These are valuable contributions to understandings of contentious politics, but they fail to answer the fundamental question of how we know democratic revolutions, electoral protests, or populist movements when we see them. Scholars are quick to label protests as "democratic," "economic," or "ethnic." Coding decisions are often subjective, based on author perceptions of events or on news reports, both of which can be biased and arbitrary (Nam, 2006; Mueller, 1974). The Social Conflict in Africa Database (Hendrix and Salehyan, 2015), the Cross-National Time-Series Data Archive (Banks and Wilson, 2015), and the World Handbook of Political and Social Indicators (Taylor and Jodice, 1983) all follow this practice. So do individual scholars: Berazneva and Lee (2013) define food riots as uprisings that international media link to food shortages; Beaulieu (2014) defines electoral protests as "opposition-initiated, election-related protest"; Brancati (2016) defines democracy protests as "mass demonstrations for which open and competitive elections are the primary goal." Yet, people in a crowd sometimes care little about the supposed goal of the protest they have joined (Beissinger, 2013; Mueller, 2013). Protests, like the societies in which they unfold, are complex "circuits of cooperation among widely heterogeneous subjectivities" (Hardt and Negri, 2017, xviii); it is not always obvious what they are "about." This problem demands "not an experimental science in search of a law but an interpretive one in search of meaning" (Geertz, 1973, 5), because the way we label political change affects how we read history (Darbon, 2014, 22).

There are epistemological and ethical reasons to uphold high standards of valid interpretation, where valid interpretation refers to studying what we think we are studying (King, Keohane, and Verba, 1994, 25). General knowledge about political events comes from analyzing not a single event but rather patterns in a group of similar events – all democratic revolutions or all electoral protests, for example. It is important to correctly interpret events so as to classify them, identify their analytically relevant features, and produce simple, useful knowledge about the complex world (King, Keohane, and Verba, 1994, 42). My emphasis on valid interpretation also stems from a moral responsibility to portray human subjects as truthfully as possible. Existing research and datasets on protest operate on categories (e.g., "pro-democracy") that one group in a particular social setting (European and American journalists and scholars) uses to describe behaviors of another group (protesters) in a foreign setting (Africa) (Emerson, Fretz, and Shaw, 2011, 131). I draw heavily on survey data and interviews, which have some disadvantages (Lieberman, Schreiber, and Oschsner, 2001) but are arguably the best tools for measuring subjects' own meanings of protests and reasons for protesting or not. My interpretive approach follows the tradition of Geertz's actor-oriented analysis (Geertz, 1973, 14), which avoids the common errors of imposing foreign categories on local behaviors or caricaturing protests as pro-democracy, anti-poverty, or otherwise. By interpreting the third wave of protests in sub-Saharan Africa, this book complements specialized political science that dismisses "mere description" in favor of explaining causality.

I have not completely stripped explanation from the book. Interpreting protests calls for explaining which grievances make people systematically more likely to start or join protests and which resources mobilize collective action. I pose causal questions: What causes some people to launch social movements? What causes others to support their initiatives? However, I am humble about my capacity to answer such questions with certainty. Protests in Africa can quickly turn violent, making it impractical and unethical to study them in a way that is both experimental and externally valid. I analyze empirical data not to make "immodest claims of causality" (Farmer, 1999) – though my analyses *suggest* causal relationships – but instead to weigh the salience of grievances and interpret what protests are really "about."

Plan of the Book

Political scientists classically refer to "waves" in the context of democratic transition (Huntington, 1991; Weyland, 2014), but waves are also a central concept in the context of social movements (Seddon and Zeilig, 2005). Waves of protest and waves of regime change are related insofar as protest spurs democratic transition, which in turn expands the freedom to protest (Scarritt, McMillan and Mozaffar, 2001). However, protests and regime change are not one and the same; this book specifically addresses the former. To allay confusion about terminology, in Chapter 2 I define what a protest wave is and reflect on the concept's analytic value. I highlight significant moments in all three African protest waves: the late colonial period from around 1940 to 1960, the uprisings leading to democratic transitions in the 1990s, and the most recent spike in unrest at the start of the twenty-first century.

The last wave stands out in terms of the substantial involvement of poor people, which I elucidate in later chapters on protest leadership and participation. To avoid selecting on the dependent variable, Chapter 2 includes a section on the "missing wave" of protests in the 1970s and 1980s when popular grievances ran high but authoritarian controls resulted in fewer protests than scholars expected to see. Beyond narrating more than eighty years of African protests, I apply sociological theories to understand why certain moments in history become protest waves.

In Chapter 3, I take a macro approach to explaining the third wave. I identify two paradoxes: first, the uneven distribution of rising incomes in Africa over the past twenty years has allowed poverty to persist amid impressive economic growth; and second, higher economic status has not guaranteed political empowerment for the new middle class. Using data on income, employment, and credit flows, I recount how new opportunities in the private sector freed a small middle class both from worries about daily survival and from the need to seek wealth from patronage. More and more Africans possess the resources, time, and political autonomy to start "post-materialist" social movements and defy incumbents who are reluctant to share power. Yet, the majority of Africans have been left behind in the course of development. Unlike the middle class, they struggle to get by and are not in a position to launch protests, despite their dissatisfaction with material conditions.

Chapter 4 contains a micro-level analysis of generals of the revolution. I start by clarifying what it means to be a protest leader, thereby laying the conceptual groundwork for describing protest leadership trends in Senegal across waves. I chose Senegal as a research site because it is the nerve center for political activism in West Africa. However, this chapter is not a country case study. The cases are individual protest leaders and their organizations, whose abundance in Senegal permits a "diverse cases" approach (Seawright and Gerring, 2008), maximizing variance along the dimensions of leader identities, strategies, and success. Senegal also has freedom of expression that facilitates research on politically sensitive topics. I show how contemporary Senegalese protest leaders are overwhelmingly middle-class and focus on constitutional democracy as opposed to economic issues. To evaluate the generalizability of my findings, I analyze original data on protest leaders' public statements from across sub-Saharan Africa.

Senegal appears to represent a widespread pattern of "prodemocracy" activism. Lastly, I study the success and failure of mobilization strategies in a trio of cases: Le Mouvement 23 Juin (The June 23rd Movement, or M23) and Y'en a Marre from Senegal and the Ufungamano Initiative from Kenya. This comparison reveals that protests last longer when leaders strategically downplay their political motives and highlight populist messages. Data sources in this chapter include historical documents, secondary interviews, and original interviews that I conducted with protest leaders in Malawi in 2011, Senegal in 2015, Burkina Faso in 2016, and Niger in 2016 and 2017.

In Chapter 5, I use nationally representative Afrobarometer survey data from thirty-one countries to show that typical African protesters fit a different profile from typical protest leaders. Unlike generals, most foot soldiers are poor and motivated not by political grievances but rather by low expectations of upward mobility. For rank-and-file activists, challenging today's institutions and power configurations is a way to secure a better economic tomorrow. This contrasts with middle-class activists seeking to express political ideologies or access state power. Objective measures of well-being, including poverty and employment status, have no measurable relationship with protest participation; neither do attitudes about the legitimacy of the incumbent regime. Corroborating other scholars' findings, I also find that people are more likely to protest if they are embedded in community networks. My individual-level analysis cautions researchers against relying on event-level protest data coded from news reports. Journalists tend to mischaracterize African protests as democratic revolutions because generals, and not foot soldiers, serve as the spokespeople for social movements. Additional analyses in the chapter address a question arising from the main results: Why are some people pessimistic about their economic opportunities, whereas others are more optimistic? A preliminary explanation points to national-level variables such as economic growth and GDP per capita.

I complement the cross-national analysis from Chapter 5 with a study of protest participation in Niger, a country where poverty and autocracy coincide and where popular uprisings helped overthrow the regime of Mamadou Tandja in 2010. I decided to conduct fieldwork in Niger in 2011 for several reasons. First, it afforded me the rare opportunity to collect surveys shortly after a major protest, mitigating bias from bandwagoning and preference falsification

(Beissinger, 2013, 5). Second, high protest participation rates ensured variation on the dependent variable in my capital-city sample. Finally, including a chapter on Niger enhanced the book's generalizability at the country level. Niger is very different from my other main research site of Senegal: It is landlocked, poorer, less democratic, more socially conservative, and experienced a less direct form of colonial rule. Previous research has ignored these differences due to a prevailing bias toward classifying African countries with linguistic or regional labels. My original survey data reveal that many citizens who joined protests "against Tandja" actually supported the president's effort to amend the constitution and serve an additional term in office. Protesters were motivated not by anti-regime passion, but instead by fears that their economic circumstances would be no better in the future. They differed from military elites whose televised messages emphasized political grievances.

In Chapter 7, I revisit my motivating question, "what explains the timing and scale of Africa's third wave of protests?" and summarize my answer: The third wave started when members of a new middle class launched opposition movements; it intensified when poor citizens joined protests for predominantly economic reasons. I discuss policy implications and recommend ways for the concepts of *generals and foot soldiers of the revolution* to advance future research on protests in Africa and beyond. The narrative of a sub-Saharan African Spring appeals to policymakers in the West who hope citizens can safeguard young African democracies. However, donors hesitate to finance social movements for fear of destabilizing politics or even triggering a coup d'état. As a result, development policy is too risk averse, occurring mostly through states and their proxies. I recommend that donors be more open to supporting non-state agents of positive change such as protesters. This would be consistent with existing initiatives to empower grassroots actors, in light of the high involvement of ordinary citizens in African social movements.

The Universe of Study

The divide between North Africa (Algeria, Egypt, Libya, Morocco, and Tunisia) and sub-Saharan Africa (the forty-nine other African countries) is ambiguous. Sahelian countries like Chad and Niger are usually considered sub-Saharan despite lying only partially south of the Sahara Desert. Furthermore, scholars widely agree that "Black African" and "Arab African" are not primordial identities but rather categories that colonial and post-colonial authorities invented or instrumentalized to exclude people from economic resources and political rights (Posner, 2005; Norval, 2001; Howard, 1995).

Concentrating a study on sub-Saharan Africa involves trade-offs. On the one hand, it risks reifying a geographic unit that is endogenous to the very power imbalances that one wishes to understand. A narrow scope might also obscure patterns that transcend regional boundaries (Branch and Mampilly, 2015, 4). On the other hand, there are valuable insights to gain from a separate analysis of protests that were not part of the Arab Spring. Conceivably, the timing of North African and sub-Saharan African protest waves was coincidental and not interdependent, in which case each wave would invite its own explanation and interpretive framework. Sub-Saharan Africa has received short shrift in journalistic and scholarly coverage of twenty-first-century protests; a regional approach could fill the gap in our knowledge about uprisings that transpired in an appreciably poorer and politically distinct environment compared to North Africa. This book therefore focuses on *sub-Saharan* Africa, although I henceforth occasionally refer to "Africa" for short. It does not challenge but instead builds on work by Zeilig (2009), Young (2012), Branch and Mampilly (2015), and others who examine broader, continental trends in popular protest and political change.

The book also focuses on urban Africa, although protests sometimes happen in rural areas (Isaacman, 1990). The vast majority of protests – both opposition and pro-regime – occur in capital cities where the seat of government is located (Hendrix and Salehyan, 2015). Cities have multiple qualities that make them effective incubators for contentious collective action: they are hubs for media activity; they are centers of labor and student organizing; and they have dense populations conducive to social networking (Nicholls, 2008). Urban proximity, moreover, generates "emotional energy" that draws people into a crowd: "Bodily presence makes it easier for human beings to monitor each other's signals and bodily expressions; to get into shared rhythm, caught up in each other's motions and emotions; and to signal and confirm a common focus of attention and thus a state of intersubjectivity" (Collins, 2004, 64). I concentrate on urban protests while recognizing that seasonal migration and ties to traditional communities blur the line between city and countryside (Hartmann-Mahmud, 2004). Protests are usually urban, but protesters may have split urban-rural identities. I take care to address the implications of urban-rural dynamics for class status and grievances.

Conclusion

It is important to understand the roots of protests because civil unrest can destabilize the status quo for both good and ill. Protests can compel dictators to liberalize (Giugni, McAdam and Tilly, 1998), or they can prompt authoritarian backlash (Beaulieu, 2014); they can pressure leaders to implement more equitable economic policies (Acemoglu and Robinson, 2006), or they can destroy an economy by damaging property and depressing investment (Goodrich, 1992). Protests are seldom inconsequential. The target audience for this book includes social scientists with a theoretical interest in contentious politics, as well as policymakers who wish to anticipate events that shape security, development, and democracy in the world's poorest region, sub-Saharan Africa.

2 | *Defining Africa's Protest Waves*

Many studies of protest in Africa highlight specific episodes of contention such as the 2000–2001 riots in Nigeria (Scacco, 2008), the Malawian political crisis of July 20, 2011 (Wroe, 2012), or violent demonstrations following Ethiopia's 2005 elections (Arriola, 2013b). These micro-level analyses signal political scientists' welcome shift away from trying to understand all of Africa at once, as if the continent were a single country. However, case studies lack context and give a misleading impression of protests as independent events unfolding in a vacuum. Sociologists make a persuasive case that protests are in fact interdependent – "they are neither understandable in their own, unique terms, nor are they merely interchangeable instances of general classes of events" (Koopmans, 2004, 19). Protests diffuse across geographic space and sectors of society through different channels: activists use social networks to exchange ideas and strategies (Diani, 2004); media broadcast information about shared grievances and the threat of state repression (Soule, 2004); people feel inspired when they witness others rising up (Tarrow, 1994). Processes of diffusion combine discrete "moments of madness" (Zolberg, 1972) into larger "protest waves" (Koopmans, 2004; Almeida, 2003; Seddon and Zeilig, 2005).[1] Studying protests as waves can shed light on triggers of social unrest that do not immediately precede a given episode – gradual changes in grievances, macroeconomic conditions, and the state's repressive capacity (Almeida, 2003). There have been three major waves of protest in African history. The first occurred from the mid-1940s to the early 1960s when students, peasants, and labor unions spearheaded the fight against colonial rule. The second wave took place in the 1990s when coalitions of students, workers, and religious leaders pressured

---

[1] The terms "protest cycle" and "protest wave" are functionally interchangeable in the social movements literature. But like Koopmans (2004), I favor the wave metaphor because it does not require that we assume levels of contention to rise and fall on a regular schedule.

autocrats to hold elections and institute multi-party politics. The latest
wave started around 2011 and seemed to arise from popular discontent
with democratic backsliding. This chapter briefly chronicles all three
waves in order to contextualize the recent protests that comprise the
focus of this book. At the end of the chapter, I apply theories of social
movements to compare features of protests across waves – frequency,
diffusion, key actors, frames of meaning, and tactics. This comparison
reveals some commonalities but also some distinct aspects of the third
wave that demand explanation.

The First Wave: Protest on the Eve of Independence

It is impossible to say just how many protests took place in Africa in the
twilight of the colonial era. Statistical record-keeping was fairly limited
at the time (Desrosières, 1998), and colonial authorities strategically
concealed information about the level of native resistance to their rule.
Europeans subjugated Africans by brute force but also through the
"theology of omnipotence," which involved convincing subjects that
any challenge to authority would be futile (Ranger, 2010, 451).
The façade of invincibility could crumble if Africans learned just how
many of their brethren were mobilizing for reforms or outright independence. Besides, there was substantial opposition to territorial con-
quest back in Europe, both within parliaments and across broader
society (Young, 1986, 28). Imperialists faced constant pressure to
secure the empire's investments. Counting protests was inimical to
assuring people in London, Paris, Brussels, or Lisbon that expensive
colonial projects were paying off.

Despite a lack of systematic data on protest frequency, numerous
historical accounts cite increased popular mobilization in the 1940s
and 1950s.[2] Colonizers were unable to stave off revolt as the world
wars diverted European resources to the home front and away from
colonial administration. The Accra boycotts and riots of 1948
prompted the British government to send Aiken Watson and three
other Englishmen to investigate the causes of disorder in the Gold
Coast. The Watson Commission begrudgingly recommended increased
autonomy for the territory, which would later become Ghana, after
concluding that colonial policies – such as forced labor and the

---

[2] See, for example, Young (1994), Rotberg and Mazrui (1970), and Bush (1999).

appointment of unpopular chiefs – had triggered large protests (Amamoo, 1958, 17).

Protests in the first wave diffused across space and social strata. Anticolonial movements typically originated in the "nationalist middle class" of white-collar colonial subjects that included teachers, journalists, nurses, and business clerks (Foltz, 1973, 147). However, these educated and salaried activists "spread the gospel of nationalism" (Rasmussen, 1974, 40) and "mobilized the masses" (Schmidt, 2005). Protest strategies that are often associated with cities – boycotts, strikes, the use of lawyers – spanned rural and urban spaces (Bush, 1999, 102). In the Gold Coast, farmers called on the colonial government to adopt fair farm labor practices and concede the right of "destoolment," or the ability to remove unpopular chiefs. When authorities refused, protesters enlisted indigenous lawyer A. G. Heward Mills to craft their legal defense (Simensen, 1974, 36). In Uganda, "the intelligentsia that organized in the 1940's ... consciously reached out to organize popular classes, peasants, and workers, by putting forth popular and democratic demands through organized forms like co-operatives and trade unions" (Mamdani, 1990, 58). In Zambia, there was a "popular basis of anticolonial protest" (Rasmussen, 1974) that radiated from cities to villages and from mining sectors to farming sectors. Rank-and-file representatives of the United National Independence Party, instead of party leaders, organized violent uprisings beyond the densely settled Copper Belt. Colonial record-keepers tried to hide the extent of rural unrest (Rasmussen, 1974, 41), but tensions escalated to the point of impelling the last Governor of Northern Rhodesia, Evelyn Hone, to send a letter to the Secretary of State for the Colonies warning of widespread political "disturbances" and nationalist leader Kenneth Kaunda's lack of control over the situation: "Kaunda himself has been bitterly disappointed that he has been unable to achieve the United National Independence Party's objectives by negotiation.... the party leadership cannot, in difficult or adverse circumstances, exercise any real control or any curb over the wild excesses of its members" (Larmer, 2011, 42). Colonial authorities responded by burning schools, killing cattle, and arresting villagers (Larmer, 2011, 41).

Protests spread from the urban elites to the rural masses in Francophone colonies, as well. There, African civil servants with university degrees rallied protesters for economic and social justice

(Wallerstein, 1961; Morgenthau, 1964). Through the centralized French education system, these *évolués*, or "evolved" Africans, studied European egalitarian movements and France's national doctrines of universal rights, liberty, and equality (Wallerstein, 1961, 45). Some went on to found the African Democratic Rally (Rassemblement Démocratique Africain, or RDA), which recruited military veterans, trade unionists, peasants, and women. The Guinean chapter of the RDA branded itself as a broad-based coalition representing ethnic minorities and the poor. Peasants began petitioning chiefs for better treatment and protesting in the streets. French administrators dismissed five village chiefs in Upper-Guinea for failing to stymie uprisings (Schmidt, 2005, 100). RDA resistance to the chieftaincy melded elite and rural interests in a nationwide social movement leading to a postwar "crisis of chiefly authority" and national independence in 1958 (Schmidt, 2005, 95). Another example of rural-urban diffusion was the Sawaba movement in what is now Niger. Under the leadership of Djibo Bakary, Sawabists used Maoist ideologies and weapons from the Eastern Bloc to marshal a peasant army that militated for complete independence from France (van Walraven, 2013).

Leaders of protests in the first wave were often members of labor unions. It is counterintuitive that formal-sector employees would challenge colonial rule while enjoying many material advantages over farmers and informal-sector merchants (Fanon, 1961/2005). Instead of striking over poverty, African workers usually went on strike over wage inequalities, sometimes advocating for reformed colonial labor laws rather than complete national independence (Bush, 1999; Henderson, 1973). Unionists were well positioned to lead protests because they were already embedded in tight social networks and had a history of successful collective action, as in the French West African railway strike of 1947 to 1948 (Cooper, 1990). Many first-wave protests that were later labeled as "anticolonial" began as strikes over workplace issues. In the 1950s, for example, the Industrial and Commercial Workers' Union of South Africa and Southern Rhodesia held assemblies and chanted slogans that non-union protesters later adopted in opposing British occupation.

Guinea epitomized the influence of organized labor on protests in colonial Africa. Employees in various industrial and civil service sectors organized general strikes to pressure French policymakers for equitable wages and better treatment on the job. One strike was led by a postal clerk, Sékou Touré, who later served nearly three decades as president. Unions representing teachers, railwaymen, medical personnel, dock workers, and domestic servants pressured Touré's RDA party to adopt a progressive and pro-independence platform that would eventually lead Guinea to become the first French colony to declare independence and the only one to reject continued alliance with Paris. Several historical factors prompted the rise of a politically vibrant and well-organized Guinean working class. France's assimilationist mode of colonial rule introduced Guineans to Western trade unionism and universalist philosophies and made Guineans aware of their subaltern status. Thus, when the Houphoüet-Boigny Law abolished forced labor in the colonies, Guinean workers were not content simply to return home from their job sites. They formed trade unions and staged strikes to advance their collective interests as workers and colonial subjects. Thus, unionism and protest in Guinea were intertwined from the beginning. Workers expanded their agendas from wage issues to national liberation and human rights, encouraging union members and non-members alike to come together to express their diverse grievances. The labor movement was also multi-ethnic, led by members of Guinea's Malinke, Peul, and Soussou groups, as well as representatives from Senegal, Guadeloupe, and other French territories. The Union of Confederated Syndicates of Guinea (Confédération Générale du Travail, or CGT) united the Guinean working class across ethnic lines. "Focusing on common ground rather than competing interests, CGT unions were particularly suited to broad-based, well-coordinated collective action" (Schmidt, 2005, 60).

Guinea's experience might give the impression that labor strikes evolved naturally into anti-colonial protests. Scholars writing during the late colonial period expected unions to "wake the lion" by unleashing anti-colonial sentiment in Africa (Woodis, 1961, xiii). In reality, though, the coalition between African workers and nationalists was precarious. Despite the outward appearance of solidarity, union leaders were torn between focusing on traditional workplace issues and joining the broader push for independence. On the one hand, many of them resented receiving lower pay and fewer workplace privileges than European workers. On the other hand, the issues that most affected union members, like wages and hours, did not affect the majority of the population. By one 1971 estimate, only about 11 percent of Africans earned formal pay checks (Henderson, 1973, 288). As a result, some union members in Africa identified more closely with workers in distant countries than with their peasant co-nationals. Adopting Marxist rhetoric of a universal workers' struggle, they chose to concentrate on industrial conditions and avoided associating with nationalist movements. Nationalist politicians and union members were sometimes suspicious of each other's motives. In Zambia, the president of the African Mine Workers' Union, Lawrence Katilungu, refused to support a day of national prayer against the colonial federation. The African National Congress, which organized the protest, criticized Katilungu and his union for abetting Britain's oppression of the Zambian people (Henderson, 1973). Workers often assembled broad-based protests, but they did so despite political differences with nationalists.

Students in colonial Africa, along with workers, were "protesters par excellence" (Sylla, 2014, 38). They felt entitled to upward mobility and challenged government systems that favored Europeans. Seven undergraduates at University College Ibadan in Nigeria founded the Pyrates Confraternity to radicalize campus politics. Spin-off "campus cults" multiplied as more universities opened, providing fertile recruiting grounds for Nigeria's first anti-colonial party, the National Council of Nigeria and the Cameroons (Ellis, 2009). In Mozambique, students organized "to spread the idea of national independence and [encourage] resistance to the cultural subjugation which the Portuguese imposed" (Mondlane, 1983, 113). The former head of the National Union of Students of Uganda described members as "committed socialists, very committed radicals who denounced imperialism and all forms of oppression" (Byaruhanga, 2006, 51). Guinean students pressured the nationalist RDA party to shift to the left and demand that the French president of the Council of Government be replaced with an elected African leader (Schmidt, 2005, 183). Student activists in Africa received support from the diaspora. The Black African Students Federation in France broke with its policy of pursuing strictly materialist interests and took up the goal to "combat colonialism in all its forms" (Diop, 1953, 115). Numerous presidents of independent African countries launched their political careers as students during the first wave of protest, including Kwame Nkrumah of Ghana, Jomo Kenyatta of Kenya, Modibo Keita of Mali, Hastings Kamuzu Banda of Malawi, and Nelson Mandela of South Africa (Nkinyangi, 1991).

Fewer founding presidents started out as religious leaders. Mosques and churches played an ambiguous role in first-wave protests, alternately encouraging and discouraging political contention. In Senegal, leaders of the Tijani and Mouride brotherhoods promoted Islam as "a rallying point for African resistance to the French" (Cellar, 1995, 6). The founder of the Mourides, Cheikh Amadou Bamba, was repeatedly exiled for organizing resistance to colonial rule. Parallel Islamic revival movements sprang up in areas that are now Mali, Sudan, and Cape Verde, as "more or less direct manifestations of hostility to colonial penetration" (Coulon, 1985, 347). Some theologists argue that Islam is inherently anti-colonial: "As a religion to which the colonized and the colonizer cannot both be committed, Islam is itself the sign of a fundamental process of differentiation and an instrument of opposition" (Balandier, 1970, 484). At the same time, fear of anti-colonial riots led colonizers to co-opt religious leaders, creating a contingent of Senegalese marabouts who accepted the status quo (Clark, 1999). The most senior marabouts generally viewed radical and nationalist movements as threatening to the traditional religious order (Hodgkin, 1962, 326). Hence, Muslim leaders in Senegal who participated in first-wave protests tended to be younger reformists operating outside the maraboutic establishment.

Religious organizations in British colonies played a similarly vague role in organizing protest. Emirs in northern Nigeria had various reactions to foreign occupation. The Mahdists considered British rule evil and resisted violently (Isa, 2010). In contrast, the Wazir of Sokoto, Muhamadu Buhari, signed a surrender to Great Britain and justified his decision with the Koranic doctrines of *muwalat* (alliance) and *taqiyya* (precaution or dissimulation). It was lawful, he reasoned, for Muslims to submit to non-Muslims due to the superiority of the British military and the necessity of self-preservation (Umar, 2006, 82). In Britain's southern colonies, some black churches sought government recognition and managed to function under apartheid, whereas others agitated for independence (Ranger, 1986, 3).

The radicalism of religious actors corresponded with the level of colonial repression that churches and mosques faced. Where Europeans were more lenient or assimilationist, religious actors did not need allies in the nationalist movement. But where colonial repression was high, it was too costly to engage in protest or civil disobedience. Only at middling levels of oppression, like in Kenya, did religious actors and political nationalists collaborate (Ranger, 1986, 3).

An alternative explanation for variation in radicalism relates to missionary influence. Some African Christian leaders denigrated pre-colonial society as "primitive" and "ignorant," even while endorsing the gradual transfer of power from Europeans to natives. Lewis Bandawe of Malawi was one such leader. Educated in missionary schools, he led the Blantyre Mission and translated the Bible into the Lomwe language. He spoke admiringly of the British in his memoirs but went on to co-found the Nyasaland African Congress, one of the most vocal opponents to the colonial government (Chanock, 1975). Churches and nationalist parties served different purposes: nationalist parties recruited adherents who experienced colonization as political or economic oppression, whereas churches recruited adherents who experienced colonization as social destruction or cultural upheaval. This division kept houses of worship on the sidelines of political protest (Buijtenhuijs, 1976, 37).

Three sets of symbols justified and dignified contentious political action in Africa on the eve of independence: new religious beliefs, pan-Africanism, and self-determination. These "frames of meaning" (Tarrow, 1994) each "generated important changes in African con-sciousness" (Bush, 1999, 102) and provided a vocabulary for protest leaders to use in recruiting activists. New religious beliefs included messianic faiths and liberation theologies that did not originate in the 1940s and 1950s but were popularized during that period. Pan-Africanism was a philosophy and transnational political movement originating in the African diaspora. The Trinidadian barrister Henry Sylvester Williams coined the term "pan-Africanism" in London in 1900 when calling on black people "to protest stealing of lands in the colonies, racial discrimination and deal with all other issues of interest to blacks" (Abdul-Raheem, 1996, 1). Pan-Africanists reclaimed the racialized concept of "African" as an empowering label denoting dignity, self-worth, and solidarity. The Pan-African Congress began meeting in 1900, but its 1945 edition in Manchester was especially significant due to increased participation by members from Africa (Young, 2004, 10). The philosophy of self-determination gained traction around the same time. President Franklin D. Roosevelt of the United States and Prime Minister Winston Churchill of the United Kingdom signed the Atlantic Charter in 1941, which asserted a principle inspired by President Woodrow Wilson: all people, including colonized people, have the right to freely choose their statehood.[3] This further justified and dignified independence movements across the colonized world. It is no coincidence that Africa's first wave of protests coincided with uprisings in Egypt, India, China, Korea, and elsewhere (Manela, 2007, 8).

Forms of protest that were once costly and rare became possible on a much larger scale during the first wave. One form involved contact between African protest leaders and diasporas in Europe and the Americas. Increasing numbers of Africans and West Indians attended university abroad and formed intelligentsias across borders. They started political organizations such as the West African Students' Union – founded by a Nigerian, Lapido Solanke – and the League of Coloured Peoples – founded by a Jamaican, Harold Moody. Leaders of these organizations initially "sought a better deal from colonial rule," but began pressing more revolutionary agendas in the 1940s and 1950s (Bush, 1999, 103). The 1945 Pan-African Congress at Manchester eased coordination between black British activists, African labor and student leaders, and American pan-Africanists like W.E.B. Dubois. It "represented a new 'militant' stage in the anti-colonial struggle" and reminded protesters in Africa that they were not alone (Bush, 1999, 225).

Journalism also expanded as a tool of protest during the first wave, although newspapers began circulating in Africa much earlier. In 1905, an Asian businessman living in Kenya published the *African Standard*, which expanded into Tanganyika as the *East African Standard*. Readers were mostly European at first, but by the end of World War II newspapers reached far into African communities; even the illiterate could access print media by listening to their friends and family read aloud. This helped set off a wave of protest in two ways: by popularizing intellectuals' subversive views and by helping people coordinate collective action. The first newspaper published in a local vernacular, the Kenyan *Mumenyereri*, became the most widely read periodical in post-war Africa (Frederiksen, 2011). Edited by future president Jomo Kenyatta, it focused on fact-checking European journalists, raising awareness about the injustice of foreign occupation, and mobilizing nationalist protests to the extent that censorship allowed. *Mumenyereri* announced community meetings and spread propaganda in support of the Mau Mau revolt

---

[3] There would be deviations from this principle, notably the wars in Vietnam.

against British rule, which raged from 1952 to 1960 and cost the empire 55 million pounds (Gerlach, 2010, 213).

Activist newspapers and pamphlets circulated on the other side of the continent, too. Angus Colin Duncan-Johnstone, the Provincial Commissioner for the Western Province of the British Gold Coast, described the native press as "scurrilous" and prone to indulge in an "orgy of insults and abuse" (Bush, 1999, 113). A group of provincial commissioners convened in 1946 and warned their superiors that African journalists "constituted a menace to the future of the Colony" (Corfield, 1960). The threat to the British empire was even greater than they acknowledged. In the 1940s, Africans and South Asians built an intricate transnational network of writers, publicists, and activists, which made it difficult for colonial authorities to identify whom to prosecute for sedition (Frederiksen, 2011).

Colonizers were targets of litigation as well as instigators. British anthropologist Geoffrey Gorer visited the Gold Coast in the late 1930s and remarked that "almost every development of public works was held up by lawsuits, while in Nigeria the 'native lawyer' was arousing Africans' aspirations" (Bush, 1999, 113). Asafo villagers solicited help from native attorneys of the Akim Abuakwa Scholars' Union to win a dispute with Ofori Atta, a traditional king who conspired with the British to increase taxes and stall local democratization efforts. Ofori Atta dropped his charges against the villagers who staged protests against him, allowing the Asofo to continue their push for representation in the State Council (Simensen, 1974). In French territories, postwar reforms expanded native control over litigation. Customary courts headed by African judges won the right to decide all civil cases in order to relieve the strained colonial court system (Jean-Baptiste, 2008). Legal action was yet another tactic in an expanding repertoire of contention during the first wave.

A Missing Wave? Protest under Single-Party Rule

Opportunities to protest contracted after independence. Early experiments with democracy petered out as the heads of new African states clamped down on political competition, co-opted labor unions and interest groups into the ruling party, and threatened violence to deter mass mobilization. By 1989, only five out of forty-seven countries in sub-Saharan Africa had multi-party systems (Bratton and van de Walle,

1997, 79). Leaders justified centralized power as necessary to shed dependence on former European rulers and stimulate economic growth. They favored import-substitution industrialization, a policy that involved increasing taxes on foreign imports and exerting state control over labor, banking, natural resources, and commodity prices (Coughlin and Ikiara, 1988). Ironically, institutions left over from the colonial era facilitated this process. Colonizers established marketing boards during the Great Depression and World War II to insulate farmers from price shocks. These boards were the only legal buyers of agricultural outputs, allowing colonial authorities to set prices artificially low during boom times and then redistribute reserved "stabilization funds" when droughts or conflicts struck (Jones, 1987). Marketing boards had the perverse effect of under-paying farmers and widening disparities in material well-being and political influence between cities and rural areas (Bates, 1981). Following statehood, incumbents biased policies toward urban manufacturing sectors out of fear that workers would revolt. Reducing food prices and creating factory jobs mollified people in the capital city, who posed a greater threat of overthrowing the regime than farmers dispersed throughout the countryside.

In the name of national self-sufficiency, post-colonial leaders maintained monopsonies and channeled agricultural surpluses to domestic industries. They concentrated wealth in state coffers, and often in their own hands. Malawi's first president, Hasting Banda, declared in 1972, "nothing is not my business in this country: everything is my business, everything. The state of education, the state of our economy, the state of our agriculture, the state of our transport, everything is my business" (Jackson and Rosberg, 1982, 165). Incumbents forestalled protests using security forces controlled through patronage (Bratton and van de Walle, 1997, 61–80). Workers and students who once led the charge against colonialism had little choice but to participate "responsibly" in official politics or else disband (Phelan, 2014). Many complied with the rules as African incumbents imitated colonial rulers by padding the civil service to "soak up the unemployed," thus weaving together the interests of the middle class and the state class.[4]

Protectionist policies seemed to work at first, but they ultimately failed to nurture technological innovation and economies of scale as

---

[4] See Grier (1987) for an account of this practice in colonial Ghana.

leaders had promised. Gross domestic product for Africa as a whole grew at an encouraging average of 2.6 percent annually between 1965 and 1974 (Mkandawire and Soludo, 1998, 6). Some countries, like Côte d'Ivoire with its 40 percent world market share of cocoa, looked like economic miracles (Klaas, 2008). However, miracles regressed into catastrophes as African economies stagnated starting around 1974. By the turn of the decade, many countries had lower per capita incomes than they did before independence. Continent-wide GDP fell by 1.3 percent per year in the 1980s, setting average growth at five percentage points below the level for all low-income developing countries (Mkandawire and Soludo, 1998, 6–7). Debt burdens and trade deficits became unsustainable. Poverty skyrocketed; fiscal crisis was acute. Leaders had neither the capacity nor the political will to deliver essential public goods (Nugent, 2012, 331). Not even petroleum-rich countries like Nigeria and Gabon were in the clear, as their economies were insufficiently diverse to withstand a sudden dip in the price of oil in 1973 (Yates, 1996).

A 1981 World Bank report, *Accelerated Development in Sub-Saharan Africa*, placed the blame for economic decline squarely on African leaders (Nugent, 2012, 334). International financial institutions began demanding that countries meet conditions before receiving aid. This prompted reforms, such as open trade and reduced government spending, that some experts now regard as disastrous (van de Walle, 2001; Easterly, 2005). It is difficult to make inferences about the causal effects of large-scale foreign aid, because grants and loans tend to flow to needy countries that might have been even worse off without intervention. But instrumental variable analyses show that World Bank and International Monetary Fund structural adjustment policies of the 1980s yielded no improvements in governance or growth (Easterly, 2005). This failure may have stemmed from the ability of African leaders to expropriate development funds. "Leakage" turned African countries into rentier states susceptible to the distortionary effects of Dutch Disease, including weak traded sectors (Rajan and Subramanian, 2011). Ghana complied better than any African country with the World Bank's conditions. Its economy underwent a brief spurt after reforms, but then stagnated once more (Lall, 1995). Some economists hold out hope for conditional aid to work in the long run (Sachs, 2014), but few deny that austerity reforms were painful for Africans. In the 1980s and 1990s, farm subsidies and civil services jobs dried up, prices inflated, and domestic producers stopped enjoying protections from foreign competitors and fluctuating global prices (Lensik, 1996).

Economic collapse in the 1970s and structural adjustment in the 1980s gave Africans more reasons to rise up just as states were consolidating their power to thwart uprisings. There are conflicting theories about how this combination of material hardship and political repression influenced the timing of Africa's second wave of protests. According to grievance-based theories of social movements, mobilization should have increased when people became fed up with deprivation and decided to challenge the status quo. In other words, opportunities to protest matter only insofar as people have the will to mobilize in the first place (Klandermans, 2004). In contrast, "resource mobilization" theories predict *less* unrest in repressive environments: "Grievances and deprivation always exist and therefore cannot explain the ups and downs of protest cycles" (Corning and Myers, 2002, 705).

Did the second wave start in the 1970s? The beginning and end points of protest waves are debatable. Does a wave begin when protests become more frequent? When they spread across geographic space and sectors of society? When they involve a certain number of social movement organizations? When political graffiti appear on walls and political songs on the airwaves? Taking all of these dimensions into account, I conclude that African protests before the late 1980s did not constitute a wave. Anecdotal data likely overestimate protest activity by highlighting rare but sensational events. People who tried to incite uprisings faced a high risk of imprisonment, exile, or death (Dulani, 2009). Protests in the 1970s and 1980s were "sporadic," as rulers "routinely managed such outburst by briefly closing institutions (usually the national university or a dissident trade union), expelling protest ringleaders, and coopting others to ensure future quiescence" (Bratton and van de Walle, 1997, 101).

Autonomous labor organizing was onerous under tight authoritarian control. In 1987, the International Labor Organization described the response of African workers to economic austerity as "cautious, at times cooperative, and at the most defensive" (International Labor Office, 1987). Strikes, which had been the go-to weapons of workers and students in the late colonial era, became "suicidal" under single-party rule (Fashoyin and Damachi, 1988). Strikes were *less* frequent during civil service layoffs and wage cuts of the 1980s than they were when economic conditions were better

(Tidjani, 1998).[5] Once-radical unions like the National Confederation of Guinean Workers came to espouse "responsible participation," prioritizing national advancement over the interests of their members (Phelan, 2014).

The Second Wave: Democracy from Below

By most accounts, Africa's second wave of protests began not in the 1970s or 1980s, but in 1990. The break-up of the Soviet Union ended arrangements whereby great powers abetted dictators in proxy battles. African leaders found it harder to contain protests as the withdrawal of foreign support shrank military budgets and upped external pressures to democratize.[6] British and American media expanded their coverage of human rights abuses in African countries. Broadcasts from the BBC and CNN reached citizens in the countryside and rendered authoritarian propaganda less persuasive (Robinson, 1994, 583). Bourgi and Castern (1992) prophesied, "if *glasnost* henceforth reigns in Moscow, the time for transparency has also come in Yaoundé and Lusaka. The winds of the east are blowing southward, and Africa, this colossal continent, cannot escape it." Nugent (2012, 376) applied the metaphor of a pendulum, which swung in favor of single-party regimes for the first thirty years of independence but "swung back again as significant sections of society weighed into politics with a gusto which had not been witnessed since the heyday of nationalism – and often exceeding it." Kenyan students marched in 1990 after President Daniel Arap Moi allegedly authorized the assassination of a rival (Bratton and van de Walle, 1997, 102). Labor unions organized general strikes in Chad, Burkina Faso, Cameroon, Ghana, and Lesotho (Zeilig, 2009, 84). Authorities shut down the University of Malawi in 1992 when students rose up to defend bishops who had circulated a letter critical of autocrat Hastings Banda (Posner, 1995). Church leadership in Malawi's pro-democracy movement marked a shift from the more ambivalent role that churches played in first-wave, anti-colonial movements.

---

[5] The Liberian teachers' strike of 1985 was a rare exception.
[6] In the twenty-first century, the international war on terror created a neo-Cold-War dynamic whereby the United States and the European Union increased support for African leaders, like Mahamadou Issoufou of Niger, who took a hard line against terrorists but had patchy human rights records.

The second wave was not just dramatic; it was effective. Popular uprisings subverted the established elite by undermining property rights, disrupting the supply of disciplined labor, and prompting international sanctions. Persistent pressure from below eventually convinced incumbents that it was less costly to grant democracy than it was to remain defiant (Wood, 2000). Sixteen out of twenty-one African transitions to democracy between November 1989 and May 1991 began with mass demonstrations (Bratton and van de Walle, 1992). Observers referred to the early 1990s as the "African Spring" (Bourgi and Castern, 1992; Bratton and van de Walle, 1992).

As critical as the end of the Cold War was for opening spaces to mobilize, it would be a mistake to attribute the second wave of African protests exclusively to changes in world politics. *Glasnost* expanded opportunities for Africans to protest, but Africans were already poised for action. Resentment about austerity measures in the 1970s and 1980s spilled over into protests of the 1990s. Zambia illustrates this. President Kenneth Kaunda tried to avoid reducing popular subsidies on staple goods like maize, but he caved to pressures from Western donors and authorized price increases, bringing an abrupt end to urban bias. Angry citizens flooded city streets, demanding that Kaunda step down. The president restored subsidies, but it was too late: a doubling of maize prices in 1989 had already devastated families nation-wide, and Kaunda's backpedaling on structural adjustment led donors to suspend aid (Walton and Seddon, 1994). Then, in 1991, Frederick Chiluba of the Movement for Multi-Party Democracy won Zambia's first open election with more than 80 percent of the vote and 123 out of 150 parliamentary seats (Mills, 1992). He ran on an anti-austerity platform, exploiting widespread impatience with leaders who cut public spending while enriching themselves. He backed up his populist message with credentials as the former head of the Zambian Confederation of Trade Unions.

Economic and political grievances overlapped similarly in other countries. Demonstrators in Zimbabwe attacked the ruling ZANU-PF party as "a further entrenchment of capitalism" and "an acquiescence to the IMF and World Bank sponsored programs" (Zeilig, 2009, 85). Workers in Niger chose May Day as the symbolic date for a parade denouncing the military regime that they associated with structural adjustment policies (Elischer, 2013). Economic frustrations simmered beneath repression throughout the 1970s and 1980s; "pro-democracy" protests boiled up in the 1990s when shifting global alliances removed the lid of authoritarian rule.

Wage earners and tuition-paying students were at the forefront of the second wave. The new weakness of autocrats allowed labor unions to re-emerge from "responsible participation" and experiment with innovative protest strategies like the "indefinite strike" (a strike with no guaranteed minimum service) and the "strike relay" (which involved launching a strike in one sector as soon as a strike in another sector ended) (Adji, 2000). Students whose stipends shrank and tuition increased under austerity programs formed their own unions that partnered with labor (Federici, Caffentzis, and Alidou, 2000). This alliance was apparent in solidarity marches that students held in support of lecturers who had walked off the job to pressure administrators for higher salaries (Nkinyangi, 1991).

Protests about bread-and-butter issues were entangled with demands for multi-party democracy, because labor and academic organizers blamed single-party regimes for their economic troubles. Women's and youth associations joined coalitions with people who had no formal education or employment (Nugent, 2012, 387). For instance, the Association of University and Secondary School Students of Mali (AEEM) protested against the Konaré government in 1993 for lower school fees and instructional improvements. At first, the general public condemned the students' violent tactics and praised security forces for cracking down on demonstrations. Two years later, the AEEM adopted a message stressing political accountability and democracy instead of narrower concerns. When the students protested again, they did so with wider public support (Smith, 1997). In the early years of the second wave, workers and students replayed their roles from the first wave as liaisons between diverse sectors of society.

Groups on the fringes of union-organized movements became alienated, however, when union leaders entered official politics. The International Labor Organization trained the heads of African labor unions to represent workers at national conferences where delegates drafted constitutions with provisions for competitive elections, checks on executive power, and civil liberties (Robinson, 1994). National conferences were ostensibly a triumph for all protesters who had fought for multi-party rule, but labor representatives based agendas on workplace issues such as the minimum wage and the right to strike. This split between protest leaders and ordinary citizens presaged the future unraveling of broad-based coalitions. For example, Nigerien unions turned out crowds of 100,000 protesters against the one-party Saibou regime in 1990 and were vocal proponents of democracy at the national conference in 1991 (Nugent, 2012, 387). By 2009, they made only a lukewarm effort to stop President Mamadou Tandja from seeking an extra-constitutional third term and acquired a reputation for being politically conservative (Elischer, 2013). In Zambia, the Movement for Multi-Party Democracy emerged from strong copper mining unions, but after the first competitive elections of 1991, leaders betrayed their base by switching from a platform centered on jobs and social services to one touting free markets and small government (LeBas, 2011, 219). African labor unions were "contingent democrats" – willing to support democracy only when it served their economic interests (Bellin, 2000). Opportunism provided a shaky foundation for young multi-party systems. African opposition parties with weak ties to grassroots activists are less able to coordinate voters across ethnic and ideological lines than parties with firmer activist roots (LeBas, 2011).

Although labor and student unions primarily served their own members, the democratic reforms that they helped to achieve spawned social movements incorporating protesters from more diverse backgrounds. Less elitist and exclusive than traditional civil society, these new associations constituted what Chatterjee (2006, 40) calls "political society" – "the entanglement of elite and subaltern politics." The poor in Harare founded residents' and ratepayers' associations that met monthly to criticize the dominant ZANU-PF party (LeBas, 2011, 125). Grassroots movements blossomed in South Africa, including the Concerned Citizens Forum in KwaZulu-Natal and the Anti-Eviction Campaign in the Western Cape (Zeilig, 2009, 120). Political dissidents, intellectuals, and businessmen formed clandestine groups opposing the Banda dictatorship in Malawi (Posner, 1995). Niger's revised 1992 Constitution of the Third Republic allowed religious organizations to proliferate, ranging from the extremist Izala Society to the humanitarian Africa Muslims Agency. Before then, the military regime of Seyni Kountché restricted religious organizing to the state-affiliated Islamic Association of Niger (Sounaye, 2009). New social movements pursued different goals and activities, but most of them coordinated protests using the language of democracy. Protest messages reached more people thanks to technological advances that were not available during the first wave. These included mobile phones, fax machines, photocopiers, and personal computers. Posner (1995, 139) describes how such technology energized Malawi's political opposition:

Independent civil society groups, businesses, and large government offices – especially those thought to have photocopiers – were targeted by the Lusaka-based opposition for the receipt of anonymous samizdat faxes. Truckers, traders, clergymen, and other mobile groups were enlisted as distributors. By the middle of 1992, Malawi was awash in a sea of anonymous faxes and photocopied leaflets containing leaked government documents supplied by disgruntled civil servants and parastatal employees, reports from foreign newspapers describing the country's economic and political difficulties, and other sorts of officially seditious material. Circulated in offices, passed among friends, or left in the night under stones in markets and at bus stops, these fragments of uncensored communication played a critical role in demonstrating, both by their content and by their very existence, that the emperor had no clothes. A series of mass arrests in May and June 1992 showed just how seriously the government took the destabilizing impact of the fax-photocopy network.

Older technology continued to play a role, too. In the 1980s, governments controlled all but nine of the ninety daily newspapers on the continent (Tettey, 2001, 9). In the next decade, private papers, some of which launched during the colonial era, started circulating once more. Independent radio also thrived. Ghana went from having no radio stations in 1993 to thirteen in 1999; eight new radio stations sprang up in Kenya between 1998 and 1999 (Tettey, 2001, 9). In addition to mass media, protesters spread their messages with "small media" – graffiti, flyers, slogans, and audio cassette tapes (Spitulnik, 2002). In the early 1990s it was still illegal to sell tapes on the streets in Kenya, but passengers on minibuses (*matatus*) toted boom boxes emitting old speeches of the country's first president Jomo Kenyatta and songs in Kikuyu lionizing political prisoners of the democracy movement (Spitulnik, 2002, 180).

The Third Wave: Protest in the Twenty-First Century

Protest rates flattened in the first years of the twenty-first century (Figure 1.1), as one might expect given political and economic milestones of the period. Activists had won major battles against single-party rule, even if the consolidation of young democracies remained uncertain

(Randall and Svåsand, 2002). Observers declared that constraints on heads of state were tightening for good (Posner and Young, 2007). Elections in sub-Saharan Africa, even if not perfectly free and fair, looked to be promoting democratic behavior among rulers and "democratic culture" among citizens (Lindberg, 2006; Gandhi and Lust-Okar, 2009). Macroeconomic conditions also looked promising. As of 2010, seventeen African countries had experienced at least fifteen years of steady economic growth (Radelet, 2010). Social movement organizations from the second wave progressively demobilized. They fell into a "security trap," wherein achieving major goals first leads to a drop in protest participation and ultimately makes social movements obsolete (Dosh, 2009, 93).

Better objective conditions did not, however, erase subjective grievances about ongoing problems like poverty and fraudulent elections. In the 2002/2003 round of nationally representative Afrobarometer surveys, 37 percent of more than 24,000 respondents across sixteen countries said they were unsatisfied with democracy. Statistics were similar in the 2005/2006 and 2008/2009 rounds. Less than a third of Nigerians gave a positive appraisal of their country's economy in 2003, a year when growth in per capita income reached 7.6 percent, up from 1.2 percent the year before. Only 35 percent believed the national economy had improved over the previous twelve months, despite objective evidence of improvement (Lewis and Alemika, 2005). With expanded civil liberties, citizens could express their concerns more freely. Thus, while protest rates stagnated in the late 1990s, they never reverted to the levels of the repressive 1980s. Major protests between the second and third waves included rallies by the Zimbabwe Congress of Trade Unions in 2003 against violations of workers' rights (*Zimbabwe Independent*, 2003) and riots in Togo after Faure Gnassingbé succeeded his father as president in 2005 (Mealer, 2005). Yet, for the most part, 2000 to 2010 saw a return to relative calm.

The jump in protests around 2011 (Figure 1.1) caught observers off guard. Suddenly, youths were spray-painting slogans on buildings in Dakar that called on unpopular President Abdoulaye Wade to step down (Fortier, 2016). Five rioters died on April 21, 2011 in Kampala amid rising food prices and the arrest without bail of protest leader and presidential candidate Kizza Besigye (Kron, 2011). Police officers shot two demonstrators at an anti-government rally in Arusha on January 6,

2011 (*BBC*, 2011). Women, children, workers, petty merchants, and retirees revolted in Ouagadougou on March 22, 2011 when five military officers were provisionally released from prison for a suspected mutiny (Chouli, 2014).

Increased protest frequency was not the only variable marking the start of the third wave. Tarrow (1994) lists a total of five "elements of cyclicity" that define a protest wave: 1) increased protest frequency; 2) geographic and sectoral diffusion; 3) social movement organizations, both old and new; 4) new "frames of meaning" (which Tarrow defines as symbols that justify and dignify contentious collective action); and 5) expanded "repertoires of contention" (which he defines as the sets of contentious actions – marches, sit-ins, vigils – that people view as possible and culturally sanctioned).

African protests after 2011 fit all of these criteria for a wave. Recalling a theme from the first and second waves, twenty-first-century protests spread across sectors of society. But this time, protest leaders forged alliances less across rural and urban spaces (contemporary protests are almost all in cities), and increasingly across class lines. Middle-class activists recruited protesters from the poorest rungs of society in a more deliberate and sustained way than *évolués* did in colonial times or salaried workers and the intelligentsia did in the late twentieth century. The next chapters of this book show how urban professionals initiated protests in response to breaches of democratic bargains that citizens and politicians forged in the 1990s. These members of the middle class were not just more motivated, but also better able to organize actions against incumbent regimes, because broader access to private capital freed them from old patronage networks.

Communication technology was central to activism in the third wave, as it had been in the first and second waves. Fahamu, an NGO founded by Kenyan activist Firoze Manji, used SMS messaging in 2005 to drum up support for the Global Call to Action against Poverty, an international confederation promoting debt relief for African countries (Asuncion-Reed, 2010). Fahamu hired a part-time programmer to set up a system whereby supporters could send a text message to a designated number and see their words of solidarity displayed on the campaign website. 2,000 messages were received overall. Since that initial experiment with mobile activism, countless other groups kicked off text campaigns advocating causes from environmentalism to women's rights (Ekine, 2010). Eventually, Twitter, Facebook,

WhatsApp, and other social media tools supplemented SMS technology. This helped protest leaders coordinate the efforts of foot soldiers and garner transnational support, especially in more plugged-in cities like Dakar and Cape Town (Olorunnisola and Douai, 2013). Incumbents, realizing the power of social media as a "coordination good" (Bueno de Mesquita and Downs, 2005), took extra pains to groom their public images. When a flood destroyed a cemetery in the capital of Niger, an anonymous activist circulated photos on WhatsApp of feral dogs rummaging through human remains. Community members raced to the scene with shovels for rebuilding grave sites; witnesses reported that even the Prime Minister lent a hand.[7] Other politicians opted to repress e-activists rather than engage with them. Authorities loyal to Niger President Mahamadou Issoufou griped about "excessive freedom of expression"[8] and ordered a string of arrests in 2016 and 2017, including that of opposition leader Ali Amadou Djibo (nicknamed "Max") for allegedly inciting people to overthrow the government.

New media complement old media; on the web, protest songs and manifestos reach disparate and dispersed audiences. In the 2001 song "*Ndio Mzee*" ("Yes Sir"), Tanzanian hip-hop artist Professor Jay caricatured politicians who make false promises to win votes. His music, which mixed Swahili and English lyrics, played on local outlets like East African Television, regional outlets like Kenya's Radio Citizen, and global outlets like YouTube (Ntarangwi, 2009, 29). It is important, though, not to overstate the promise of new media as "liberation technology" (Diamond, 2010). While techno-optimists celebrate "the Facebook revolution," techno-pessimists warn about "slacktivism" and the weakening of ties among protesters (Gerbaudo, 2012). Social media allow people to connect across great distances, but virtual connections threaten to replace face-to-face interaction that is more effective at increasing political participation (Gerber and Green, 2000). Malcolm Gladwell (2010) quipped, "the revolution will not be tweeted."

Some principal actors of the third wave were veterans of traditional civil society – labor and student unions, religious associations, and former single parties – while others came from newer organizations – consumer coalitions, collectives of rap artists, opposition parties, and

---

[7] Interviews on July 5, 2017.   [8] Interviews in July 2017.

"new citizen" groups that provided alternatives to official politics. Frames of meaning expanded from pan-Africanism and constitutionalism to encompass democratic renewal (Cheru, 2012), social mobility (Dawson, 2014), and economic equality (McConnell, 2014). Senegalese activists rallied around the concept of *un nouveau type de sénégalais* (a new type of Senegalese) who would defend majority interests against the corrupt elite. Citizen groups calling themselves "Coalitions against the High Cost of Living" staged demonstrations in Niger in 2010 and Benin in 2010 and 2011 (Bonnecase, 2013; Engels, 2015).

Table 2.1 summarizes characteristics of the third wave of African protests in the context of previous waves, using Tarrow's typology. It confirms what other scholars have observed: recent protests in Africa are a mix of tradition and innovation (Branch and Mampilly, 2015; Zeilig, 2009). Yet there is no consensus on why the third wave started when it did or why so many people participated in it. Analysts alternately describe third-wave protests as democratic revolutions (Harsch, 2012; Dibba, 2013; Sowore, 2013) and bread riots (Smith, 2013; Berazneva and Lee, 2013; Macatory, Oumarou, and Poncelet, 2010; Adam, 2008). In the remaining chapters, I ask: who leads and joins protests in twenty-first-century Africa? What are their most salient grievances? And how do aggrieved people overcome collective action problems?

Conclusion

My use of the term "wave" diverges from standard usage in the political science literature. For many readers, the word might call to mind Samuel Huntington's *The Third Wave: Democratization in the Late Twentieth Century* (1991) and texts inspired by that influential work (e.g., Haggard and Kaufman, 2012; Berg-Schlosser, 2009; Markoff, 2009; Kurzman, 1998). Waves of protest often precede waves of regime change (Collier, 1999), but they are not the same thing, even if the literature tends to conflate them. Protest waves reflect transformations in society, not government – transformations involving increased protest frequency, new links between actors across sectors and space, innovative tactics for collective action, and revised mental frames for understanding the world and one's place in it.

Table 2.1 *Defining Features of Africa's Protest Waves*

Wave	Increased Frequency	Geographic and Sectoral Diffusion	Social Movement Orgs.	New Frames of Meaning	Expanded Repertoires of Contention
First Wave (1940s–1950s)	evident in colonial documents and policy changes	urban to rural, elite to popular	labor unions, student groups, some mosques and churches	messianic faiths, pan-Africanism, self-determination	mass demonstrations, contact with diaspora, journalism, litigation
Second Wave (1990s)	1,867 major protests (Hendrix and Salehyan, 2015) after repression in previous two decades	urban to rural, limited diffusion from elite to popular	labor unions, student groups, mosques and churches, musicians	democracy, constitutionalism	national conventions, strikes, marches, rallies, hip-hop
Third Wave (2010s–)	19,816 major protests in 2011–2016 after stagnation at turn of the century (Raleigh et al., 2010)	elite to popular, limited diffusion from urban to rural	labor unions, student groups, musicians, political parties, "new citizen" groups	democratic renewal, equality, upward mobility	private capital, social media

Waves of protest do not happen in a vacuum; they "happen in inherited contexts" of earlier mobilization (Chalcraft, 2016, 6). This chapter chronicled how three major waves of protest unfolded in sub-Saharan Africa: one on the eve of independence, roughly from 1940 to 1960, one in the 1990s surrounding transitions to multi-party democracy, and one that began around 2011 and was still evolving when this book was published. There are some continuities across waves, such as urban-rural diffusion and the involvement of labor unions. There are also idiosyncrasies of the third wave that invite further explanation, namely cross-class alliances and the shifting salience of political and economic grievances during a time of aggregate prosperity.

3 | *Paradoxes of Prosperity*

Seventy thousand people gathered at the University Cheikh Anta Diop in Dakar, Senegal in February 2011 for the World Social Forum, a week of protests against globalization and human rights violations. The theme of the event, "another world is possible," echoed the message of anti-government demonstrators in Egypt who were concurrently attempting to overthrow President Hosni Mubarak. Although Forum organizers vocally sympathized with the plight of the unemployed poor, most of them were teachers, communication professionals, and managers of NGOs (Pommerolle, 2014). Their calls to reform governments and international organizations did not resonate much with ordinary residents of Dakar, who saw such goals as serving only elite interests. Nevertheless, thousands of poor locals did turn out to protest, voicing their own concerns about hunger and unemployment. A survey revealed that almost none of the Senegalese attendees were paid members of activist organizations and that many worked in the informal sector (Pommerolle, 2014). Crowds grew large enough to attract foreign media attention, thanks to the participation of people from across social strata.

The 2011 World Social Forum illustrates how present economic conditions in sub-Saharan Africa produce two important ingredients for a wave of protest: an economically marginalized lower class and a politically marginalized middle class. This chapter describes those conditions, laying the foundation for subsequent chapters on the behavioral responses of the rich and the poor. It explains two paradoxes: first, the uneven distribution of rising incomes has allowed poverty to last amid impressive economic growth; and second, prosperity has not equaled more political power for the new middle class.

More Africans than ever are achieving middle-class levels of income, wealth, and education. By some estimates, there are now as many middle-class people in Africa as there are in fast-growing parts of

Asia like India and China (Mahajan, 2009). Upward mobility poses a dilemma, though. Higher economic status has increased people's feelings of entitlement to political power without making incumbents more willing to share power. Unlike previous generations of middle-class Africans, today's university graduates, entrepreneurs, and salaried workers tend to align with opposition parties. This orientation prompts resistance from presidents who try to change constitutional term limits or restrict party organizing. Members of the middle class ostensibly have more reasons than most Africans to be optimistic about the future, but they remain frustrated with the state of democracy. Some start protests in an effort to change existing policies, institutions, and power arrangements. A *New York Times* headline encapsulates this ironic blend of prosperity and protest: "'Africa Rising'? 'Africa Reeling' May Be More Fitting Now" (Gettleman, 2016). Middle-class restlessness in sub-Saharan Africa resembles the climate in North Africa and the Middle East in 2010–2011, when the middle class led uprisings that toppled several dictatorships.

It would be erroneous, however, to equate Africa's third wave of protests with the Arab Spring. A majority of Africans south of the Sahara continue to suffer material deprivation that dwarfs poverty in middle-income countries like Egypt or Tunisia. The percentage of people living under the World Bank poverty line of $1.99 a day is 41 percent in sub-Saharan Africa and just 2.3 percent in the Middle East and North Africa. The poor face a different paradox from the one confronting the new middle class: economic growth has coincided with increased inequality, leaving middle-class status out of reach for most. Skyscrapers are pushing African cities upward at the same time that squatter communities are pushing urban slums outward. As Darbon (2014, 19) observes, the rise of a new middle class has corresponded with the rise of "new poverties." Although the poor overwhelmingly favor democracy (Bratton and Mattes, 2001), they are often less concerned about gaining political influence than they are about achieving economic mobility. Their motivations to protest are usually different from those of the middle class, whose material well-being is more assured.

The first part of this chapter describes two macroeconomic trends in late twentieth and early twenty-first-century Africa: income growth and rising inequality within countries. It focuses on the people left behind in the course of economic development, presenting evidence of lingering

poverty and constrained prospects of upward mobility for the majority
of people. The second part documents the emergence and political
marginalization of Africa's new middle class as compared with middle
classes of previous generations. Combined, these first two sections challenge the absolutist perspectives of "Afro-pessimism" and "Afro-
optimism." Current development trends in Africa are both negative
and positive at the same time; it just depends whom you ask.
The chapter concludes with a case for redefining Afro-pessimism and
Afro-optimism to reflect the attitudes of Africans themselves and not just
the assessments of distant onlookers.

"You Can't Eat Growth"

The feature story in the May 11, 2000 edition of *The Economist*
magazine was "The Hopeless Continent." On the cover was a youth
holding a machine gun, superimposed on an outline of Africa.
The article summarized a general consensus among economists and
policymakers: hunger, disease, violent conflict, and dictatorship were
intractable problems in the region. The authors floated the possibility
of United Nations peacekeeping missions giving up on Africa
altogether.

The Economist changed its tune in March of 2013 by publishing
a special feature entitled, "A Hopeful Continent." The report opened
with a scene at an upscale coffee shop on the shore of Senegal where
slave ships once sailed for the Americas. Students lounged while sipping
cappuccinos and reading a newspaper on a tablet computer. They told
the journalist they were optimistic about Africa's chances to escape
problems that seemed so insurmountable thirteen years before.
The article went on to cite encouraging statistics: a spike in foreign
direct investment from $15 billion in 2002 to $46 billion in 2012,
a continent-wide life expectancy increase of 10 percent, and declines
in malaria deaths by 30 percent in some countries.

The scholarly literature on African political economy reflected this
shift from resignation to hope. Before 2013, standard fare in political
science and development economics courses included *The Politics of
Africa's Economic Stagnation* (Sandbrook, 1985), *African Economies
and the Politics of Permanent Crisis, 1979–1999* (van de Walle, 2001),
and *Africa's Stalled Development: International Causes and Cures*
(Leonard and Straus, 2003). Gradually, students became more likely

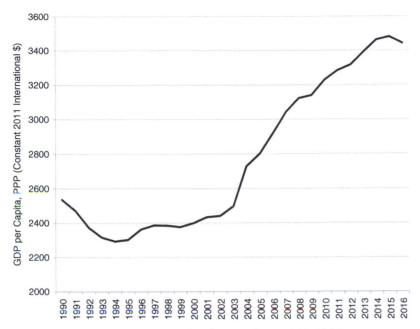

Figure 3.1: GDP per Capita in Sub-Saharan Africa, 1990–2016
Data are from the World Bank's World Development Indicators.

to read *Emerging Africa* (Radelet, 2010), *Africa Emerges* (Rotberg, 2013), and *Yes Africa Can: Success Stories from a Dynamic Continent* (Chuhan-Pole and Angwafo, 2011). Academics and journalists express more optimism about Africa than they have since a brief period in the 1960s when most African countries shed colonial rule.

This optimism seems justified if one considers that total income in sub-Saharan Africa climbed steadily starting around 1995 (Figure 3.1). Region-wide GDP per capita was $2,536 in 1990 and $3,480 in 2015, according to World Bank estimates. There was a slight dip in 2016 to $3,440, but the censored data conceal whether this was a local aberration or the start of a longer-term decline.[1] Regional trends reflect widespread growth at the national level. Only one African country, South Sudan, has recorded negative average annual income growth

---

[1] There is no guarantee that the upward trend will continue, as African economies are susceptible to sudden fluctuations from wars and commodity price shocks (Milanovic, 2016b, 173).

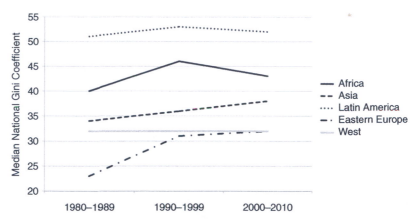

Figure 3.2: Inequality by Region over Time
Data are from the All the Ginis (ALG) Dataset (Milanovic, 2016a). Reflecting data availability, African averages are calculated from 16 sub-Saharan countries in the 1980s, 30 in the 1990s, and 43 in the 2000s.

since the year 2000.[2] Every other country on record has seen at least modest positive growth in per capita income, and many have fared even better. Eighteen African countries grew 3–5 percent each year on average from 2000 to 2016, and fourteen averaged more than 5 percent. Seven countries, including the former war zones of Mozambique and Rwanda, grew more than 7 percent annually on average, putting them on par with the "Asian tigers" of the 1980s (Rispens, 2009).[3]

The hopeful tone in recent publications glosses over the fact that incomes have not been distributed evenly within African countries. Figure 3.2 summarizes changes in median intracountry inequality, measured by the Gini coefficient,[4] over recent decades in sub-Saharan Africa, Asia, Latin America, Eastern Europe, and the West. The graph does not go farther back than 1980, because very few observations

[2] South Sudan has only been a state since 2011, but its "war-produced economy" (Elnur, 2009, 93) was probably no better before independence than after. Somalia has likely also experienced negative growth, but it does not report income data.

[3] Some fast-growing countries, like Nigeria and Angola, are oil-producing states. Oil can have adverse effects on democracy, peace, and women's rights (Ross, 2012), making income growth a potentially misleading metric of well-being.

[4] The Gini coefficient is the most widely available measure of disproportionality in shares of income across households. It ranges from 0 to 100, with higher numbers denoting higher inequality.

were available for sub-Saharan Africa before then. There are also few observations in any given year, so I summarize data at the decade level. Inequality in African countries increased sharply at the end of the twentieth century. In the 1980s, the median African Gini coefficient was forty. In the 1990s, it rose to forty-six and then fell between 2000 and 2010, but not back to 1980s levels. In absolute terms, inequality remains higher in Africa than in all other regions except Latin America. According to the World Income Inequality Database, six of the most unequal countries in the world are African: Lesotho, South Africa, Botswana, Sierra Leone, Central African Republic, and Namibia. This trend extends beyond the distribution of income. Africa is also seeing rising inequalities in education, health, and nutrition (Cogneau et al., 2006; Christiaensen, Demery, and Stefano, 2002; Frankema and Bolt, 2006; Okojie and Shimeles, 2006). Scholars have long acknowledged high inequality in Latin America (Greskovits, 1998), but they have tended to perceive inequality in Africa's largely agrarian societies to be low and of little consequence for poverty reduction (Fields, 2000). Contrary to this assumption, poverty in "emerging Africa" is a problem of distribution and not of production. If incomes were distributed evenly, no African would be poor by the World Bank's standard of living on less than two dollars a day (Firebaugh, 2003, 13).

What causes this "immense chasm between the rich and the poor people in Sub-Saharan Africa" (Karinge, 2013, 437)? A long intellectual tradition links domestic inequality with colonialism, which restricted consumption by the masses (Marx, 1846/1963; Hobson, 1902/1965; Luxemburg, 1913/1963; Lenin, 1916/1999). Geography influenced the intensity of colonial resource extraction, as natural endowments of rich soils and warm climates in some areas gave rise to plantation-style economies – sugar in the Caribbean, groundnuts in West Africa – that impoverished all but a small elite (Sokoloff and Engerman, 2000). Capitalism before and after independence disproportionately benefited Europeans: "the governing class," wrote Fanon (1961/2005, 5), "is first and foremost those who come from elsewhere, those who are unlike the original inhabitants, 'the others.'" Colonial and neo-colonial rule also cultivated an indigenous elite of bureaucrats and "rural aristocrats" (Sklar, 1979; Boone, 1992). After independence, the African governing class extracted large surpluses from primary commodity sales and selectively distributed revenues as patronage (van de Walle, 2009).

An alternative explanation for inequality is corruption (Karinge, 2013; Acquaah-Gaisie, 2005). Transparency International rates African countries as some of the most corrupt on earth (Transparency International, 2012). Corruption in Africa tends to be of the disorganized, decentralized type that creates uncertainty and economic inefficiency. It is also linked with inequality. A one-point bump in the Corruption Perceptions Index is associated with a seven-point increase in the Gini coefficient (Gyimah-Brempong, 2002, 186).

Rising inequality in countries around the world discredits the long-accepted Kuznets theory, which predicted that inequality would decline as countries got richer. Contemporary economists argue instead that inequality stems from economic growth itself (Milanovic, 2016b). The logic is as follows: when the average income in a society is extremely low, as in much of Africa during the twentieth century, increasing inequality would require elites to hoard enough economic surplus to drive the lowest-income people below the point of starvation. As the average income grows, more "space" opens for the rich to capture surplus while the majority lives hand to mouth. Inequality in Africa has room to creep even higher than current levels, especially in richer countries with larger unclaimed surpluses. Take South Africa, with a Gini coefficient of 57.3 and a GDP per capita of $13,225 ($8,508 above the regional mean). There, elites have extracted only about two-thirds of the maximum feasible Gini coefficient of 90.8, meaning the highest inequality under the condition that no person has an income lower than subsistence (Milanovic, Lindert, and Williamson, 2007).

No matter the origins of inequality, most Africans have enjoyed few tangible improvements in their living conditions even while aggregate economic activity expands. "You can't eat growth," goes a popular saying in West Africa.[5] A jump in national income of 10 percent translates into a decrease in poverty of 35 percent under conditions of perfect equality but a decrease of only 4 percent at a moderate level of inequality (Gini ≈ 40) (Fosu, 2008). That is because unequal access to health, education, credit, and insurance traps people at the bottom rungs of society (Fanta and Upadhyay, 2009; Ravallion, 1997). Poverty-growth elasticity, meaning the percent change in poverty rates for

---

[5] Nor can you eat the physical infrastructure that growth allows governments to buy. Variations on the saying in Bamako, Mali include, "You can't eat a monument," and "You can't eat a bridge."

a given percentage of economic growth, is less than 10 percent in Central African Republic and Sierra Leone (Fosu, 2008, 565). In Kenya, Nigeria, and Tanzania, real expenditures among the poorest decile of the population fell between 1983 and 1991 despite reduced poverty nationwide (Demery and Squire, 1996).

For a minority of Africa's population, economic growth has been a ticket to higher education, stable employment, and material comforts. As the next sections describe, improved economic status imbued this nascent middle class with a desire for political influence that incumbents are often reluctant to concede. But having a say in policies and institutions is a lower priority for subsistence farmers and the "informal proletariat" in ballooning urban slums.[6] Economic growth has not eradicated hunger and disease, and there is no guarantee that replacing an autocrat with a democratically elected leader will solve those predicaments. It is apparent in Africa's rural hinterlands and poor urban neighborhoods that most boats do not rise with the tide. Such a climate gives ordinary people ample reasons to join protests. They do not necessarily protest against inequality, per se – indeed, Chapter 6 shows perceived inequality to have relatively weak ties to protest participation. Rather, protesters may express a variety of grievances about material conditions that emerge in an unequal society, including low expectations of upward mobility.

Mixed Blessings for the Middle Class

The Westgate mall in Nairobi was literally a playground for Kenya's rising middle class. Crime and crumbling infrastructure in the city limited the number of green parks and safe public spaces for children. The upscale shopping complex, located where tin-roofed houses once stood, served as an oasis for well-to-do parents to meet for coffee and host family play dates. On any given Saturday, Kenyans and expatriates queued up to purchase the latest Apple products. Riding the escalators or browsing racks of designer clothes, it was easy to forget that this was Nairobi and not San Francisco.

---

[6] The informal proletariat is "the sum of own-account workers minus professionals and technicians, domestic servants, and paid and unpaid workers in microenterprises" (Portes and Hoffman, 2003, 54). See Davis (2004) for more on this concept.

Rocket-propelled grenades leveled the mall on September 21, 2013. Somali fighters from the Shabaab extremist group gunned down at least sixty-seven patrons, targeting children. The Kenyan military launched a counter-attack during a four-day showdown that stopped the massacre but could not restore public perceptions of Westgate as a sanctuary from Kenya's political turmoil. Nairobi Governor Evans Kidero vowed to "ensure the mall is restored to its former glory" (Kamau, 2015), but subsequent terrorist attacks and hundreds of casualties across the country stirred outrage about the failure of President Uhuru Kenyatta's administration to improve domestic security (Stewart, 2015). Activists organized an "Occupy Kenya" movement to denounce government inaction, rallying protesters on Twitter with the hashtag #Tumechoka, meaning "we are tired" in Swahili (McConnell, 2014). Nairobi became a stage for several large marches. On February 3, 2015, seven hundred teachers demonstrated in front of the parliament building, beseeching the government to transfer them from posts near the Somali border to safer regions (Odula, 2015).

The middle class in Kenya and elsewhere in Africa has reasons for both hope and fear. On the one hand, there are more economic opportunities available to more people than ever before. Roughly a quarter of Africa's 900 million inhabitants are "middle-class" according to the World Bank's definition of earning between $2 and $20 per day (Rotberg, 2013, 6),[7] and that number is projected to triple by 2060 (African Development Bank, 2014, 3). Although the middle class comprises different proportions of the population in different countries (Figure 3.3),[8] almost every African country has seen increased sales of cars, refrigerators, and television sets in recent years (African Development Bank, 2014, 24).

On the other hand, violence and ineffective governance still trouble large parts of the continent. The extremist groups al-Shabaab, Boko Haram, and al-Qaeda in the Islamic Maghreb terrorize East and West Africa. Electoral violence is common, notably in Kenya in 2007 and

[7] This benchmark is well below middle-class incomes in the United States and other rich countries, which economists usually set at around $13. Nevertheless, an income of $6 to $10 puts a person near the 80th percentile of the income distribution in much of Africa (Banerjee and Duflo, 2008, 6).

[8] The figure uses income data, which does not capture my entire working definition of the middle class as *the stratum of Africans who meet their basic material needs with income from sources outside the state.* However, income data are available for many countries and therefore facilitate a basic comparison.

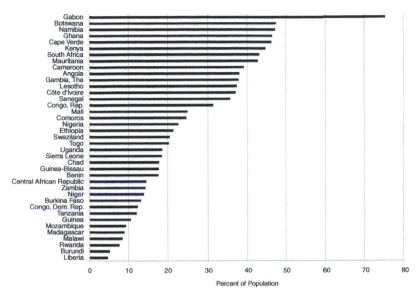

Figure 3.3: Middle Class Population by Country (Measured by Income)
Data are from the African Development Bank (2008). Middle class is defined as
earning a daily income of $2 to $20 per day.

Burundi in 2015. Religious riots have plagued Nigeria and the Central
African Republic. Walled residences and personal security guards cannot provide complete protection from these "public bads" – problems
that seem endless and that touch almost everyone in some way. There is
also plenty to vex the middle class even during times of peace: corrupt
bureaucrats demand bribes (Blundo and de Sardan, 2006); weak property rights prevent entrepreneurs from building economies of scale
(Keefer and Knack, 2002); and democratic backsliding denies citizens
a say in government (Kapstein and Converse, 2008).

Clients Become Capitalists

These problems are not new, and neither is the presence of a middle
class in Africa (West, 2002). What is new is the tendency of university
graduates, professionals, and entrepreneurs to challenge leaders who
fail to provide solutions. Up until the late twentieth century, the African
middle class was smaller and comprised mainly of people on the
government payroll whom incumbents co-opted into ruling cadres.

With support from Western donors, state-driven development schemes like import-substitution industrialization squeezed most private enterprises from the economy (Meier and Steel, 1989). Salaried jobs were scarce outside of parastatal firms, as most private economic activity was informal and agricultural. Employment growth in the formal sector contracted during the 1970s in every African country that kept records (Becker, Hamer and Morrison, 1994). State-centric economic policies hit some countries especially hard. Cameroon's annual employment growth rate halved in the 1970s from about 3 percent to less than 1.5 percent. Even Côte d'Ivoire, which initially had one of the strongest post-colonial economies, saw a decline in jobs growth from 6.6 percent to 2.9 percent (Becker, Hamer and Morrison, 1994, 137).

With private sector opportunities dwindling, universities attracted more young people seeking civil service careers. Rural families who sacrificed to afford tuition hesitated to denounce government employers who wrote their children's paychecks, despite urban-biased policies that devastated farmers, such as crop price ceilings and overvalued currency (Bates, 1981). Graduates were equally strategic with their political allegiances. When General Yakubu Gowon began drawing up plans to reconstruct Nigeria after the Biafran War in 1970, "academicians began to present well researched papers pointing to the fact that military rule was the better preferred since the civilians had not learned any lessons sufficient enough to be entrusted with the governance of the country" (Ayittey, 2006, 428). Middle-class Africans, for the most part, did not bite the hand that fed them.

State leaders co-opted the bourgeoisie along with intellectuals and the working middle class. People who owned means of production, some of whom spearheaded anti-colonial efforts, lost their political autonomy soon after independence. Single-party rule was the dominant form of government from the 1960s through 1980s, which allowed party bosses to control banking almost completely (Arriola, 2013a). The state was the sole purveyor of credit, capital, and subsidies. Capitalists, albeit free from discriminatory colonial policies, relied financially on post-colonial incumbents. They behaved as rentiers, drawing their income from "trading in state-controlled markets, business activity carried out under state-created monopolies, obtaining government contracts awarded on a non-competitive basis, bribes and kickbacks" (Boone, 1998, 188). They tended to invest their income in non-productive activities like real estate, because official regulations discouraged other forms of investment and limited returns on private capital (Boone, 1998, 191). Civil servants provided contracts, loans, and subsidies in exchange for political support. This bargain was a good deal for patrons and clients alike, as it avoided costly repression.[9] Economic and political elites were so intertwined that scholars started referring to them collectively as the "state class" (Keller, 1991a) or the "political class" (Boone, 1998). At one point in Cameroon, 79 percent of business managers had previously served as high-ranking government ministers (Ngayap, 1983).

Before the 1990s, both wage-earning and business-owning members of the African middle class mostly accepted the status quo, because they owed their material well-being to the non-programmatic distribution of goods. This reflected deliberate tactics by leaders of the time. Daniel arap Moi, who served as Kenya's president from 1978 to 2002, used bribes to induce opposition members to defect to the ruling Kenya African National Union (KANU) (Holmquist and Ford, 1994). KANU officials promised patronage to citizen groups or formed their own "popular" associations to mobilize votes (Tripp et al., 2009, 84). In Senegal, the administration of Léopold Sédar Senghor doled out loans to members of the Socialist Party and demanded repayment only from the least loyal (Boone, 1992). Julius Nyerere of Tanzania dismantled the Tanganyikan Federation of Trade Unions in 1964 and absorbed workers' organizations into the state bureaucracy (Friedland, 1969). For almost thirty years, the middle class remained a "hapless bystander as government after government transitioned to one form or another of autocratic rule" (Lofchie, 2015, 38). Incumbents avoided pressures at home and from abroad, as Cold War rivalries led foreign powers to grant practically unconditional aid to their African allies.

When the Cold War ended, so did the West's justification for backing autocrats. Bilateral and multilateral donors started insisting that recipient governments legalize opposition parties, loosen control of banks, and privatize parastatal companies. Cash-strapped leaders had no choice but to comply with structural adjustment programs. They sold off state-owned industries, often to foreign buyers (Ariyo and

---

[9] Some rulers preferred repression over co-optation. For example, Zimbabwean president Robert Mugabe ordered the repeated jailing and beating of opposition leader and former industrial plant supervisor Morgan Tsvangirai until finally allowing Tsvangirai to become prime minister in 2008.

Jerome, 1999). Nineteen countries instituted multi-party politics and adopted tighter constraints on executive authority between 1990 and 2000.

Not all regimes liberalized to the same extent; leaders of more aid-dependent countries had less leverage to maintain their grips on power (Arriola, 2013a). In general, though, political and economic liberalization advantaged the business-owning and wage-earning segments of African society. The amount of domestic credit available to the private sector, and therefore to political entrepreneurs and coalition formateurs, rose considerably when structural adjustment accelerated in the 1980s and 1990s (solid line, Figure 3.4). It remained high, notwithstanding sporadic dips following shocks like the September 11th terrorist attacks and the financial collapse of 2007–2008; a post-collapse slump looked to be slowing or even reversing as of 2016. The increase in credit from banks, denoted by the dashed line, indicates reduced state discretion over issuing loans. Investment patterns changed in response to credit availability. Young African entrepreneurs started directing private capital into productive enterprises (Konings, 2011), distinguishing themselves from the rentiers of earlier generations who consumed more than they invested (Boone, 1998).

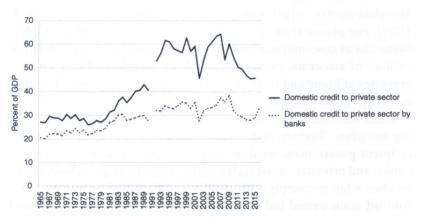

Figure 3.4: Domestic Credit to the Private Sector in Sub-Saharan Africa, 1965–2016
Data are from the World Development Indicators (2017). No data are available for 1991 or for domestic credit to the private sector in 2016.

Private sector growth also transformed the job market. Across Africa, the share of employment comprised of work in private firms rose from 20 percent to 24 percent between 2000 and 2009 (Strode et al., 2015, 89). This is not a dramatic change, but it is larger than the 1.4 percent increase during the 1990s. Economists consider having a steady, well-paid, and salaried job as the most important difference between the middle class and the poor (Banerjee and Duflo, 2008, 19).

Fluctuating employment patterns had political consequences. In the short term, workers protested over losing their jobs from the sale and downsizing of parastatal firms (Rachleff, 2001). Pressure from the United States, the World Bank, and the International Monetary Fund forced incumbents to scale back bureaucracies that were bloated from decades of clientelistic hiring practices. International advisors encouraged African policymakers to embrace free markets and dismantle marketing boards (institutions left over from colonial times that empowered the state to set prices for agricultural products). Conditionalities compelled leaders to end their longstanding habit of underpaying farmers for crops as a way of subsidizing urban food prices. Economic liberalization was initially painful for a middle class built on patronage and urban bias.

But in the long term, the middle class flourished. Domestic investors were finally able to accumulate private capital, which they began using to fund competitive party coalitions in former single-party strongholds like Kenya and Zimbabwe (Arriola, 2013a; LeBas, 2011). Taylor (2012) cites several cases of African "cronies gone good." For example, Burkinabè businessman Seydou Idani overcame his reputation as an inveterate rent-seeker[10] to found the profitable Nouvelle Espace Technologies, which earned praise from the Peace Corps and the Lion's Club. Liberalization interrupted African leaders' discretion to set prices and allocate credit, terminating old bargains with clients (Lofchie, 2015; Arriola, 2013a; Becker, Hamer, and Morrison, 1994; Bates and Block, 2013). Intellectuals, business owners, and salaried professionals subsequently became the engines behind opposition movements, biting the hand that no longer fed them (Cheeseman, 2014; Fichtmüller, 2014).

---

[10] The World Bank investigated him in 2004 for colluding with corrupt Bank officials to award contracts on a no-bid basis in Senegal, Burkina Faso, and other countries.

Hapless Bystanders No More

The realignment of the middle class with opposition movements involved organizing protests and not just financing political parties. In regimes where multi-party systems are still new and unpredictable, opposition leaders commonly fall back on a form of contentious action with a longer record of effecting change in Africa: mass mobilization. Policymakers and political scientists studying democracy tend to focus on electoral rather than non-electoral politics to the point of perpetuating what Schmitter and Karl (1991) call an "electoral fallacy," equating democracy with elections. But in many African countries, citizens' ability to influence policies and institutions historically rests on actions in the streets, not in the polling booths (Bratton and van de Walle, 1997). Financing parties is just one option in an activist's repertoire of political behaviors. Another choice, and often the more obvious one in an African context, is starting a protest. The M23 social movement in Senegal, which challenged President Abdoulaye Wade's bid for a third term in 2011, had a budget of $115,000 for expenses ranging from transporting protesters to printing T-shirts (Demarest, 2016, 70). White-collar Nigerians who made their fortunes in banking, telecommunications, and entertainment were prominent in the Occupy Nigeria movement of 2012 and the #BringBackOurGirls social media campaign of 2014 to recover 276 girls who were abducted by the terrorist group Boko Haram (Orji, 2016). Middle-class realignment during the twenty-first century was not limited to Africa. In Russia, middle-class professionals from the private sector became significantly more likely to mobilize against electoral fraud than their counterparts who remained in the state sector (Rosenfeld, 2017).

Political and economic liberalization in Africa did more than provide outlets for latent middle-class grievances. Ruling-party loyalists turned into opposition leaders in part because the nature of their most salient grievances changed. The ability to accumulate private capital and invest in productive activities not only released the middle class from patronage arrangements; it sped up economic growth and provided more lucrative sources of income relative to government rents. Put simply, the struggle for survival became less pressing to this minority of the African population. In a survey of middle-class Ugandans, Fichtmüller (2014) found that nearly two-thirds of respondents had no confidence in political leaders and that less than 20 percent voted for the ruling party. Most felt no sense of obligation to a government whose health and education services they did not use anyway.

Consider as well South Africa, which went from having zero black-run corporations listed on the Johannesburg Stock Exchange in 1990 to almost 10 percent black-run corporations in 1996 (Handley, 2008). After apartheid ended in 1994, institutions such as the Foundation of African Business and Consumer Services, the National African Federated Chambers of Commerce, and the Black Economic Empowerment Commission stepped up efforts to privatize the economy to the benefit of black citizens. The Conference for a Democratic South Africa, which was established to negotiate the transition to democracy, pledged to guarantee the independence of the South African Reserve Bank. Leaders of the rising African National Congress party attended executive training courses held by international financiers, economists, and business professors. Economic privatization and Africanization were controversial and imperfect; the benefits were concentrated in a small segment of society. Nevertheless, investor confidence soared near the turn of the century (Handley, 2008, 77). For the first time, business "was not dependent on the government for its profitability and there was very little overlap between the country's political and economic elites ... [B]usiness occupied an 'autonomous [economic] sector, an area of political and economic significance which is beyond the reach of the state'" (Handley, 2008, 93). Private income let the middle class become a more outspoken critic of government. President Thabo Mbeki published a letter on September 10, 2004 in his party's newsletter, *ANC Today*, accusing business people of "bad mouthing our country" and spreading rumors about political risk:

All of us are aware that business in our country has flourished in the last ten years, our First Decade of Liberation. The reality is that business people in our country have never had it so good. It has therefore been difficult to understand why important business people would continue to hold and communicate negative views about our country, regardless of the actual and real situation in the country, which they know very well, and from which they benefit handsomely (Mbeki, 2004).

The incredulous Mbeki failed to draw a connection between prosperity and middle-class autonomy to speak out against the regime. White-collar professionals in contemporary Africa are both more independent from state power and richer than the rentier class of the 1960s through 1980s. No longer preoccupied with meeting their basic material needs or chasing state patronage, middle-class Africans have started pushing more politicized agendas. Another example is Women in Nigeria (WIN), founded by a group of academics in 1982. WIN became increasingly militant as it asserted financial independence from the state, funding its activities through private grants, membership fees, and the sale of publications and T-shirts. It joined with sympathetic organizations to launch a media campaign for protesting human rights abuses under military rule and helped achieve a return to civilian government in 1999 (Tripp et al., 2009, 84). Tripp et al. (2009) elaborate on additional cases of "new African women's movements" that became progressively outspoken toward the turn of the twenty-first century.

Figure 3.5 illustrates a shift in the grievances or protest organizers. The solid line denotes the percent of annual protests surrounding

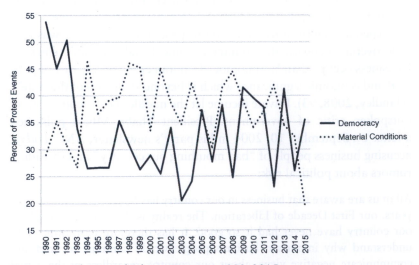

Figure 3.5: Themes of African Protests, 1990–2015
Data are from the Social Conflict in Africa Database (Hendrix and Salehyan, 2015). The solid line denotes the percent of protests surrounding democracy and related issues (elections, human rights, etc.); the dashed line denotes the percent of protests surrounding material conditions (economy, jobs, subsistence, etc.). Other protest categories not shown. Average number of protests per year is 231 (standard deviation = 74).

democracy and related issues (elections, human rights, etc.); the dashed line denotes the percent of protests surrounding material conditions (economy, food, subsistence, etc.). Data are from the Social Conflict in Africa database (Hendrix and Salehyan, 2015). Coders used news reports to identify the main issue of each demonstration, riot, or strike,[11] so the theme of a given event does not necessarily reveal the motivations of the majority of demonstrators, but rather those of people who led the protests and acted as spokespeople. Democracy was the dominant themes of protests in the early 1990s at the height of the pro-democracy movement (the second wave). Once democracy became more widespread around 1994, economic issues increased in relative salience and remained the focus of popular mobilization for about a decade. Protest themes were more mixed after 2005, and there was an overall drop in the percentage of uprisings surrounding material conditions.

These patterns reflect social and economic changes in the twenty-first century. The middle class has expanded to include many *nouveaux riches* who have never derived their wealth from patronage or state employment. They lack nostalgia for the clientelist single-party era and are sometimes willing to challenge leaders they perceive as violating democracy (Ayittey, 2006).[12] Ayittey (2006, xx) calls this cohort the "cheetah generation":

They do not relate to the old colonialist paradigm, the slave trade, nor Africa's post-colonial nationalist leaders such as Kwame Nkrumah, Jomo Kenyatta, Kenneth Kaunda, or Julius Nyerere. The cheetahs know that many of their current leaders are hopelessly corrupt, and that their governments are ridiculously rotten and commit flagitious human rights violations. [...] Unencumbered by the old shibboleths over colonialism, imperialism, and

---

[11] In total, the database includes fourteen categories of issues. I collapsed them into three categories: democracy, material conditions, and other. To avoid clutter, Figure 3.5 does not display the percentage of protests in the "other" category. I highlight democracy and material conditions because they are the issues most commonly cited as reasons for African protests.

[12] I do not want to give the impression that all middle-class people become protest leaders. In societies around the world, only an exceptional few people choose to invest their time, money, and emotional energy into mobilizing protests. The new middle class may be especially risk averse, a condition known as "panic theory" (Rallings, 1978; Fichtmüller, 2014). See Chapter 4 on what distinguishes protest leaders.

other external adversities, they can analyze issues with remarkable clarity and objectivity.

When incumbents show signs of reneging on democratic bargains – for instance, by amending the constitution to become president for life – the "cheetah generation" is not afraid to speak out. Popular uprisings unseated leaders in Niger in 2010 and Burkina Faso in 2014, both times after the president tried to stay in office beyond constitutional term limits; similar drama unfolded in Burundi and Congo in 2016. Constitutions may be constraining African executives more than ever before, but democracy is still far from certain in most cases (Posner and Young, 2007; Cheeseman, 2015). Maikoul Zodi is employed as a teacher but also organizes the Niger chapter of a transnational social movement called Tournons La Page (Let's Turn the Page). He describes his campaign as "the expression of a generation concerned about the future of Africa, which today is fragile and humiliated by dictatorships and a façade of democracy" (*ActuNiger*, 2017). There is little evidence in Figure 3.5 to suggest that improving the economy is the primary goal of most protest leaders in contemporary Africa. Instead, as I detail in Chapter 4, activists like Maikoul Zodi prioritize strengthening democracy.

By underscoring the political impetus for middle-class mobilization, I loosely echo the argument of Ansell and Samuels (2014, 7): "Typically, economic development brings about the rise of new economic groups, whose members are wealthier on average and who have growing economic interests to protect, but who lack political rights. Given their precarious political position, these rising elites will invest in changing the political regime, in an effort to rein in its expropriative authority." However, I advance a slightly different theory of middle-class protest leadership not requiring us to assume, cynically, that the middle class pursues democracy only as a tool for economic expropriation. My interviews with dozens of African protest leaders leave the impression that the middle class includes some sincere democrats who use their economic privileges to pursue a more just system of government. Many, like Abdourahmane Insar of Niger's Action Framework for Democracy and Human Rights (Cadre d'Action Pour La Démocratie et Les Droits de l'Homme, or CADDRH), have served prison time for speaking against the ruling regime. In the short run, at least, they lose, not gain, from their involvement with social movements. Some "pro-democracy" militants probably seek to enrich themselves, but according to Afrobarometer surveys, Africans tend to value democracy for intrinsic and not instrumental reasons (Bratton and Mattes, 2001).

Historical anecdotes indicate a long-term change in the grievances of African protest leaders from economic to political. The ousting of Ghanaian president Hilla Limann in 1981 focused on populist economic demands. Coup plotter Jerry Rawlings seized power after leading students and workers in protests that eroded Limann's legitimacy. Rawlings was the son of a chemist and graduated from the elite Achimota School in Accra, which produced three other Ghanaian heads of state. Despite this middle-class pedigree, he staffed his administration with radical leftists and implemented redistributive economic policies until the start of Washington-prescribed market reforms in the late 1980s (Haggard and Kaufman, 2012, 510). Income per capita temporarily spiked when Rawlings devalued the cedi and boosted subsidies to the coca industry, but economic grievances flared once more when growth slowed. Rioting over cuts to student loans shut down universities nationwide for four months in 1989, and Rawlings faced multiple coup attempts for complying with World Bank austerity measures and seeming to betray the populist revolution (Federici, Caffentzis, and Alidou, 2000). Critics of the ruling People's National Defence Council stressed economic woes. Ghana represented a regional trend: opposition protests across Africa in the 1980s commonly took on anti-austerity themes (Walton and Seddon, 1994).

In contrast, African coups of the early twenty-first century have centered more on constitutional democracy. Chrysogone Zougmoré is a lawyer who became a spokesperson for the movement to thwart President Blaise Compaoré's 2014 bid for re-election in Burkina Faso. He left no doubt in a statement to the press that democracy was his primary concern: "any project that has as its aim to allow Blaise Compaoré to rule for life poses a serious threat to the peace and democratic freedoms of our country. Compaoré's mandate comes to an end in November 2015 and he will have to leave" (Penny and Bonkoungou, 2014). Likewise, opposition leaders in Niger chose the Constitutional Court as a symbolic venue for assembling thousands of citizens to protest against the regime of Mamadou Tandja in 2009. Tandja dissolved the Court in a last-ditch attempt to circumvent term limits. Attorneys responded with a 24-hour strike, propelling two months of demonstrations in the capital. As in Burkina Faso, there was little question about the main grievances of the mostly middle-class protest organizers who declared themselves democratic revolutionaries.

These examples seem consistent with recent critiques of a classic thesis advanced by Acemoglu and Robinson (2006), Boix (2003), and others, which states that protests – and eventually regime change – are a function of preferences for redistribution. Testing this theory with a novel dataset, Haggard and Kaufman (2016) find only half of democratic transitions from 1980 to 2008 to contain elements of distributive conflict. Rather, mass mobilization "appears to hinge on political factors: how exclusionary or co-optive authoritarian regimes are and the extent to which publics are capable of mobilizing grievances into the political arena" (Haggard and Kaufman, 2016, 3).[13]

Haggard and Kaufman ran into difficulties when trying to code a number of African cases for the presence of distributive conflict. One source of ambiguity was the class composition of protests: "protest included or was even dominated by middle and in some cases upper-middle-class groups, calling into question the class dynamics of the model even if we allow for cross-class coalitions including the poor" (Haggard and Kaufman, 2016, 46). For instance, demonstrations in Niger under the regime of General Ali Saibou opposed structural adjustment programs but involved very few poor people. Opposition emanated mostly from civil servants who represented only about 6 percent of society. While coding cases, Haggard and Kaufman also struggled "to separate redistributive demands from grievances that focused on generalized dissatisfaction with authoritarian incumbents, issues such as poor economic performance and corruption or nationalist claims." They were unsure whose grievances among the many in a crowd ought to define what a protest is "about."

In the remainder of this book, I offer solutions for both of the above challenges of interpreting mass mobilization in Africa. First, I chart the class composition of African protests over time and document how protest coalitions gradually became more inclusive. Second, I dissect the multiple grievances motivating people to initiate and participate in protests, and estimate which are most salient. Chapter 4 shines a light on

---

[13] See Ansell and Samuels (2014) for another critique of the distributive conflict thesis.

the regime-related concerns of middle-class protest leaders; Chapters 5 and 6 reveal that economic motivations dominate among the poor. In other words, protests can be distributive *and* political at the same time. Haggard and Kaufman may have puzzled over African protests because they used the following criterion for coding distributive conflict: "The mobilization of redistributive grievances on the part of economically disadvantaged groups *or* representatives of such groups (parties, unions, NGOs) posed a threat to the incumbency of ruling elites" (my emphasis). We fail to see the full picture of social movements when we amalgamate the often divergent mindsets of generals and foot soldiers of the revolution.

Conclusion

Commentary on Africa's economic growth of the last twenty years often conveys optimism and pessimism on the same page, from one sentence to the next. World Bank chief economists Chuhan-Pole and Devarajan introduce *Yes Africa Can: Success Stories from a Dynamic Continent* (2011) with this ambivalent message: "[…] the prevailing discourse on Africa's economic development has shifted from *whether* the region will develop to *how* the region is developing. Yet, there are still causes for concern" (Chuhan-Pole and Devarajan, 2011, 1). They proceed to list grim statistics about infrastructure deficits, pandemic disease, and weak democracy. Policy analysts, donors, and development personnel are simultaneously hopeful about Africa's rising GDP per capita and worried about ongoing problems. Research on African political economy of development has become a tug-of-war between so-called "Afro-optimism" and "Afro-pessimism."

African intellectuals criticize this debate for ignoring or even vilifying African experiences while valorizing Euro-American engagements with Africa (Zeleza, 2006). Western assessments of Africa's trajectory can help us understand aid flows, American and European foreign policy, or the investment decisions of multinational corporations. However, the optimism and pessimism of non-Africans cannot explain the timing and scale of Africa's third wave of protest. This book focuses on two dependent variables: 1) why some people in Africa start protests and others do not; and 2) why some people in Africa join protests and others do not. Explaining those outcomes requires paying attention to the optimism and pessimism of Africans themselves, who experience varying degrees of material want and well-being.

This chapter outlined the economic and political circumstances of people in contemporary Africa – those who have benefited from economic growth as well as those who have been left behind. It makes a step toward shifting the center of analysis from foreign opinions about Africa's political economy to Africans' own perceptions. Economic growth and market liberalization have engendered substantial material gains for the middle class, but not commensurate gains in political power. For the poor majority, inequality precluded any major improvements in daily life. The remaining chapters show how these disparities influence Africans' desire and ability to launch or join protests.

4 | *Comparative Protest Leadership: Theories, Trends, and Strategies*

"By mobilizing the masses ... the Y'en a Marre movement raised mixed emotions: hope and fear, attraction and distrust, admiration and suspicion. In any event, the passion that it stoked left no one indifferent." – Savané and Sarr (2012, 6)

In 2015, the physical infrastructure of Senegal's seaside capital city offered constant reminders of the protests that helped thwart President Abdoulaye Wade's bid for an extra-constitutional third term in 2011. Nearly every public wall, expressway overpass, and monument bore spray-painted messages such as "*Je vote Macky 2012*" in support of Macky Sall, the opposition candidate who defeated Wade in a run-off to become Senegal's fourth president. The paint still looked fresh when I visited Dakar three years after the election. Opposition slogans covering the barriers of the congested "VDN" boulevard seemed to mock Wade's faded 2012 campaign poster hanging outside the Senegalese Democratic Party headquarters. In the United States and Europe, graffiti are stereotypically associated with gang violence and urban poverty, but in Senegal, political graffiti blanket middle-class neighborhoods like Les Almadies, Mermoz, and Sicap Karack.[1] It is from such neighborhoods that many Senegalese protest leaders hail.

This chapter expands on the previous one by showing how protest leadership works beneath the level of the collective middle class. Rather than viewing the middle class as a unitary actor, I examine how its individual members act as generals of the revolution – how they build cross-class coalitions and inspire the poor to raise their voices. I

---

[1] I define middle-class neighborhoods based on my ethnographic observations of how Dakar residents describe them, supplemented by a focus group that I attended in Dakar on July 11, 2015 about the meaning of the middle class. Neighborhoods with a reputation for being "*classe moyenne*" often feature considerable socioeconomic diversity. See Dimé (2010) and Antoine and Fall (2004) for details on the precariousness and "pauperization" of some middle-class corners of Dakar.

structure my analysis around several related questions: Who, specifically, launches and organizes protests in Africa? How do their socio-economic backgrounds, motivations, and constraints shape their strategies? And why are some instigators of unrest more successful than others at sustaining contentious collective action? I answer these questions by profiling protest leaders – their paths to activism, their rhetoric, and their behaviors. A biographical approach is appropriate because the "schemes of action, perception, and evaluation" that people enact in the streets reflect people's lives *prior* to contentious episodes (Auyero, 2003, 3). I highlight examples from Senegal, a young democracy[2] whose numerous high-profile activists and freedom of political expression[3] facilitated my research in Dakar during the summer of 2015.

Dakar is an ideal location for studying not just Senegalese protest leaders, but also their counterparts from neighboring countries who are attracted to the city through transnational activist networks. Living in the Sicap Karack neighborhood for two months allowed me to embed myself in the communities of people who had recently founded social movements in Senegal and Burkina Faso. Dakar also hosts an assortment of artists and intellectuals who are chronicling Africa's latest wave of uprisings as it unfolds. Filmmakers and scholars granted me access to their works in progress, including unreleased documentary footage and survey data. Newspapers, social media, and archived interviews complemented my ethnographic research. I attempt to balance depth and breadth of analysis. This chapter focuses on Senegal but draws on comparative case studies and field notes from other African countries. I conducted additional interviews with protest leaders in Burkina Faso in 2016, Niger in 2016 and 2017, and Malawi in 2011.

Protest leaders in contemporary sub-Saharan Africa are disproportionately middle-class in terms of upbringing, education, and occupation – even those who say their goal is to serve the material interests of the poor. These generals of the revolution, unencumbered by extreme deprivation of their own, strive for political change in

---

[2] There are many ways to measure democracy, but the popular Polity IV index of regime types classifies Senegal as a democracy starting in the year 2000, when Abdoulaye Wade's Senegalese Democratic Party defeated the Socialist Party that had dominated national politics since independence (Marshall, 2013).

[3] According to Freedom House (2015), Senegal has greater freedom of expression and belief than any African country except South Africa.

regimes they perceive as undemocratic. However, the more successful generals downplay their ideological motivations and appeal to bread-and-butter concerns of the masses. They use their entrepreneurial skills of communication, recruitment, and management to forge cross-class alliances that sustain participation and a good public profile. In contrast, protest leaders who concentrate on political issues tend to alienate the poor and become co-opted into state cadres. A comparison of protest waves across history suggests that recent uprisings have grown larger and more frequent due to the emergence of a middle class in the true sense of the term – one that is neither extremely poor nor a part of the established elite that derives its wealth from state patronage. Members of this stratum initiate protests in response to political shocks and then enlist crowds by attending to chronic economic hardships that might not affect them personally. An organizer of the Burkinabè movement Le Balai Citoyen (The Citizen's Broom) stressed, "When big political events happen we address them, but we are fundamentally interested in daily problems."[4]

In the first part of the chapter, I theorize what it means to be a protest leader. I then describe protest leadership trends in Senegal across waves. Original data on protest leaders' public statements from across sub-Saharan Africa indicate that Senegal represents wider patterns in "pro-democracy" activism. Finally, I analyze the success and failure of mobilization strategies in a trio of cases: Le Mouvement 23 Juin (The June 23rd Movement, or M23) and Y'en a Marre (Fed Up) from Senegal, and the Ufungamano Initiative from Kenya.

What Makes a Protest Leader?

Heads of state are reelected, coaches of sports teams memorialized, and business managers promoted based on their ability to improve conditions for their citizens, athletes, and shareholders. The last part of this chapter will address what makes a protest leader effective, but before getting there it is necessary to define what a protest leader is, apart from how well someone performs that role. The social movements literature identifies three general attributes of a protest leader: visibility, mobilizing behaviors, and professionalization. In short, a protest leader is a decision-maker who spends significant amounts of time organizing

[4] Interview on June 1, 2016.

collective action and representing rank-and-file protesters outside the movement.

Visibility

Visibility (or audibility) means the extent to which an actor is the face (or the voice) of a protest. This criterion relates to the management of "symbolic resources" including public speeches, Facebook posts, slogans, signs, and popular music (Morris III and Browne, 2001, 1), which in Africa are largely the domain of the middle class. A protest leader deploys such resources outside a movement as well as inside, addressing audiences that are variously sympathetic and hostile: "In the one function, that of mobilization, he breathes the fire and brimstone of enthusiastic mission. In the other function, that of articulation, he pours the oil of bargaining, compromise, and the common culture" (Gusfield, 1966, 141). Protests play out in the streets, but protest leaders also negotiate with their targets in order to translate mass mobilization into concrete concessions (Wood, 2000). They act as spokespeople when courting diplomatic and financial support to sustain their movements (McCarthy and Zald, 1977). They speak to mass media, publish manifestos, and go on tour.

Researching for this book, I sometimes struggled to catch protest leaders for meetings in between their frequent public relations trips. While I was in Dakar in 2015, the founders of Y'en a Marre were away in Ouagadougou networking with their comrades from Le Balai Citoyen; while I was in Ouagadougou the next year, a delegation from Le Balai Citoyen left for Dakar to receive the Ambassador of Conscience Award from Amnesty International. Roving protest leaders tend to switch the SIM cards in their phones when crossing state borders, making phone tag a common wrinkle in fieldwork. A head of communications for Le Balai Citoyen explained that international travel is a major piece of his organization's activities. Partnering with activists in other countries lets him circumvent political barriers that prevent the spread of the ideals of democracy and engaged citizenship.[5] For example, the Gambian government would not accept visits from Y'en a Marre due to conflicts with the Senegalese government over trade routes, so representatives of Le Balai Citoyen went on

[5] Interview on June 1, 2016.

their behalf. Being a visible point person allows a protest leader to foster alliances and push an activist agenda in ways that ordinary protesters cannot.

Some protest leaders are so visible as to become synonymous with the movements they spearhead – think Thomas Sankara and Martin Luther King, Jr. This is not to say that they are the only ones facilitating collective action; different types of leadership can occur at multiple levels (Gusfield, 1966). Often, the individuals who mobilize support at the grassroots or behind the scenes – knocking on doors, answering phones, and sorting pamphlets – are critical to a movement's success but go unrecognized. These invisible figures are also more likely to be women.[6] The dichotomy between generals and foot soldiers of the revolution is a convenient tool for simplifying complex protest dynamics, but it risks oversimplifying. Many degrees of involvement lie between the casual protest participant and the vanguard of social and political change.

The coordinator of national resources for Le Balai Citoyen manages the group's central office in Ouagadougou. She explained that the rules for registering a local chapter of Le Balai Citoyen had recently changed in 2016 to require two women per fifteen-member club, but that she remained the sole woman in the core of the organization.[7] Most people who attend the marches, concerts, and community clean-up events that she facilitated were unaware of her efforts. This individual does not "count" as a protest leader according to the criterion of visibility, despite the essential role she plays as an ally of her movement. I stress that my criteria for identifying protest leaders are a way to organize empirical facts, not a normative statement about the best way to arrange any particular group. The reason I include visibility in my working definition is because the visible leaders of a movement have disproportionate influence on how protests are perceived – rightfully or not. If we consider a protest to be "pro-democracy" or "anti-govern-ment," it is probably because of something that a spokesperson said into a microphone at a rally or to a reporter at a press conference. Visibility comes naturally to activists who were celebrities before enter-ing politics, and audibility comes naturally to "men and women of words" (Nasong'o, 2007a, 21). It is no accident that hip-hop artists

---

[6] See Rowe (2006) on protest leadership as a performance of masculinity.
[7] Interview on June 1, 2016.

and journalists became prominent in African social movements of the second and third waves, from Dakar to Dar es Salaam (Fredericks, 2014; Casco, 2006).

Mobilizing Behaviors

Mobilizing behaviors include any action that enables people to come together in the streets. These do not always involve direct contact with potential protesters; they can also work indirectly, when a protest leader makes a first move that triggers a cascade of people asking one another to participate (González-Bailón et al., 2011). A Malawian lecturers' union leader affirmed, "it takes a while to organize protests, but once that current starts, history has shown it cannot be stifled."[8] Chapter 1 listed ways in which protest leaders help the masses coordinate and cooperate. To recap, coordination tactics include disseminating information and providing transportation; cooperation tactics include distributing selective incentives, monitoring free-riders, and maintaining morale. In practice, these tactics take myriad forms. For example:

• **Holding concerts and television or radio shows:** These are more than self-promotional events; they are also occasions to publicly announce the place and time of a demonstration, drum up enthusiasm to participate, and garner sympathy. In a survey the week before a scheduled nationwide vigil in Malawi,[9] 98 percent of three hundred respondents said they knew about the vigil, and 80 percent had heard about it on the radio. Some protest leaders spend thousands of dollars arranging for demonstrations to be televised (Demarest, 2016, 70). They may ask protesters to carry signs written in English to reach a broader public (Sindic and Condor, 2014, 48). Images of repression are one way to galvanize international reinforcement, as in 2009 when U.S. Secretary of State Hillary Clinton rebuked Guinean soldiers who were photographed murdering and raping peaceful protesters in Conakry's football stadium. "When the

---

[8] Interview on August 18, 2011.
[9] This study was a partnership with Kim Dionne, Amanda Robinson, John Kadzandira, and Jimi Adams, in August 2011. The vigil was to commemorate the victims of government repression during protests earlier that year. Surveys took place in Blantyre, Lilongwe, and Zomba.

whole world is watching, that which could normally demoralize a movement's supporters might instead mobilize them further" (Gamson, 1990, 157).

- **Posting on social media:** Motivational messages can convince aggrieved people that change is possible and encourage foot soldiers to withstand setbacks. A July 8, 2016 Facebook update from the Zimbabwean opposition group Tajamuka (We Have Rebelled) read, "[Former president of the Zimbabwe National Student Union] Promise Mkwananzi has been arrested and detained by the ruthless Mugabe regime. We will not stop and tire until prosperity returns to Zimbabwe."
- **Hiring vehicles:** This makes protests accessible to people who live far from the locus of action. An internal document from opposition party leaders in Senegal revealed a budget of 25,500,000 CFA (about 100,000 USD) for cars to transport residents of Dakar's sprawling suburbs into the center of town during the uprisings of 2011 (Demarest, 2016, 70).
- **Giving gifts:** Offering "swag" at a protest can attract participants who would not have attended otherwise. Senegalese politicians hoping to replace President Wade in 2012 provided food, water, and political party paraphernalia at rallies, mainly purchased with private funds (Demarest, 2016).
- **Distributing clothing:** T-shirts emblazoned with unifying slogans help people feel like part of a community. "Our numbers are our might," say the shirts dotting crowds of Le Balai Citoyen supporters. Many supporters of Le Balai Citoyen buy their own shirts for 2,000 CFA each, suggesting that the shirts provide a psychological benefit as opposed to a material incentive to rise up.
- **Showing up to protests:** Joining the crowd displays solidarity with the rank and file. The Selma to Montgomery march of 1965 would not have made as powerful a statement in the American civil rights movement without Martin Luther King, Jr. marching on the front line of 25,000 followers. King knew that participating in protests is a fundamental part of leading them. Contemporary African protest leaders often tweet selfies from the front lines.

According to modern revolutionary theory, leaders contribute the strategy for protests, whereas followers contribute the tactics (Hardt and Negri, 2017). Strategists possess the forethought and intellect to help the masses set aside their impulses for the greater, lasting good; tacticians possess knowledge about the immediate space and time but tend to be shortsighted. Hardt and Negri (2017, 15) thus compare a social movement to a centaur, a mythical being with the head of a human and the body of a beast. As Machiavelli (1532/2005) observed, balancing reasoned authority with animal instincts is necessary for representing the popular will. A protest leader with total power will neglect general interests, but a completely horizontal organization will crumble under a lack of structure. The failure of the Bolshevik vanguard party and the "leaderless" Occupy Wall Street movement attest to the dangers of each extreme.

Professionalization

Organizing protests can be all-consuming. People who drop their normal routines to become full-time organizers exhibit the third criterion of protest leadership: professionalization. McCarthy and Zald (1973) noticed in the 1970s that social movements were changing. No longer were protesting crowds comprised just of people who immediately benefited from resisting the status quo. Rather, the people leading the crowds were career activists who spent considerable time, material resources, and skills assembling nominal supporters who were not all invested in the same goal. Between 1955 and 1975, American scientists struggled to reconcile their employers' expectations of objectivity with their own intensifying opposition to the war in Vietnam. They decided to draw boundaries between life at the lab and life in a radicalizing society, launching new public interest science groups founded on the premise that it is impossible to be both a radical and a scientist at the same time (Moore, 1996). At first, the groups were distinct from professional workplaces, but they began incubating protest leaders who were increasingly specialized in mobilization tactics and more adept at building coalitions beyond the scientific community – in a word, more professional. The trend toward professionalization continued into the 1990s when Meyer and Tarrow (1998, 14) observed that "core activists today support themselves through social change efforts, as organizing becomes a career option and social movement-related organizations differentiate."

Professional protest leadership implies social distance from ordinary protesters, usually in the form of higher education, and savings or a salary that can sustain activism on a full-time or nearly full-time basis. It also entails heightened levels of sacrifice and risk compared with being just one in the crowd. Alternative Espaces Citoyens is an organization in Niger that uses protests, forums, and journalism to "create a society based on equality of human rights and gender rights, concerned with the preservation of the environment, the promotion of youth, and enhancing solidarity among peoples."[10] The director describes the boundaries between him and the pastoral village where he grew up. The only member of his family to attend Western schools, he is "not like most other people" who follow their parents into farming. "It's random that I am who I am today," he says about activism as a vocation.[11]

The face of Le Balai Citoyen is another example of social distance between generals and foot soldiers of the revolution. Serge Bambara (better known by his stage name, "Smockey") was born to a Bissa father and a French mother in what is now Burkina Faso. After building a successful career as a hip-hop artist in France, the political assassination of Burkinabè journalist Norbert Zongo inspired him to return to Ouagadougou (Bellot, 2016). He then took up an activist style of rap that segued into founding Le Balai Citoyen, which was instrumental in toppling the regime of Blaise Compaoré in 2014. With co-founder and fellow musician Sams'K Le Jah, Smockey espoused the philosophies of former revolutionary president Thomas Sankara: self-sufficiency, anti-colonialism, and the integrity of citizens (Smith, 2014). Emphasizing unifying principles made Smockey seem less distant from other Burkinabès, but his distinct social privileges helped him organize a mass movement capable of withstanding an intransigent regime.

Professionalism can go too far, verging on elitism and alienating leaders from the rank and file. In South Africa at the turn of the twenty-first century, labor union organizers started dressing more formally and speaking only standard English instead of pidgin English or indigenous languages (Buhlungu, 2010). A spokesman for the National Union of Mineworkers (NUM) grumbled, "I am a leader by myself. The challenge here at branch level [is that] the members are not trained, they don't have information on how to deal with issues ... some have a literacy problem, some they did not even go to school ... " (Botiveau,

[10] http://www.alternativeniger.net/a-propos/.
[11] Interview on May 26, 2016.

2015, 215). The eagerness of NUM leaders to exhibit a conservative version of professionalism could explain the organization's ultimate decline in membership (Botiveau, 2015). Some leaders of the Congress of South African Trade Unions left the labor movement to use their organizational and communication skills in government positions or private business (Buhlungu, 2010).

Despite the risks of factions and alienation, protests can benefit from having professional leaders at the helm (Hardt and Negri, 2017). Shaffer (2000, 123) found full-time members of environmental groups to be more involved in coalitions than occasional volunteers, because they had more time to nurture relationships. Studying the American pro-choice movement, Staggenborg (1988) noted that activists without day jobs were more likely to preside over financially stable organizations. Professional leaders can also help settle confusion about the credibility of public statements. The Facebook page for the Tajamuka campaign in Zimbabwe reads, "For the avoidance of doubt, #Tajamuka only issues statements through the official channels and the designated spokesperson. #Tajamuka will not issue statements through political parties or individuals." Some foreign donors try to professionalize protest leadership by requiring regular reporting, accurate financial accounting, and transparent project management (Tripp et al., 2009, 101).

Nonprofessional activists, in contrast, are part-time aides who "are compensated for some or all of their time, but are not career activists" (Staggenborg, 1988, 587). They are people like the aforementioned coordinator of national resources for Le Balai Citoyen, who shares the group's mission and lends logistical support but hopes to return to lecturing at the University of Ouagadougou as soon as she finds an opportunity. The communications director of that organization also fits the description of a nonprofessional activist. When I asked whether his position with Le Balai Citoyen is full-time, he replied that he earns his living as a newspaper reporter. "You can integrate your daily work with activism," he maintained.

In sum, protest leaders are more than charismatic public figures; they are skilled community organizers and professional activists with "the material means of power and prestige" (Diani, 2003, 8). Protest leaders emerge not through innate wisdom or courage, but through their position in society (Stutje, 2012; Melucci, 1996). Leader status is hence a function of class status. This is true even in Africa, where class is often assumed to be irrelevant.

Changing of the Guard: Protest Leadership in Senegal across Waves

Senegal is the nerve center of political activism in Francophone Africa, its rulers having relaxed authoritarian bans on public organizing in the 1970s, two decades before most countries in the sub-region.[12] This allowed a robust "culture of protest" to flourish, especially in densely populated Dakar and its suburbs (Sylla, 2014, 23).[13] Dakar is the operating base for Y'en a Marre, a movement that animated the 2011 campaign against Abdoulaye Wade's third presidential term and remained active thereafter. Between 2011 and 2015, Y'en a Marre inspired numerous foreign offshoots: Le Balai Citoyen in Burkina Faso, Ça Suffit Comme Ça (That's Enough of This) in Gabon, Halte au Troisième Mandat (Stop the Third Term) in Burundi, Trop C'est Trop! (Too Much is Too Much!) in Chad, Sauvons Le Congo (Let's Save the Congo) in Congo-Brazzaville, and Filimbi (Whistle) in Congo-Kinshasa (Boisselet and Roger, 2015). Senegal's "yenamarristes" toured Africa to lend expertise and moral support to pro-democracy activists, with their efforts landing several of them in a Kinshasa prison in March of 2015 and sparking a pan-African Twitter campaign to #FreeSylvain, #FreeFred, #FreeYves, and #FreeFilimbiYouth (Roger, 2015). As one Dakarois expressed with both pride and regret, "we don't have oil or other natural resources; all we have to export is our voices."

Y'en a Marre represents a resurgence of protest following a stretch of relative calm. Senegal experienced periods of social upheaval in the twentieth century surrounding fights against colonialism and single-party rule. Unrest then ebbed after President Abdou Diouf instituted a

---

[12] President Abdou Diouf tolerated public organizing seemingly in an effort to mollify groups outside his own weakening Socialist Party (Diop and Diouf, 1990).

[13] Migration from Senegal's struggling agricultural regions makes Dakar seventy-five times denser than the average city in the country, at approximately 12,510 inhabitants per square kilometer as of 2013 UN estimates. New arrivals are so frequent that in 2015 I met some taxi drivers who could not yet navigate well-traveled parts of the city.

multi-party system in 1981,[14] giving rise to new parties that progressively displaced protesters from the political scene. Protests demobilized in the 1980s and early 1990s, although student and labor unions continued to strike for improved study and work conditions (Diouf, 1996, 233). Civic organizations of the time routinely exchanged political support for government favors. Groups did little to hide this fact with names like The Association of Friends of Jean Collin for the Support of President Abdou Diouf.[15]

The demobilizing trend reversed in the years approaching the landmark 2000 national election in which Abdoulaye Wade unseated Diouf to end forty years of Socialist Party rule. Citizens, most of them young and unemployed, took to the streets more frequently and in greater numbers than they had in a generation. The annual rate of major strikes, marches, sit-ins, and boycotts increased 134 percent between 1996 and 2000, from 73 to 171 (Ndiaye, 2013, 465). Disturbances continued for the length of Wade's twelve-year presidency, as people who once staged pro-Wade rallies switched to calling for *Goorgui* (Old Man) to govern better or step down.

The second decade of the twenty-first century saw the rise of Y'en a Marre, M23, Fekke Ma Ci Boole (I Am Involved), Bes du Nakk (A Day Will Come), and many other opposition-leaning movements whose political weapon of choice was public demonstrations. The emergence of these groups "was not a sudden mutation, but another phase in a long tradition of Senegalese participation in modern democratic processes and institutions that began during the French colonial era" (Gellar, 2013, 119). Despite some historical continuity, this new wave of protest activity stood out from earlier waves by virtue of the prominent roles that middle-class musicians, journalists, and businesspeople played in mobilizing the masses around democratic renewal. Below, I chronicle how Senegal arrived at this juncture after two waves of elite-led protests against France and the Socialist Party.

---

[14] This system was formally multi-party, but competition remained limited. Socialists dominated Senegalese politics until the 2000 national elections.

[15] Jean Collin was a former French colonial administrator who became a Senegalese citizen after independence and served in the Senghor and Diouf presidential administrations (Gellar, 2013, 122).

Protest Leadership in the First Wave: Elites Tepidly Resist Colonialism

Rioters left one room untouched when they ransacked the Azalai Hotel Indépendance in Ouagadougou, the capital of Burkina Faso, on October 30, 2014. Their eagerness to topple the authoritarian regime of Blaise Compaoré did not eclipse their respect for a suite where the Senegalese writer and filmmaker Ousmane Sembène used to regularly stay for the biennial Pan-African Film and Television Festival of Ouagadougou.[16] Sembène's cultural importance beyond his native Senegal was among the only points of agreement between Compaoré's now-deposed government and the ardent opposition. Burkina Faso's Minister of Territorial Administration and Decentralization immortalized the late author in 2009 by renaming a section of road in Ouagadougou L'Avenue Ousmane Sembène. School children across Burkina Faso still read Sembène's 1960 classic *Les Bouts de Bois de Dieu* (*God's Bits of Wood*), based on an actual railroad workers' strike that took place in 1945 in what was then French West Africa.

The plot of *Les Bouts de Bois de Dieu* illustrates how protests in colonial Senegal suffered from a lack of middle-class leaders to serve as intermediaries between indigenous elites and the poor. In the novel, railwaymen go on strike to pressure the French government into establishing a *cadre unique*, or a single pay-scale, to replace the hierarchy between African and European workers. This marginalizes peasants and informal-sector merchants, who do not earn regular wages and who resent trade unionists for seeking to assimilate into the French-educated class of *évolués*. The railway strike does not gain broader support or win concessions until the end of the story, when a group of poor women volunteer to march on Dakar in solidarity with the striking workers.

Recounting the true events inspiring Sembène's novel, Frederick Cooper (1996) explains that the French colonial model divided Senegalese society into two main socioeconomic classes: *paysans* (peasants) and *évolués*, or "evolved" Africans who attained French education

---

[16] Interview with a Burkinabè activist on June 22, 2015. Audience members repeated this story at a screening of the documentary *Sembène!* at the West African Research Center in Dakar on June 26, 2015.

and adopted French religious and sartorial customs.[17] Each of these groups served a strategic role in the empire – peasants for generating crop revenues and *évolués* for administering colonial law. French authorities withheld capital from would-be indigenous business owners to maintain a monopoly on textile and groundnut production and prevent independently wealthy nationalists from organizing against the government (Boone, 1992, 10). The middle class was therefore effectively non-existent outside a small community of Lebanese traders (Lofchie, 2015).

The 1945 railway strike is one of the most significant examples of protest from colonial West Africa, because it affected communities all along the 1,287-kilometer rail line between Dakar, in what is now Senegal, to Koulikoro, in what is now Mali. Unlike urban protests that typically escaped notice in the vast hinterlands of French-controlled territory, the strike of 1945 was impossible for people in rural villages to ignore. Railwaymen followed orders from the Indigenous Workers' Union of the Dakar-Niger Railroad (Syndicat des Travailleurs Indigènes du Dakar-Niger, or STIDN) to vacate depot towns and return home to their families while labor negotiations wore on (Cooper, 1996, 95). Peasants shouldered the burden of housing and feeding idle workers who went without pay for five months.

Leaders of the strike showed little empathy for the poor even as they agitated for equality with Europeans. The original architect of the strike, STIDN Secretary General François Gning, was a stalwart of the French Socialist Party and an *évolué* par excellence. He fashioned the STIDN as a politically moderate union that eschewed radical anti-colonial ideologies (Roche, 2001, 103). Gning undermined his own legitimacy by proposing a railway shutdown after refusing to back a 1945 general strike to advance the rights of lower-class and nonsalaried workers. On May 23, 1946, a thousand STIDN members rallied in Thiès, seventy-two kilometers east of Dakar – not against French employers, but against their own Secretary General (Cooper, 1996, 86). Ibrahima Sarr and several other railroad office clerks replaced Gning in the mutiny. Like their predecessor, the new leaders struggled to mobilize collective action beyond union ranks despite being

---

[17] Although French remains the language of state and big business in Senegal, there was a post-colonial revival of traditional dress among Senegalese professionals. President Macky Sall upset journalists by requiring Western-style suits at state press conferences (Interview with a Senegalese member of the Associated Press on July 3, 2015).

relatively more sympathetic to ordinary citizens. The fact remained that the STIDN had shunned the 1945 general strike, which earned the union paltry support from wider society. There are no records of major solidarity protests or attempts to turn the quest for a *cadre unique* into a broad-based social movement. The women's march on Dakar in Ousmane Sembène's novel *Les Bouts de Bois de Dieu* was mere fiction.

A careful reading of history suggests that clashes between rulers and subjects on the eve of Senegal's independence in 1960 were not anti-colonial protests at all, but rather struggles of African elites to improve their standing in the existing colonial social order. Elites formed what Linz (1973, 193) calls a "semi-opposition," advocating for a different emphasis in policy but not long-run regime change. The four communes of Dakar, Saint-Louis, Gorée, and Rufisque had official status as extensions of France according to an 1848 decree of the French Second Republic. Subjects born in the communes who mastered the French language received opportunities to study in Paris and vote in metropolitan elections. Lamine Guèye, one of several Africans to become deputies in the French National Assembly,[18] proposed a law to extend citizenship to all nationals of France's overseas territories. The law known as La Loi Lamine Guèye took effect in 1946. It is telling that protests broke out in Dakar only when a rumor spread that La Loi Lamine Guèye might be reversed less than a year after implementation (Roche, 2001, 69). Leaders of these protests were salaried workers and heads of leftist political parties who had the most to gain from assimilationist legislation. Thus, the expansion of citizenship through the law "did not produce a demand for separation but instead prompted further mobilization for inclusion" (Lawrence, 2013, 114). Gellar (2013, 121) elaborates that "ideological differences and debates over French colonial policy were the concern of the tiny western-educated elite" and that political pacts, not popular uprisings, set the terms for Senegalese statehood.

Generations later, Senegalese society is still coming to terms with the history of collaboration between indigenous elites and French colonizers. Every twenty-sixth day of August marks the anniversary

---

[18] Another was Léopold Sédar Senghor, who ran for the National Assembly at Lamine Guèye's urging and later became the first president of independent Senegal in 1960 (Hymans, 1971).

of a protest in 1958 during General Charles de Gaulle's visit to Dakar. Senegal's capital was one stop on the French president's multi-city tour ahead of a referendum on September 28, 1958 that would present colonial subjects with two choices: immediate independence or continued economic and political ties with the metropole through membership in the new French Community. De Gaulle reluctantly issued the referendum after France suffered heavy losses in World War II that made it economically impractical to maintain a colonial project. The war also produced the diplomatic conditions for African self-rule, as de Gaulle could not as easily justify denying sovereignty to Senegal after his own country celebrated liberation from German occupiers in 1944. Creating the French Community was a strategy for France to preserve its influence in Africa after decolonization, but France's leader first had to convince Africans to join it. Senegalese elites, including Mamadou Dia and Léopold Senghor, anticipated popular support for immediate independence and left Dakar during de Gaulle's stopover in order to avoid an awkward confrontation. Taking advantage of their absence, members of the communist African Independence Party (Parti Africain de l'Indépendance, or PAI) met the French delegation at the Place Protêt ("Protest Place," now the Place de l'Indépendance) with signs reading, "*Diotsarew!*" and "*Momsarew!*" – Wolof phrases both translating roughly to, "Take back our country!" (Seck, 2005, 50). De Gaulle dared the crowd: "hear me now: Let those who want independence seize it on 28 September!" The *porteurs de pancartes* (sign wavers) were a fringe of Senegal's population and suffered a sound defeat in the September referendum. Only decades later did mainstream politicians lionize them. During the 2013 and 2014 anniversaries of the 1958 protest, historians set the record straight on former Gallophiles who changed political stripes (Faye, 2013; Gaye, 2014). Madické Wade, an early PAI militant and ardent *indépendantiste*, inveighed against elites who once backed the "neocolonial" Senegalese Progressive Union (Union Progressiste Sénégalaise, or UPS)[19] for "appropriating this historic day by claiming that they were waving signs at the Place Protêt, without even mentioning the PAI" (Gaye, 2014). "This makes me nauseous," he wrote.

[19] Pro-independence Senegalese labeled the UPS neocolonial for its collaboration with France (Meredith, 2011, 269). The party was unpopular yet had a powerful say in the terms of statehood. This contradiction was emblematic of weak cross-class coalitions in the 1950s.

Prelude to the Second Wave: The Age of Repression

Senegal became independent in 1960 despite elites' tepid resistance to colonialism. Senegalese voted, along with all of the French West African colonies except Guinea, to join the French Community. Afterward, France's military and treasury backed President Léopold Sédar Senghor in implementing a clientelist system that insulated the new regime from protest (Boone, 1990; Brian and O'Brian, 1967). Senghor stacked his coalition, the UPS,[20] with veteran civil servants from the existing *évolué* class. Mimicking French administrators, Senghor focused on stifling the growth of a middle class that might furnish opposition movements with capable leadership. He accomplished this with three approaches. First, he founded credit agencies that nominally promoted private enterprise but issued loans according to political criteria that rewarded the UPS old guard (Boone, 1992). Second, he handpicked loyal Senegalese businessmen to replace French managers of commercial enterprises under the guise of "Africanizing" the private sector (Boone, 1998). Third, he undercut labor unions, which represented the privileged 4 or 5 percent of the population that earned regular wages and had the organizational infrastructure to start opposition movements (Phelan, 2014). The first two approaches – restricting credit and installing businessmen – recycled colonial practices already in place. The third approach departed from the French tolerance for labor organizing. Senghor's hostility toward unions reshaped protests in Senegal during the 1960s by limiting the size, duration, and frequency of strikes. Senghor required all unions to join the National Confederation of Workers of Senegal (Confédération Nationale des Travailleurs du Sénégal, or CNTS) in order to more easily co-opt them into the ruling Socialist Party. The organizing philosophy of the CNTS was "responsible participation," which involved obeying party dictates and transmitting party propaganda.[21] The president denounced

---

[20] The UPS was renamed the Socialist Party in 1976.

[21] Responsible participation became the dominant model for labor unionism throughout Francophone West Africa in the 1960s (Lô, 1987; Phelan, 2014). A few autonomous unions continued operating in secret and staged protests, undeterred by the high risk of government repression. One notable example is the uprising of 1963 in Dahomey (now Benin). Rogue unionists took to the streets to oppose a 10 percent cut in public workers' pay. The state-run General Union of Workers of Dahomey protested in solidarity, setting in motion a coup d'état (Phelan, 2014, 351). Weaker governments like Dahomey's were less able to discipline labor than stronger foreign-backed governments like Senegal's.

as selfish any pleas for workplace reforms. Gains for privileged workers, he argued, "no longer came at the expense of France but rather at the expense of the new nation" (Phelan, 2014, 347). Senghor adopted the same stance toward student unions that advocated for lower tuition fees and higher stipends. He dissolved the Democratic Union of Senegalese Students and used military force to put down campus demonstrations. Violating the strict ban on protesting could result in a penalty of full dismissal from the University of Dakar (Ndiaye, 2000). Co-opting the central labor union and repressing other unions seemed to significantly curb protest activity in the 1960s. There are no comprehensive quantitative data on protests from the period, but numerous qualitative accounts point to the Senghor regime's effective control of labor and student protesters (e.g., Lô, 1987; Ndiaye, 2000; Boone, 1990; Fatton Jr., 1986).

Senghor's formula for single-party dominance was the same one that sustained colonial rule: a two-tiered society comprised of a small co-opted elite, an unorganized lower class, and an absent middle class. Senghor adapted this formula to dominate the agricultural sector, aware that the threat of opposition protests was not confined to cities. He dispensed patronage to rural aristocrats as a way of funneling farm revenues into the state's circular network and not into productive investments that might generate wealth for entrepreneurs (Boone, 1992, 24). Patronage typically consisted of inflated crop prices and salaries for large-scale peanut producers who were powerful Sufi leaders known as marabouts. The marabouts reciprocated by issuing a *ndiguël*, or decree, to their followers to vote for the UPS (Beck, 2008). Senghor was a double minority as a member of the Catholic faith and the Serer ethnic group, so clientelism was also a way for him to appease leaders who held sway over Senegal's majority Muslim and Wolof population. Co-opting and suppressing activists helped the UPS remain Senegal's de facto single party until 2000, even after Senghor allowed limited multi-party competition in 1979 (Osei, 2012, 585).

Protest Leadership in the Second Wave: The Individualist Ethos of Bul Faale

Like many African countries, Senegal implemented structural adjustment in the 1980s with encouragement from the World Bank and the International Monetary Fund. The downsizing of the public sector was swift and painful. The government dismantled rural development agencies, privatized inefficient industries that were nationalized in the 1970s, and liberalized prices. Fertilizer subsidies plummeted from 75,000 tons in 1980–1981 to 22,000 tons in 1987–1988. Purchasing power in cities dropped by 30 percent between 1985 and 1989. Thousands of public sector jobs evaporated through measures to reduce bureaucratic bloat. Researchers from the U.S. House Subcommittee on Africa admitted in a 1989 report to the Foreign Affairs Committee that Senegalese people were suffering from hasty economic reforms (Seissman et al., 1989).

Senghor voluntary resigned in 1981, giving Senegal a gloss of democracy even though Socialist hegemony endured under President Diouf. This created an opening for labor unions to rethink responsible participation and protest structural adjustment. Representatives from 26 unions signed a manifesto a month after Senghor's resignation, entitled "Union Revival." They touted "shared participation" and outlined plans to establish a central union capable of "taking into account the diversity of all people comprising the labor movement, in order to prioritize the collective interests of workers" (Lô, 1987, 72). But the manifesto was difficult to put into practice, because the labor movement was divided between clans of elites that could either "unite or perish" (Diop, 2010, 145). Union leaders set aside their differences barely long enough to militate for concessions from the government, such as ceilings on prices of staple consumer goods and tax exemptions for factories that were under pressure to slash payrolls. Students also went on strike and took to the streets, convincing incumbents to increase scholarships (Seissman et al., 1989, 14). Such actions chipped away at the state's repressive capacity and paved the road for an eventual second wave of protests.

For the time being, though, the largest trade union confederation remained aligned with the ruling party and many students still dreamed of civil service jobs upon graduation. Political limits on credit were stubbornly tight, because the Central Bank of West African States was powerless to monitor credit management, and because Senegalese authorities did not agree to a World Bank audit of the banking system until 1987 (Berthélemy, 1997). This kept the middle class hostage to state and religious patrons. Supporters of the liberal Senegalese Democratic Party (Parti Démocratique Sénégalais, or PDS) rioted over alleged fraud in the 1988 elections, but the Socialists held on to their legislative majority and Diouf won reelection with three quarters of the vote (Creevey, Ngomo,

and Vengroff, 2005, 482). Diouf declared a state of emergency to sup-
press electoral protests and jailed key opposition figures including
Abdoulaye Wade and Amath Dansokho (Young and Kante, 1992, 70).
Co-opted marabouts continued dictating voters' choices through the
ndiguël (Galvan, 2001, 59).

The second wave of protests ignited in earnest in the 1990s, with the
ascent of hip-hop. Rappers Didier Awadi (alias "DJ Awadi") and
Amadou Barry (alias "Doug-E-Tee") used their freedom as political
outsiders to launch a social movement that would challenge Diouf and
the Socialist regime from a new angle. Awadi was born in the posh
Amitié 2 neighborhood of Dakar to schoolteacher parents from Benin
and Cape Verde. Barry was raised in the manicured Liberté 6 precinct
by an Air Afrique employee and a businesswoman. The two began
independently experimenting with hip-hop and break dancing in the
1980s. One of Awadi's first bands was Syndicate, a name that evokes
the French word *syndicat*, meaning labor union. Syndicate battled with
Barry's band, the King MC's, until an impromptu duet at a mutual
friend's birthday party led the former rivals to collaborate and form
Positive Black Soul. The duo went by "PBS," as a play on the acronym
for the main opposition party at the time, the PDS (Le Gendre, 2008).
Their cassette Boul Falé[22] (Don't Worry) debuted to wide acclaim in
1994. The album's American-flavored rhythms and slang made it easy
to forget that unlike American and French hip-hop, Senegalese hip-hop
has bourgeois roots (Havard, 2001, 65).[23]

Foreshadowing his third-wave successors Smockey and Sams'K Le
Jah, DJ Awadi considered himself the spiritual son of Thomas Sankara
and dropped out of university to take on the mantle full time
(Ahougnon, 2016). He and Doug-E-Tee rhymed in Wolof about corruption within the Socialist government and encouraged youth to vote
Senghor's heirs out of office (Mbaye, 2011). In French, they placed
themselves at the center of the fight for democracy: "Salaam, power to
the people / A true democracy / The knowledge of PBS governs the code

---

[22] This is the French spelling of the Wolof phrase *bul faale*.
[23] "People thought we were crazy, trying to be little Americans," recalled Awadi
(Le Gendre, 2008). American-style hip-hop followed a similar progression in
other African countries, starting in the middle class and eventually spreading to
the masses. In Tanzania, the first people to embrace rap during the late 1980s
and early 1990s were the children of well-off families with diaspora connections
(Casco, 2006).

of the rappocracy."[24] In English, they championed anti-colonial ideology: "Haters always try to false my identity / Showin' an African continent ain't no destiny / Don't want black people to live in community / And teachin' white is right, black is wrong and all that."[25]

The members of Positive Black Soul reserved their boldest criticism for the Sufi brotherhood, whose political authority dated back to precolonial times. The power of the *ndiguël*, or religious voting directives, was noticeably weaker in the 1993 presidential election when Diouf won but by a lower margin (58 percent) than in 1988 (73 percent) (Galvan, 2001, 60). At a New Year's Eve rally in 1999, citizens booed the marabout Serigne Modou Kara for endorsing the Socialist Party (Havard, 2001, 76). This signaled Bul Faale's evolution from a rap sensation into an ethos that academics credited with "rewriting the Senegalese social contract" (Havard, 2001, 76). Senegalese philosopher Alpha Amadou Sy characterized DJ Awadi as "an emblematic figure of Senegalese hip-hop … a political animal in the Aristotelian sense of the term, which is to say a social part of governing the Polis, the City" (Sy, 2012, 84). Awadi also reflected politics beyond the polis by exuding an individualism that blossomed around the world after the fall of the Berlin Wall. He expounded on the deeper meaning of Bul Faale beneath the phrase's literal translation of "don't worry": "That basically means 'do things for yourself, be yourself.' It's about taking matters into your own hands" (quoted in Le Gendre, 2008).

No one personified the individualist ethos of Bul Faale more than Mohammed Ndao, a star of traditional Senegalese wrestling who nicknamed himself Tyson after the American boxer Mike Tyson. Captivated with the archetype of the self-made man *à l'américaine*, he was known for entering the competition arena wrapped in stars and stripes, and jumped at chances to recount his journey from rags to the pinnacle of Senegal's nepotistic wrestling hierarchy. He popularized Bul Faale dance moves and the Bul Faale hairstyle (short on the top with three shaved lines) (Havard, 2001).

Ultimately, however, Tyson came to symbolize the limits of Bul Faale's popular appeal and, more generally, of protest leaders who cannot afford to refuse patronage due to their socioeconomic disadvantage. In the 1990s, rap was still a medium that spoke mainly to

[24] From "Président d'Afrique" ("President of Africa") (1995).
[25] From "Return of Da Djelly" (1995).

Senegal's middle class. Lyrics by PBS and other groups focused on political ideologies more than on the daily struggles of the poor; individualist messages suggested that the poor should help themselves. Tyson began to bridge class divides as a Bul Faale icon with humble beginnings, but his economic background also made him vulnerable to political co-optation. He graced billboards selling everything from milk to office supplies and agreed to the Socialist Party using his image to attract young voters in the 2000 presidential election. This led fans to write off Tyson as a traitor, and dimmed Bul Faale's popular appeal even as a presidential win for PDS candidate Abdoulaye Wade interrupted 40 years of Socialist rule.

Diouf buckled under civil unrest as the pains of structural adjustment deepened. In 1994, France caved to pressure from international financial agencies to stop subsidizing the CFA franc (the currency of several former French West African colonies, which was then tied to the French franc and later to the euro). After devaluation, prices of food and medicine doubled in parts of Senegal, and skyrocketing labor costs induced wage freezes. Trade unions representing numerous sectors responded with strikes. Protests by thousands of people turned violent, killing five police officers and civilians (Noble, 1994).[26] Diouf's chief rival rode this wave of activism into power. In the run-up to the 2000 vote, Wade's underfunded campaign used caravans to reach the electorate around the country, mounting amplifiers on trucks and blaring 20,000 watts of popular music to draw enormous crowds of supporters out into the streets (Foucher, 2007). Advocates for *sopi* (change) wore blue, the color of the PDS, and waved their party membership cards as they danced. Senegalese newspapers called these events "blue marches" and portrayed Wade as the people's savior. No candidate won a majority of votes in the first round of the election, but Wade won the second round with 58 percent.

Protesters changed their message soon after turnover. Chants for *sopi* morphed into shouts of "*nopi*" (Havard, 2004). Youths who had rioted against the Socialist Party, braving tear gas and beatings at the hands of the state's Mobile Intervention Group, felt unrewarded for their sacrifices (Dimé, 2014, 16). Wade mismanaged public services

---

[26] The CFA once again became a target for protest in 2017 when Franco-Beninese activist Kémi Séba was arrested and expelled from Senegal for burning a CFA note in an anti-colonial demonstration.

and finances, resulting in frequent electricity outages and urban floods. He commissioned a $27 million African Renaissance Monument that thousands protested as a waste of money. Wade offended his opponents further by trying to position his son, Karim, to succeed him. Karim served as a powerful minister under his father until being sentenced to six years in prison for corruption. Among the tracks on DJ Awadi's 2005 solo album were "Stoppez Les Criminels" ("Stop the Criminals") and "Le Cri du Peuple" ("The People's Cry"). Mass mobilization during Wade's presidency kicked off a third wave of protests in Senegal. This ongoing wave features new actors and a thematic shift from individualism to collectivism.

Protest Leadership in the Third Wave: The Collectivist Ethos of Y'en a Marre

Wade won reelection in 2007 after one round of voting – an outcome that his opponents viewed with suspicion given that polls closed amid a jump in unemployment and a flare-up of secessionist conflict in the Casamance region. Protests did not abate in Wade's second term. Imams in Guédiawaye agitated over deficient public services. Residents rose up in areas affected by the dumping of toxic waste. Students revolted in Kédougou when mining projects failed to generate jobs. Women of the Front Siggil Sénégal opposition coalition marched against "the constitutional manipulation of the PDS." Informal-sector merchants rioted at Dakar's Sandaga market. Arsonists attacked bureaus of the national electricity utility. Hospital workers went on strike (Diop, 2010).

The largest and most publicized protests broke out on June 23, 2011 surrounding Wade's bid for a third term. The president pledged in 2007 not to stand again for reelection but reneged, citing the ambiguous Article 27 of the 2001 constitution limiting a president to two five-year terms. Wade and his supporters claimed that Article 27 did not apply because Wade assumed office the year before the constitution was adopted by referendum (Kelly, 2012). An executive-appointed Constitutional Court authorized Wade's candidacy, precipitating demonstrations around Dakar, including at La Place de l'Obélisque and La Place de Soweto outside the National Assembly. Thousands of demonstrators clashed with anti-riot police (*Le Monde*, 2011). Over several days, citizens ransacked symbols of the state such as government buildings and ministers' homes. At least eight died in the chaos.

Ruling party defector Macky Sall partnered with fellow opposition politicians Moustapha Niasse, Ousmane Tanor Dieng, and Idrissa Seck to create a formal institution for mobilizing the public. He named it Le Mouvement 23 Juin, or M23. Experienced at running political organizations, the statesmen professionalized M23 complete with a general assembly, a coordination committee, a secretariat, and commissions of finance and diaspora relations (Demarest, 2015, 19). They joined forces with the Y'en a Marre movement, which was founded the previous January by three journalists – Fadel Barro, Aliou Sane, and Denise Sow – and three members of the successful rap group Keur Gui – Fou Malade, Thiat, and Kilifeu. M23 and Y'en a Marre agreed to hold a protest on the twenty-third of every month to honor the people's victory on Jun 23, 2011 (Lo, 2014, 33).

Y'en a Marre means "fed up." The movement's leaders conveyed this sentiment in a series of anthems that they produced, performed at rallies, and released into the public domain. The song "Faux! Pas Forcé!" translates literally to "Fake! Forced Step!" and is homophonous with "faut pas forcer," meaning "don't push." It takes Wade to task for failing to uphold his duties as president:

> Abdoulaye! Don't push it!
> I swear! Don't push it!
> Abdoulaye, stay true to your word, I swear! Don't push it!...
> Juggling with the constitution of our mother country/We won't let
>   you get away with it
> We're dealing with an old liar
> We will make you swallow your mistakes ...

Another song, "Daas Fanaanal" ("Sharpen Your Weapon"), inspired a voter registration campaign of the same name. Keur Gui and Fou Malade's verses urged youth to brandish their voter cards as arms to defeat Wade through democratic means:

> The voter card gives you power/Choose and see where to go
> In 2012 shoot a bullet to the thug/ Wake up! You are sleeping/
>   Register for your card
> Move to another level
> Dare to impose your charter
> This is the sound of the alarm/ Sharpen my weapon the night before!

My voter card is my weapon
Sharpen my weapon the night before! It is what is going to wipe my
  tears![27]

If the pioneers of Bul Faale rewrote the Senegalese social contract around
an ethos of self-sufficiency, Y'en a Marre rewrote it anew around an ethos
of citizenship. The yenamarristes promoted their own vision of "a new
type of Senegalese" who would wage a collective fight against "social
injustice, corruption, and bad governance" (Haeringer, 2012). Fadel
Barro, who had by then retired from journalism to concentrate on community organizing full-time, declared as Y'en a Marre's mission to "place
citizens' concerns at the heart of political action" (Cailhol, 2014). This
emphasis on national solidarity constituted a "clear rupture" with the
individualism of Bul Faale (Dimé, 2014, 23). Y'en a marre leaders sought
"a new values system based on individual and collective responsibility
and on citizenship ... which clashed with the cultural nihilism of the Bul
Faale generation" (Awenengo-Dalberto, 2012, 50). In April 2011, a
newspaper noted the symbolism of Mohamed Ndaw Tyson losing a
wrestling match to a sixteen-year-old rookie, Bala Gaye. The headline
read, "Bul Faale is dead! Long live Y'en a Marre!" (Fall, 2011). The
founders of Y'en a Marre were in their thirties, yet by criticizing the
gerontocracy they galvanized Senegal's predominantly young population
to defy the cultural norm of age deference (Lo, 2014, 27). Acting as
"identity entrepreneurs," they managed "to construe themselves, along
with those they wish to mobilize, as part of a common category" of
disaffected youth (Reicher et al., 2001, 186). Thiat and Barro confessed
that they had once militated for Wade's rise to power. Thiat started the
band Keur Gui while on strike with the National Union of Senegalese
Students in 1996 (Thiat and Cissokho, 2011; Haeringer, 2012).
Although he voted for Wade in 2000, he came to see the corrupt PDS
as more insidious than the repressive Socialist Party (Thiat and Cissokho,
2011). Keur Gui was the first hip-hop group in Thiat's home region of
Kaolack to have an album censored for addressing the faults of politicians (Lo, 2014, 29). Barro recalled his own political conversion:

I even remember an anecdote about Abdoulaye Wade. He encountered me
once in Kaolack. It was in 1993. He was campaigning. He found us there; we
were in the process of blocking the route. He gave us 50,000 francs and told

---

[27] Translation from Wolof by Gueye (2013).

us, "Fight. You are on the right track." But unfortunately after his arrival in power he betrayed the entire dream that he represented. He abused turnover. Turnover became a nightmare .... We told ourselves at a certain point: We traded Abdou Diouf for Abdoulaye Wade in 2000, but in the end nothing changed except that things got even worse (quoted in Haeringer, 2012).[28]

The youth of Y'en a Marre and the politicians of M23 were not the only actors organizing protests. A host of other movements emerged around the same time, proclaiming variations on the goals of defending constitutional democracy and improving material conditions for ordinary citizens. Despite subtle differences in their aims, the list in Table 4.1 shows that nearly all the leaders of these groups took an anti-regime stance and had middle-class backgrounds.[29] This profile led onlookers to exaggerate comparisons between uprisings in Dakar and the Arab Spring (e.g., Gopaldas, 2015; Genova, 2012). Some Senegalese protesters reinforced the image of north-south contagion by chanting, "Get out, Wade!" – a version of the slogan from Tunisia's Jasmine Revolution, "Get Out, Ben Ali!"

However, leaders of Y'en a Marre rejected that message. They were adamant that civil disobedience should remain peaceful and that participatory democracy and social justice were bigger issues than a single president's transgressions (Awenengo-Dalbert, 2012, 52). "Today, Tunisia is in flames," Barro remarked. "They have gotten rid of Ben Ali, but have they changed the fundamental system? We think the system is still there and they are in a dead end. It is the same thing in Egypt, and now look what is happening in Libya. Y'en a Marre does not want this kind of solution" (Gueye, 2013, 30). The courtyard of Fou Malade's hip-hop center in Guédiawaye displays murals of Thomas Sankara, Sékou Touré, and Kwame Nkrumah, showcasing the sub-Saharan inspiration for contemporary Senegalese protest leaders (Bryson, 2014, 47).[30] Indeed, several of the movements in Table 4.1 predate the Arab Spring. They arose from the Assises Nationales of 2008 and 2009, a gathering where 140 civil society and political party

---

[28] The idea of continuity across presidents resurfaced in a 2014 track by Keur Gui entitled "Diogoufi" ("Nothing Has Changed"), which targeted the government of Macky Sall.

[29] See Gellar (2013) for details on each movement.

[30] That inspiration is also evident in the names of local clubs comprising Le Balai Citoyen: Club Thomas Sankara, Club Mandela, Club Cheikh Anta Diop, and others.

Table 4.1 *Third-Wave Social Movements in Senegal*

Movement Name	Stated Objectives	Leadership
Y'en a Marre	Reform the political system with citizens' concerns at the center; promote civic education, non-violent protest, and improved living conditions; nurture a "new type of Senegalese" who would be more involved in public affairs; oppose Wade	Journalists Fadel Barro, Aliou Sane, and Denise Sow; rappers Fou Malade, Thiat, and Kilifeu
Le Mouvement Juin 23 (M23)	Defend the constitution and democratic values; oppose Wade	Opposition party leaders, especially Macky Sall, Moustapha Niasse, Ousmane Tanor Dieng, and Idrissa Seck; Alioune Tine, head of the African Assembly for the Defense of Human Rights
Bes du Nakk	Provide moral support to citizens and local government officials protesting high electricity prices and low quality of public services; within the Assises Nationales framework, help opposition parties and civil society unite around a single candidate to run against Wade	Mansour Sy Djamil, a progressive Tijani Sufi marabout who returned to Senegal in 2007 after working for the Islamic Development Bank
Fekke Ma Ci Boole	Oppose Wade, but not in cooperation with the Assises Nationales; raise citizen awareness	Youssou Ndour, a globally renowned singer with humble origins
Yamalé	Fight corruption in government contracts	Bara Tall, president of the large construction

Table 4.1 (*cont.*)

Movement Name	Stated Objectives	Leadership
		company Jean Lefebvre Sénégal
Luy Jot Jotna	Promote the presidential candidacy of Cheikh Tidiane Gadio	Gadio, a journalist and head of a pro-democracy NGO with a doctorate in communications
Collectif des Imams et Résidents de Guédiawaye	Protest poor living conditions in Guédiawaye and low government accountability; draw attention to high electricity prices, power outages, flooding, dirty drinking water	Local imams including Youssoupha Sarr, a retired civil servant

actors launched the Front Siggil Senegaal (Senegal First Initiative) to address political, economic, and social crises facing the country (Wade's party declined an invitation to participate). The Assises Nationales culminated in "citizen constitutions" for renewing democracy. Yenamarristes stressed that the Arab Spring was about democratic birth, not renewal. Tunisia and Senegal "don't have the same realities," Barro said. "The forms of our struggles are different. Because here we have a pseudo-democratic regime, with freedom of expression, whatever one might claim" (quoted in Haeringer, 2012).

Senegalese protest leaders are representative of their counterparts in other African countries, who tend to claim democracy as their main concern. This is evident when analyzing data on the stated motivations of protest spokespeople. The bar graph in Figure 4.1 summarizes the percentage of leaders from eighty protests between 2005 and 2014 who declared missions prioritizing: 1) democracy and human rights; 2) economic conditions; or 3) foreign affairs and other issues. Protest event data are from Branch and Mampilly (2015), and I coded motivations from news reports. The vast majority of protest leaders branded

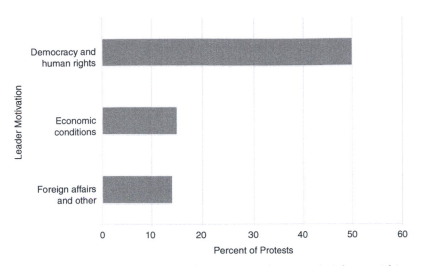

Figure 4.1: Public Motivations of Protest Leaders in Sub-Saharan Africa, 2005–2014
N = 80. Public motivations are coded from leaders' statements in news reports. Protest event data are from the Branch and Mampilly (2015).

themselves to the international media as defenders of democracy. Relatively few said they were advocating for economic justice or changes to foreign policy. Some left no doubt about their focus on democracy and human rights. In Tanzania, for example, leaders of the opposition Chadema Party called citizens to the streets in response to the National Assembly's plans to draft a new constitution in 2014. They objected in a press release, "the new constitution is being written under the barrel of a gun" (Ng'wanakilala, 2014). Other leaders sent more equivocal messages. Sikelela Dlamini of the Swaziland United Democratic Front professed multiple goals including government accountability, higher salaries, and other reforms (Rice, 2011). In these vaguer cases, I made a best effort to discern leaders' top priority from reporters' accounts. Coding was inherently subjective, so the breakdown of motivations in Figure 4.1 gives only a rough picture of the distribution. Nevertheless, democracy and human rights dominate protest leaders' agendas even within a wide margin of error. This corroborates findings by Cheeseman (2014) and Fichtmüller (2014) that the emerging middle class in Africa overwhelmingly holds pro-democratic attitudes and supports the opposition.

When hearing protest leaders' pro-democracy statements, it is instinctive to assume that rank-and-file demonstrators share the same political motivations. The rest of this book dispels the assumption of a single-minded crowd. Motivations and grievances are often heterogeneous across a society, such that democratically motivated and typically middle-class African protest leaders must tune their rhetoric to energize people who prefer democracy to autocracy but care foremost about their pocketbooks. The challenge for generals of the revolution is to transform economic frustration into collective action that can advance a political agenda. This applies to protest leaders worldwide. In Brazil, for example, "leaders in social movements face a delicate balancing act as they invest both in the collective goals and projects of their organizations and in their own personal life projects and ambitions" (Mische, 2001, 137).

What Makes a Protest Leader Effective? Cross-Class Coalitions as a Leadership Strategy

Cross-class coalitions distinguish third-wave African protests from protests of earlier waves, but coalitions are neither universal nor guaranteed; they are precarious and prone to dissolve when foot soldiers and generals of the revolution cannot reach common ground. The African middle class is chameleon-like: "it can be swept to activity by the masses at a time of revolutionary tide; or be driven to silence, fear, cynicism, withdrawal into self-contemplation, existential anguish, or to collaboration with the powers-that-be at times of reactionary tides" (Ngugi, 1986, 22). As Marx theorized, intellectuals are best positioned to lead social movements but risk becoming "generals without an army" if they impose their own ideas on reluctant people whom they make no attempt to understand (Avineri, 1967, 276). An effective protest leader, in other words, is an empathetic one (Dunlap, 2004).

Empathy may have some genetic determinants (Knafo et al., 2008), but viewing a situation from another person's point of view can also be a deliberate strategy for recruiting followers. For instance, a protest leader could decide to amplify economic grievances while suppressing their own sincere concerns about advancing a political ideology or obtaining personal power. They might use different rhetoric when addressing potential recruits as opposed to peers, government officials, or reporters. Social movement scholars refer to this code-switching as the psychological "framing" of movement goals (Benford and Snow, 2000), which can wed people around shared principles (Keck and Sikkink, 1998). Leaders who fail to tailor their rhetoric sacrifice legitimacy. Their movements eventually "die from the inside" as recruits burn out, drop out, split into factions, or lose commitment. An internally weak movement, in turn, has little defense against the external threats of co-optation and repression (Davenport, 2015). Members of Africa's new middle class increasingly possess the resources and political autonomy to mobilize the masses. Having already met their basic material needs, they have the luxury to pursue "ego rents"[31] and postmaterialist ideals like representation, human rights, and environmentalism (Inglehart and Abramson, 1999). Effective protest leaders downplay such interests when rallying foot soldiers who are preoccupied with just getting by.

M23 and Y'en a Marre illustrate different modes and outcomes of protest leadership. M23 leaders focused on regime-related problems, whereas Y'en a Marre leaders strategically folded bread-and-butter issues into their messages and programs. M23 became absorbed into the government and lost much of its grassroots following, whereas Y'en a Marre radicalized and grew its support base.

Variation in leadership and protest outcomes can also occur within a single movement over time. In Kenya, the Ufungamano Initiative began as an egalitarian alliance with a strong popular mandate, but it dissolved when leaders abandoned their populist platform.

The press and academics characterized all three of these movements – M23, Y'en a Marre, and the Ufungamano Initiative – as "pro-democracy," echoing language that protest leaders used on the global stage. Analyzing differences in protest leaders' rhetoric on the *local* stage lets us draw inferences about the reasons for movement success or failure. Table 4.2 outlines this analysis.

Strategies of M23: "Seek Ye First the Political Kingdom"

The leaders of M23 adopted strategies reflecting their experience as veteran politicians: bureaucratic organization, office-seeking, and elite-centered rhetoric. Their bureaucracy consisted of headquarters in

---

[31] Non-pecuniary benefits from holding a position of power (Besley, 2006, 40).

Table 4.2 *Cases of Protest Leadership Examined in this Section*

Movement	Country	Approximate Duration	Leaders Highlighted	Populist Message
M23	Senegal	2011–2012	Macky Sall, Ousmane Tanor Dieng, Idrissa Seck, Moustapha Niasse, Abdoulaye Bathily	Weak
Y'en a Marre	Senegal	2011–	Fadel Barro, Fou Malade, Thiat, Kilifeu	Moderate
Ufungamano Initiative	Kenya	1999–2005	Mutava Musyimi, Kivutha Kibwana, Phoebe Asiyo, Julia Ojiambo	Strong, then weak

Dakar and departmental "cells" that staff set up using contacts lifted directly from political party lists (Demarest, 2015, 13). Senior activists delegated public outreach to deputies rather than engaging citizens in person. M23 founders Moustapha Niasse, Ousmane Tanor Dieng, and Abdoulaye Bathily "missed roll call" at a gathering in Touba where they had promised to rebut a campaign speech that Wade had delivered there the previous week. Instead, the founders dispatched junior partisans to represent M23 at the event (Ndiaye, 2011). Fund-raising was likewise bureaucratic. The group's finance commission solicited donations from members of affiliated opposition parties – Niasse's Alliance of the Forces of Progress, Dieng's Socialist Party, Idrissa Seck's Rewmi, and Macky Sall's Alliance for the Republic. When grassroots fund-raising fell short, M23 leaders drew from their parties' reserves to keep up offices, transport and pay protesters, and televise demonstrations (Demarest, 2015).

It became ambiguous whether M23 was a social movement or a political campaign, as one leader after another declared his candidacy for president. Sall, Niasse, Seck, and Dieng practically stopped organizing protests once they entered the presidential race. They had in fact been campaigning unofficially for years, seeking out government posts that would position them for the highest office. Sall canvassed for

Wade's reelection in 2007 and then served as president of the National Assembly before splitting from the PDS over scandals involving Wade's son. Niasse was appointed prime minister under the first Wade administration as a reward for helping defeat Diouf in 2000. Seck had his own turn as prime minister until Wade dismissed him for alleged corruption. Dieng, a Socialist, was never Wade's ally but spent decades in politics as an advisor to presidents Senghor and Diouf. Approaching the February 2012 election, only minor candidates continued "beating the pavement" for M23, insecure about their electoral odds against the incumbent (Dalberto, 2012, 8). Rumor had it that Niasse deserted an M23 meeting to attend a campaign event by himself (Dakaractu, 2012a) and to avoid venturing into Dakar's rougher neighborhoods (*Senexbar*, 2012). Niasse's associates denied the report (Dakaractu, 2012b), but not before people started doubting M23's cohesion. Rank-and-file activists began losing faith in men who appeared to be manipulating protests for political gain. The skeptics were vindicated when Sall became president and installed former M23 principals in his cabinet. The famous saying of Ghanaian independence leader Kwame Nkrumah encapsulates the strategies of M23: "Seek ye first the political kingdom, and all else shall be added unto you."

Senegalese economist Ndongo Samba Sylla published a controversial op-ed on the eight-month anniversary of the June 23 uprisings. He claimed that citizens desired basic dignity and improved living conditions, not to restore a constitution that most of them had never read in their lives. Employing the language of class conflict, he described the protests that M23 organized as "impopular":

Impopular because the working classes feel excluded and because they do not identify with the fight that demagogues pursue in their name. The poorest and most vulnerable members of society would have loved for someone to speak to them about solutions to the cost of living, massive youth unemployment, floods, housing shortages, and strikes that have paralyzed the education system. But those who have designated themselves the mouthpieces of the people have other words: 'Don't touch my constitution' for example (Sylla, 2012, 2).

"Impopularity" stalled the efforts of M23 leaders to mobilize the masses. By declaring victory after June 23, movement spokespeople failed to address deep-seated problems such as inflation and joblessness. They praised demonstrators for showing "unprecedented maturity" in fighting for abstract principles like constitutional democracy instead of material goods like bread and electricity. "Passing off an elite affair as an affair of the people" was a self-defeating strategy (Diome, 2014). Radicals fled the cause, M23's partnership with Y'en a Marre dissolved, and militants who refused to be corralled by elites broke off to form M23 Authentique and M23 Patriotique. When I tried to call the M23 headquarters for an interview in 2015, I reached a man on his mobile phone. "I'm not involved with that anymore," he brusquely informed me and hung up.

Using the Arab Spring as an organizing template damaged M23's legitimacy. The movement's leaders had no viable strategy for inspiring youth who were suspended in "waithood," – a pan-African condition that Honwana (2015) defines as the period between childhood and an economically independent adulthood. Two-thirds of Senegal's population is younger than 30. This demographic faces onerous hurdles to a steady paycheck, a home outside the family compound, and other markers of adult and middle-class life. Job shortages induce an existential "*mal*" (Antoine and Fall, 2004), which in French connotes a blend of illness, pain, and evil. The percentage of unemployed university graduates in Senegal climbed from 16 percent in 2005 to 31 percent in 2011 (Hathie, 2014). This enlarged the "precariat," – a stratum of young and often well-educated people who lack forms of labor-related security including adequate income-earning possibilities, upward social mobility, and opportunities to make use of their competencies (Standing, 2011).

Contrary to Michael Bratton's view of civil society as an arena for all classes (Bratton, 1989), Senegalese protest leaders from civil society – including labor unions and political parties – have historically advocated mainly on behalf of salaried workers. They trumpet messages about party representation that are "increasingly irrelevant to much of the population" (Resnick, 2013, 626). Street vendors recast the M23 battle cry of "Don't touch my constitution!" as "Don't touch my table!" when M23 sympathizers tore through Dakar burning the first flammable objects they could grab. Singed wooden stalls became a metaphor for M23's aborted coalition with the poor. Middle-class activists treated materials that were valuable to the lower classes as expendable props in their post-materialist revolution. "Social movement partyism" has emerged in some contexts, especially in Latin America where protesters and party members formed coalitions during austerity reforms in the 1990s (Almeida, 2010). However, this model of protest organizing requires considerable overlap between party and social movement membership (Almeida, 2010, 176). Overlapping memberships are less common in Africa, because prolonged single-party rule demanded full party loyalty and sought to "monopolize associational life" (Manning, 2005, 714).

Senegalese youth of the informal sector showed their disregard for formal politics by turning out in droves at protests but in trivial numbers at the polls. Citizens between the ages of eighteen and twenty-three were under-represented in the 2012 election, even though a million of them had become eligible to vote since Wade's reelection in 2007. Turnout was low overall, at 44.8 percent compared with 55.1 percent five years earlier (Resnick, 2013, 636). M23 candidates suffered hard losses in the first round of voting, especially the "Independence Square candidates" who took the most radical stance on democratic revolution. Seck garnered 7.9 percent of the ballot, Cheikh Abiboulaye Dièye 1.9 percent, Ibrahima Fall 1.8 percent, and Cheikh Tidiane Gadio 0.98 percent (Diome, 2014, 401). The opposition rallied around Sall in the second round, but Sall was a default victor who could not shake public suspicion that politicians were using protests for their own professional benefit. M23 proved to be an "event alliance," organizing protests only around the specific event of Wade's bid for a third term. In contrast, M23's former ally, Y'en a Marre, became an "enduring alliance" by using strategies to engage people even after Wade backed down.[32]

Strategies of Y'en a Marre: Popular Engagement

Most of the Senegalese who rose up in 2011 lived hand to mouth and had modest expectations of upward mobility (Dimé, 2010). M23 failed to win them over with conventional statecraft: an M23 rally on September 24, 2011 attracted only hundreds of protesters as opposed to the thousands who flooded Dakar three months earlier (Demarest, 2015, 15). After taking oaths of office, the creators of M23 were unable to claim credit for the demonstrations that outlasted the February election and spilled beyond Senegal's borders.

---

[32] See Levi and Murphy (2006) on the differences between event and enduring alliances.

Sall was unpopular from day one, transforming from an instigator of protests into a target of them. His Bennoo Bokk Yaakaar coalition, made up of M23 leaders, kept mum as Sall's administration neglected to carry through its promises of creating jobs and resuscitating the economy. Citizens accused the lapsed activists of doing "the same as Wade without Wade" (Diome, 2014, 406).

The leaders of Y'en a Marre used a different play book based on musical performance, popular outreach, and decentralization. Thiat insisted that his music was for the people, not his own enrichment (Lo, 2014, 36). Barro recounted how Y'en a Marre was originally a response to material deprivation under the Wade and Sall regimes:

> It was the 16th of January. We were in a living room, in what has become our common neighborhood because the group Keur Gui, a rap group that comes from Kaolack, and I, with some other journalist friends, have made the habit of meeting there to chat as childhood friends …. Anyway, we were there on the 16th during a 20-hour power outage. We told ourselves, 'Folks can't continue to just sit back and watch this excess, this injustice, without doing anything.' And that same night we drafted a declaration calling on all of Senegal's driving forces, the youth, the street vendors, the workers, the executives, etc. from all sides to join us so that together we could take this step forward and overturn the political class (quoted in Haeringer, 2012).

This narrative became mythical through frequent retelling – mythical not in the sense of dubiousness, but in the sense of providing "a narrative-based representation of intangible experiences that are evocative because they are unconsciously linked to emotions such as sadness, happiness and fear" (Charteris-Black, 2011, 23). Citizens can identify with the adversity of a power outage whether or not they have read the constitution. Barro divulged that his populist language was strategic: "… when the same guy who respects [the] codes within his religious community or his family or his ethnic group comes to Dakar and you talk to him about the Constitution, he has no idea what you're talking about. To him, the Constitution has nothing to do with the people, it's a matter for the intellectuals, it's not his concern" (quoted in Nelson, 2014, 15).

On other occasions, the leaders of Y'en a Marre emphasized democracy and rule of law instead of material grievances. A prominent example is when U.S. President Barack Obama met with Barro and other representatives of Senegalese political society for a summit on democracy, rule of law, and government transparency at the Gorée Institute on June 27, 2013. Outside such elite spaces, repeating their origin myth was a better strategy for transforming popular anger about material conditions into mass mobilization. A nationally representative Afrobarometer survey showed in 2013 that three-quarters of Senegal's population felt the government was doing "very badly" or "fairly badly" at improving living standards of the poor; nearly as many deemed the government weak at providing a reliable electric supply. The coordinators of Y'en a Marre listened for popular grievances that could serve as rallying points. They adopted twin priorities: democracy *and* economic justice.

These priorities appeared side-by-side in a petition that Y'en a Marre circulated during Wade's run for a third term. Tens of thousands of Senegalese signed a memorandum that took swipes against government "hypocrisy" and "demagoguery." The petition also contained a long list of materialist complaints: "I am sick without access to basic care … I am a teacher with a meager salary … I am a street vendor and constantly badgered … I just want a place to earn a living." Dieng (2015, 85) dissects the rhetoric and concludes, "The Y'en a Marre movement shone in protest, certainly because of its capacity to explicitly express the difficulties that the majority of Senegalese live." In other words, a broad agenda incorporating solutions to the chronic hardships of power outages, unemployment, and poverty sustained Y'en a Marre years after the main threat to the constitution dissipated. Experiments from Zimbabwe confirm a causal link between people's emotions and their propensity to join pro-democracy protests (Young, 2016b). In harnessing this power of emotional appeals, yenamarristes distinguished themselves from their old allies in M23 and the new political opposition. Barro dismissed "Mackymètre," a website for tracking Macky Sall's presidency, as "too elitist" and "not inviting for ordinary people" (Nelson, 2014, 19).

Effective protest leaders engage with a large cross-section of society. They tailor their rhetoric when talking to allies, rivals, the media, and potential recruits (Mische, 2001, 140). Y'en a Marre's decentralized structure and informal communication style contrasted with M23's hierarchy and arm's-length mobilization tactics. In Senegal, hip-hop eventually expanded beyond the middle-class enclaves where Positive Black Soul broke onto the scene in the 1990s. By the early twenty-first century, Fou Malade and Keur Gui could use live concerts and online music distribution for reaching the masses directly.

Hip-hop's influence on Senegalese youth was no secret. Wade exploited it to mobilize counter-movements, subsidizing artists who produced records in support of his 2007 reelection campaign and threatening physical reprisals against those who released inflammatory tracks (Lo, 2014, 29). In 2011, youths who remained loyal to Wade rallied around rapper and avowed PDS supporter Pacotille. They called themselves Y'en a Envie (I Want It). Pacotille vouched, "Today, you cannot have musical protests without rap" (quoted in Coulibaly, 2007). Y'en a Envie and Y'en a Marre both embodied hip-hop culture, but the resemblance stopped there. Besides taking opposite stances toward the president, Y'en a Marre and Y'en a Envie differed in their degrees of political autonomy: Y'en a Envie was inseparable from the ruling party, whereas Y'en a Marre refused to endorse candidates or accept political donations.

Protest leaders in other African countries emulated Y'en a Marre's independence. After Le Balai Citoyen staged demonstrations that brought down Burkinabè president Blaise Compaoré in 2014, members of opposition parties tried to associate themselves with activists who looked to be on the right side of history. Le Balai Citoyen reacted with a public statement denying any partisan attachments. The movement's communication director justified this nonpartisan stance: "You can't be in Le Balai Citoyen and also be a politician. That would diminish our legitimacy."[33] A few African hip-hop artists did trade activism for politics, including Tanzanian emcees Joseph Haule (popularly known as Professor Jay) and Joseph Mbilinyi (known as Sugu). Mbilinyi entered a fistfight to defend a fellow opposition member that security guards had tried to eject from the Parliament chamber for refusing to sit down. Former fans expressed disappointment with his behavior (*The Citizen*, 2013).

Y'en a Marre was not immune to legitimacy problems. Despite being nominally leaderless, the movement had a "hard core" of intellectual founders who made the bulk of decisions. Like most professional activists, the original yenamarristes drew "a line of separation between a thinking minority and an acting majority" (Savané and Sarr, 2012, 74). At the same time, they tried to counter perceptions of elitism by

---

[33] Interview on June 1, 2016.

stepping up efforts to extend their local and regional presence. Leaders established satellite organizations called *esprits* (roughly translated, "the spirit of Y'en a Marre"). Similar to the clubs of Le Balai Citoyen, *esprits* hosted civic education workshops and vocational skills clinics (Nelson, 2014). Such projects provided opportunities for highly educated, middle-class protest leaders to connect with street vendors and farmers from poor urban neighborhoods and rural villages. Barro praised this inclusive approach to social organizing:

Just yesterday, there was someone from the Kaolack *esprit* who came to the coordination meeting to present an agricultural project to us. He saw and opportunity in his area to grow sesame and sell it to a group of Chinese merchants. He presented his idea to us, and now he is working with Julien, who is a young yenamarriste with a master's in political science. So this young yenamarriste who's a farmer comes from Kaolack with an idea for a project, and he can work with Julien, who has done advanced studies, to define a project, study the feasibility, and put it all down on paper so that we can examine it and see how to move forward together. The structure of Y'en a Marre allows that collaboration to happen (quoted in Nelson, 2014, 23).

Esprits can be tools of political activism without appearing overtly political. They distribute community services while doubling as venues for deliberating about elections, the meaning of citizenship, and governance at national and local levels. During the summer of 2011, yenamarristes organized caravans to encourage more people to join *esprits*. They performed anti-Wade anthems and held community meetings in town squares (Fredericks, 2014, 142). More than 300 *esprits* arose from this effort and continued convening in response to salient issues. In 2016, for example, they mobilized citizens to vote down a referendum for approving a slate of constitutional amendments that included reducing presidential term limits from seven to five years, with an exception for President Sall. The *oui* votes ultimately prevailed, but yenamarristes nimbly shifted their focus after the defeat. On June 26, 2016, spokespeople disseminated a "call to mobilization" on Facebook to oppose the release of Wade's son from prison.[34] Their demands underscored the injustice of poor citizens enjoying fewer legal protections than government insiders.

Y'en a Marre transcended geographic as well as class borders. *Esprits* sprung up in Paris and New York. Planners of the 2013

---

[34] Karim Wade was under corruption charges.

World Social Forum in Tunisia requested a yenamarriste to represent the African Committee alongside delegates from Occupy Wall Street, the Arab Spring, and Canadian student unions. Global encounters shaped Y'en a Marre's strategies. Like the organizers of Le Balai Citoyen in Burkina Faso, yenamarristes encouraged demonstrators to tidy up the streets after protests. This practice reinforced a sense of collective responsibility and paid homage to earlier waves of activism, namely the *Set/Setal* (Clean/To Clean Up) movement of the late 1980s, which encouraged trash removal and the "moral cleanliness" of Senegalese citizens (Diouf, 2005). Y'en a Marre may have departed from Bul Faale's individualist ethos, but it retained elements of other movements from the past.

Strategies of the Ufungamano Initiative: Popular Engagement, Then a Retreat to the Political Kingdom

Some social movements disband after living out their purpose, as part of a natural protest life cycle (Giugni, McAdam, and Tilly, 1998; Dosh, 2009; LeBas, 2011). But the Ufungamano Initiative in Kenya never became obsolete. Rather, it deflated because its leaders pivoted from inclusive to elitist organizing strategies. The Ufungamano Initiative dates back to the cusp of the third wave (1999–2005), providing a glimpse into the long-term evolution of leadership in African protests. It is also a useful case for examining trends beyond Francophone West Africa. Kenya is a more ethnically and religiously fragmented country than Senegal and thus illustrates how domestic divisions interact with protest leadership. Social movements are like armies; they may have multiple generals whose goals do not necessarily align. Modes of leadership in the Ufungamano Initiative changed over time as the balance of power vacillated between competing interests. Within-movement variation makes it possible to analyze how different strategies influence success while holding constant factors that vary across movements and countries.

Kenya has undergone multiple rocky periods of constitutional revision, including ad-hoc negotiations in 1992 to set the terms of multi-party elections, a modification of the constitution in 2002 to ease a truce between rival parties, and another set of reforms in 2008 to address post-election violence (Kramon and Posner, 2011). In 2017, Kenya's Supreme Court nullified national election results citing procedural irregularities, raising fears of a constitutional crisis. At each stage, ordinary Kenyans have fought to join diplomats and legal scholars at the bargaining table. Whereas political elites tend to emphasize "the lawyer's paradise in constitution-making" and the minutiae of "crafting structures of good governance and free, fair and peaceful elections," citizens stress "the preoccupations of the people" and matters of "material survival" (Mutunga, 1999, 19–20).

On December 15, 1999, members of Kenya's religious community and their secular supporters assembled at the Ufungamano House, also called the Christian Students' Leadership Centre, near the University of Nairobi. They aimed to forge a people-driven constitutional reform process to balance the elite-driven process occurring under the direction of President Daniel arap Moi. Roughly four hundred individuals representing churches, human rights organizations, women's groups, and opposition parties deliberated for two days and then released a declaration asserting that "the constitution is ultimately the expression of the sovereign will of the people." The Ufungamano Initiative emerged as a rare unified movement in an otherwise ethnically, religiously, and economically divided society (Mati, 2012b). Its name derives from the Kiswahili word *fungamana*, meaning "to join together." Leaders were a mix of middle-class urbanites, poor students, and politicians with a "government-in-waiting" complex (Mutua, 2008, 123). They elected Oki Ooko Ombaka, a lecturer in humanitarian law, as their chairman.

These unlikely allies set about mobilizing the lower classes. They drew inspiration from the theology of Martin Luther King, Jr., who warned that "any religion that is not concerned about the poor and disadvantaged, the slums that damn them, the economic conditions that strangle them, and the social conditions that cripple them, is a spiritually moribund religion awaiting burial" (quoted in Mati, *2012a*, 167). Leaders of the Ufungamano Initiative organized the people hardest hit by economic decline. They toured churches, mosques, and temples to poll public views on revising the constitution (Nasong'o, 2007a, 46). They built a sizable corps of foot soldiers and attracted national attention (Mati, 2012b, 75).

President Moi insisted that public input on the constitution was superfluous on top of advice from foreign and domestic experts. In 2000 he created the state-run Constitution of Kenya Review Commission (CKRC) and pushed for a merger with the Ufungamano

Initiative. Activists from the human rights group Muungano wa Maguezi (Movement for Change) were quick to reject the proposed merger, which they viewed as a co-optation tactic that would undermine the purpose of the Ufungamano Initiative as a voice of the people. They further denounced it as a scheme to divide the movement's leadership.

There were already signs of fissures within the Ufungamano Initiative. Leaders representing the National Convention Executive Council (NCEC) butted heads with clergy who they believed were siding with the ruling KANU party. Each of these factions was also internally divided. Bishop Lawi Imathiu supported KANU while fellow Methodist Bishop Nthamburi did not. Reverend Mutava Musyimi was branded a traitor for agreeing to negotiate a merger with the chair of the CKRC, constitutional law professor Yash Pal Ghai. The NCEC split over whether to abide by state regulations on public assembly. When one camp announced a rally against the government's boycott of constitutional dialogues, another scheduled a rival demonstration (Latumanga, 2000, 24). Many rank-and-file members of the NCEC were students who had joined the organization in the late 1990s to take their fight against tuition hikes to the national level. Solomon Muruli, the Vice Chairman of the Kenya University Students' Organization, was locked in his dorm room and burned alive in 1997. The circumstances of the murder were mysterious, but some sources blamed a senior cabinet member (Klopp and Orina, 2002). Ignoring students' resultant distrust of politicians, NCEC spokesman Kivutha Kibwana joined parliament in 2002 and became counselor to the president in 2007 (Nasong'o, 2007b, 111). Kibwana alienated the backbone of his movement when he "abandoned mass action as a strategy to pressurise for constitutional reforms" in 2000 (Amadala and Lumwamu, 2000).

The Women's Political Caucus also broke up amid constitutional quarrels. One of its main figures, Phoebe Asiyo, left the Ufungamano Initiative for a commissioner post in the Parliamentary Select Committee. Another, Julia Auma Ojiambo, used activism as a springboard to launch her political career as the running mate of presidential candidate Stephen Kalonzo in 2007. The Ufungamano Initiative was a "movement of movements" whose leaders came to deeply mistrust each other (Mati, 2012a). It was as if "for every [civil society organization] agitating for reform, there was a corresponding one working in the opposite direction" (Nasong'o, 2007b, 106).

Enough leaders of the Ufungamano Initiative reversed their strategies from confrontation to co-optation that it was only a matter of time before the entire movement took a conservative turn. The merger with the CKRC became official by an act of parliament on May 8, 2001, spelling the beginning of the end for the Ufungamano Initiative. After the merger, the NCEC and allied groups abandoned the movement, while public participation in constitutional debates waned (Mati, 2012a, 307). The CKRC adopted some practices of the People's Commission of Kenya, such as working through committees. However, committee meetings became less inclusive, and Ufungamano Initiative activists who joined the CKRC grew more conservative as their government salaries rose. By 2005, the Ufungamano Initiative ceased functioning as a unified voice of the Kenyan people, five years before a new constitution was finally pro-mulgated. Weak cross-class coalitions extinguished the campaign for bottom-up reform.

Conclusion

Success in the political kingdom and success in the streets are compet-ing goals for protest leaders. On the surface, this is a classic tale of co-optation: Achieving state power means relinquishing popular legiti-macy. On a deeper level, the rise and fall of African social movements reflects ongoing changes in the African middle class that make some protest leaders more outspoken against incumbent regimes than others. M23's loss of legitimacy stemmed in part from strategic missteps but also from the fact that the group's leaders began their careers in politics and sought to claim executive power for themselves. Leaders of Y'en a Marre had already established private-sector careers before devoting themselves to political causes. They were therefore relatively more successful at mobilizing the masses over a longer period. The Ufungamano Initiative in Kenya at first mirrored Y'en a Marre but later came to resemble M23, as conservative leaders overshadowed the radical wing of the movement. This last example indicates that patterns in Senegal are not unique to one country.

Money, time, and charisma are not enough for protest leaders to sustain collective action. Such resources must come without political strings attached if leaders are to challenge the state class and build coalitions with the poor. In Senegal, recovery programs after the 1994 currency devaluation gave rise to more than 2,000 microfinance institutions issuing loans to small-scale entrepreneurs (Taylor and Zahka, 2004). It became easier for citizens to earn a living outside the civil service and to protest the government. Even so, the burgeoning middle class remains small across sub-Saharan Africa. A political career is still in many cases more lucrative than work in the private sector (Ncube and Lufumpa, 2015). As a result, not all third-wave protest leaders are equally effective, as this chapter showed. The next chapters delve further into why some people and not others follow leaders into protest.

5 | *Comparative Individual Participation in the Third Wave*

Why do some people heed protest leaders' calls to action whereas others do not? Journalists and African politics scholars have inconsistent answers to that question. As the third wave of protests swept across Africa starting around 2011, the international media alternated between attributing protest participation to anger over autocracy (Dibba, 2013; Sowore, 2013) and attributing it to frustration with poverty and income inequality (Smith, 2013; Berazneva and Lee, 2013). It might be tempting to view third-wave protesters as democratic revolutionaries in light of the finding from Chapter 4 that key spokespeople of the third wave professed a goal of defending democracy. Prominent protest leaders such as Fadel Barro in Senegal trumpeted rule of law and condemned elected leaders they perceived to be reinstating autocracy. Journalistic portrayals of demonstrators as hungry rioters or as part of global "occupy movements" are equally understandable in the context of enduring poverty and rising inequality (see Chapter 3).

In the current chapter, I adjudicate between the above explanations for variation in protest participation, addressing the question: what makes people in Africa join protests – dissatisfaction with political regimes, materialist concerns, or something else? This puzzle is distinct from the one that I explored in the preceding chapter, of why some people launch protests and others do not. Reviving an approach of C. L. R. James (1969) and Pearl Robinson (1994), I entertain the possibility that what motivates ordinary protesters differs from what motivates protest leaders. I also allow for the possibility that protest spokespeople misrepresent the attitudes of the masses, either unwittingly or strategically.

Analyzing nationally representative Afrobarometer survey data from thirty-one African countries between 2002 and 2015,[1] I show that

---

[1] I include data going back to 2002, on the cusp of the third wave, to maximize the number of observations. I include survey round fixed effects in my statistical models to control for long-term changes in political context.

different grievances influence protest participation to different degrees. Political grievances are not as salient as materialist concerns in general, and some in particular are associated with increased protest propensity while others are not. People who expect their economic circumstances to decline in the near future are more likely to protest than their more optimistic peers, controlling for other factors. In contrast, poverty and perceived inequality have no measurable relationship with protest propensity. These results are counter-intuitive, because they suggest that people in Africa are not too oppressed and disenfranchised to challenge the status quo; they are too optimistic. Next, I discover that ethnic grievances also correlate with protest participation: a person's chance of protesting is about 25 percent higher if that person feels the government has treated her or his ethnic group unfairly. The magnitude of this relationship is almost twice as large as that between protest participation and low expectations of upward mobility, suggesting that ethnicity remains an important root of social conflict in Africa, though not the only one. Correlations do not constitute evidence of causal relationships; I address potential endogeneity bias with a combination of process tracing and references to the social psychology literature on sources of grievances.

My analysis underscores how people express multifarious grievances in the common behavior of protesting. Groups that form for the express purpose of challenging a regime, such as guerrilla organizations and vanguard parties, are unusual. Most groups that mobilize during protests are preexisting organizations such as mosques, student associations, and labor unions (Goldstone, 1994, 148). Particularly in Africa's third wave of protest, many social movement organizations owed their existence to democratic openings achieved during the second wave (Chapter 2). Once group leaders initiate protests, the people who join them may have grievances that only loosely connect with dominant protest narratives (Beissinger, 2013; Beissinger, Jamal, and Mazur, 2012; Mueller, 2013). Protest leaders often reveal their grievances in public statements, but the grievances of protesting crowds are heterogeneous and not immediately observable.[2] For example, journalists investigating South Africa's "#FeesMustFall" movement

---

[2] The heterogeneity of grievances has implications for the duration of protest waves. Social movements that involve participants of "mixed motives" are more sustainable because they are less likely to succumb to the "security trap" that results when a movement meets its main goal (Dosh, 2009).

at a student march in October 2015 discovered that protesters sought more than affordable tuition; they also called for "the 'decolonization' and 'transformation' of higher education institutions, the insourcing of outsources workers ... and the release of their classmates arrested earlier in the week" (Baloyi and Isaacs, 2015). One demonstrator demanded further that the president step down, waving a sign saying, "Zuma must fall."

The chapter proceeds as follows. In the first section, I review theories about the link between grievances and protest participation and develop hypotheses from them. In the second section, I describe data and methods that I use in statistical analyses of grievances and protest participation. In the third section, I analyze Afrobarometer surveys to construct a profile of the average African protester, comparing my inferences about who protests with descriptions of protests in the media and events databases. I then present the main regression analyses of protest participation, along with tests of robustness and model sensitivity, and an analysis of what determines expectations of upward mobility. The final section concludes with a summary of findings and implications for policymakers.

Grievances and Protest Participation

Grievances are feelings of resentment about injustice, which some theorists argue will naturally lead people to rise up (della Porta and Diani, 2006, 87). Scholars in the tradition of Gurr (1970) and Berkowitz (1972) describe protest as an expression of "moral outrage" about perceived economic deprivation or political oppression (Martin, Brickman, and Murray, 1983; Olson and Hafer, 2001). They stress that "it is ultimately perceptions of reality," and not objective conditions, "that drive people to take certain actions or display certain behavior" (Langer and Smedts, 2013, 4). According to grievance theories, people protest fundamentally because they are upset.

Other theorists debate whether outrage will necessarily result in contentious action. Observing that grievances are widespread whereas protest participation is rare, "resource mobilization" theorists emphasize the opportunity rather than the desire to protest (McCarthy and Zald, 2002; Klandermans, 1984; Corning and Myers, 2002). They argue that people take to the streets not because they are upset, but instead because they are able to coordinate collective action and overcome the temptation to free-ride on other people's willingness to bear the sometimes mortal costs of challenging authorities. The paragraphs below outline both schools of thought.

Grievance Theories

Grievance theories highlight anger, frustration, and desire to change the status quo. They also address why many people seem to accept rather than resent objective deprivation (Olson and Hafer, 2001; Shapiro, 2002). In this framework, the ability to act collectively matters only if people have the will to release psychological tension or make power-holders aware of their discontent: the "Olsonian logic of collective action," which focuses on people's inability to overcome coordination and cooperation problems, "provides an explanation for why people do not participate, but fares poorly in explaining why people do participate" in protests (Klandermans, 2004, 363). Experimental and observational studies show grievances to influence protest participation separately from cost-benefit calculations (Stürmer and Simon, 2009; Opp, 1988). Case studies of protest events also reveal that aggrieved individuals occasionally protest even without resources and organizational help from "social movement entrepreneurs" (Piven and Cloward, 1991; Scacco, 2008).

Reenock, Bernhard and Sobek (2007) predict that subjective "basic needs deprivation" will fuel conflict when poverty lingers amid general economic development, as is presently the case in many African societies. As I described in Chapter 3, sub-Saharan Africa has undergone remarkable growth since the 1990s, but not necessarily pro-poor growth. Under such circumstances, perhaps citizens "will not only notice deprivation more readily, but also, given the greater social surplus, will deem it more unacceptable, provoking radical demands for redistributive justice" (Reenock, Bernhard, and Sobek, 2007, 685). The following hypothesis summarizes this theory:

Hypothesis 1:   People who perceive their living conditions as bad are more likely to protest than people who perceive their living conditions as good. (Absolute Deprivation Hypothesis)

Gurr (1970) identified relative deprivation, as opposed to absolute deprivation, as a precondition for revolution. He predicted that the disadvantaged will remain politically quiescent as long as they see themselves as better off than their peers.

Hypothesis 2: People who feel that they are disadvantaged relative to other people are more likely to protest than people who do not feel disadvantaged. (Egoistic Relative Deprivation Hypothesis)

Scholars have empirically tested Gurr's theory. Some estimate that relative deprivation has little or no effect (Sayles, 2007), whereas others find only certain types of relative deprivation to matter. Motivated by the theoretical literature distinguishing "egoistic" from "fraternal" relative deprivation,[3] Dubé and Guimond (1983) and Walker and Mann (1987) observed that personal dissatisfaction with one's relative social position (egoistic relative deprivation) has less of an effect on protest behavior than dissatisfaction with the social position of one's identity group (fraternal relative deprivation).[4] Fraternal relative deprivation may be especially salient in Africa, where, according to conventional wisdom, colonial histories and political institutions reinforce horizontal inequalities (Cederman, Weidmann, and Gleditsch, 2001; Østby, 2007; Stewart, 2010) and politicize ethnic identities (van Stekelenburg and Klandermans, 2013; Posner, 2005). In an article entitled "What Is behind Ethiopia's Wave of Protests?" a journalist conjectured, "what we are seeing is an accumulation of years of frustration from ethnic groups who say they have been marginalised by the government" (BBC, 2016a).

However, some evidence casts doubt on the assumption that protests in plural societies stem from ethnic grievances. As Lindberg and Morrison (2008, 112) assert, "recognizing the significance of ethnicity in politics does not allow us simply to assume that it matters also for voters at the polls" (or, presumably, for protesters in the streets). In their survey of more than 3,000 voters in the 2000 Ghanaian presidential election, no respondents said they had voted for the winner because he was Ashanti. Voters expressed little concern for candidates' ethnic identities despite the prevalence of ethnic stereotyping in newspapers and public debates. I extend Lindberg and Morrison's analysis to explore whether African citizens are more likely to protest if they perceive systemic ethnic injustice.

---

[3] See Crosby (1976), Olson et al. (1995), and Runciman (1966).
[4] See Klandermans et al. (2002) and Opp (2009) for more on how collective identity motivates protest participation.

Hypothesis 3:   People who feel that their ethnic group is disadvantaged relative to other ethnic groups are more likely to protest than people who do not perceive such injustice. (Fraternal Relative Deprivation Hypothesis)

In addition to egoistic and fraternal relative deprivation, some researchers highlight "temporal relative deprivation" or "backward-looking framing effects," whereby individuals assess their deprivation relative to their own well-being in the past (Reenock, Bernhard and Sobek, 2007; Shapiro, 2002). The "J-curve theory" holds that people will protest when a sharp decline in living conditions interrupts a prolonged period of improvement (Davies, 1962).

Hypothesis 4:   People who feel that their current living conditions are worse than their past living conditions are more likely to protest than people who perceive no decline over time in their living conditions. (Temporal Relative Deprivation Hypothesis)

Temporal relative deprivation can be forward-looking as well as backward-looking (Shapiro, 2002). In other words, people might compare their present well-being not to their past well-being, but instead to the well-being they anticipate for the future. Hirschman and Rothschild (1973) theorize that people will be less inclined to oppose the status quo if they expect their status to improve. The authors use an analogy of a two-lane tunnel where heavy traffic, all heading in the same direction, slows to a standstill; the tunnel is too long to see the exit. If a driver suddenly notices cars beginning to accelerate in the neighboring lane, the driver will not initially become jealous, but rather interpret nearby movement as a sign that traffic in her or his own lane will also accelerate soon. This acceptance of one's current suffering is called "the tunnel effect." But if traffic in the driver's lane does not begin to speed up after a long while, then the driver will get angry and switch lanes despite the risk of a crash or a fine for reckless driving. Thus, when the tunnel effect wears off, the immobile "experience the turnaround from hopefulness to disenchantment," a situation that "clearly contains much potential for social upheaval" and "might even qualify as a theory of revolution" (Hirschman and Rothschild, 1973, 552). Yet as long as people expect mobility, they will not protest against the status quo. Using a formal model, Bénabou and Ok (2001) illustrate how this theory is compatible with rational choice.

Several empirical studies have validated the relationship between expectations of upward mobility and preferences for redistribution. Ravallion and Lokshin (2000) observe that Russians with higher expectations for their future well-being are less supportive of government limits on the incomes of the rich. This relationship holds even if respondents' incomes are below average. Alesina and La Ferrara (2004) similarly find that Americans who expect improvements in their families' living conditions are less likely to support redistribution than more pessimistic Americans. Jaime-Castillo (2008) and Bjornskov et al. (2010) find evidence of the same phenomenon in other countries. Checchi and Filippin (2003) conducted a laboratory experiment in which subjects chose levels of income redistribution after viewing simulations of how different tax rates might change their incomes over time. Respondents who saw a matrix depicting higher probabilities of upward mobility consistently preferred lower tax rates.

Social scientists ever since Alexis de Tocqueville have noted that perceived social mobility affects political attitudes (Piketty, 1995), but they have generally ignored the effects on political *behavior*. Perceived social mobility relates to the study of protest participation because it provides a source of grievances that can motivate people to protest. People might tolerate or even embrace high levels of inequality because they see other people's advancement as a sign of their own imminent advancement. They might also accept the rich getting richer if they view elites as sources of patronage (Daloz, 2013). As a result, even the most objectively dismal living conditions will not necessarily fuel people's desire to challenge the status quo if people believe that they will become better off eventually. This would help explain widespread political quiescence in extremely poor and unequal societies. Conversely, people who are pessimistic about their economic opportunities may be less tolerant of the status quo and more inclined to protest.

The literature on "aspirations failures" contradicts the literature on expectations of upward mobility by suggesting that people who expect declines in their living conditions will see prosperity as so far out of reach that they will lack the motivation to "contest and alter the conditions of their poverty" (Appadurai, 2004, 59). Duflo (2012, 38) elaborates: "the anticipation of likely failure (or at least a severe limit to the extent of possible success) could lead an individual to rationally decide to hold back his or her efforts, avoid investment, and thus achieve even less than he or she could otherwise have attained." These theories imply that pessimistic people will not rise up, but instead resign themselves to their expected fate (Bernard, Dercon, and Seyoum Taffesse, 2011; Ray, 2006; Dalton, Ghosal and Mani, 2013). In sum, the jury is still out on the following hypothesis:

Hypothesis 5:   People with low expectations of upward mobility are more likely to protest than people with high expectations of upward mobility.

I operationalize political, as opposed to economic, grievances as attitudes about state legitimacy. In an earlier analysis of Afrobarometer data, Kirwin and Cho (2009) found that people were more likely to say they had protested if they regarded the state as illegitimate: "without positive perceptions about state legitimacy, people do not believe that they ought to follow rules or commands issued by their state. As legitimacy of the government decreases individuals become increasingly less likely to follow the rule of law which could lead to higher levels of violence" (Kirwin and Cho, 2009, 7). Based on these prior findings, I hypothesize as follows:

Hypothesis 6:   People who view the state as less legitimate are more likely to protest than people who view the state as more legitimate.

Resource Mobilization Theories

Resource mobilization theorists propose that there is little or no connection between grievances and protest participation, reasoning that "grievances and deprivation always exist and therefore cannot explain the ups and downs of protest cycles" (Corning and Myers, 2002, 705). Olson (1971) popularized the idea that members of a group will free-ride if they expect others to bear the costs of mounting a social movement. If the primary goal of protesting is to win a public good such as democracy or an increase in the minimum wage, then a rational person will prefer to consume the good without shouldering any cost of obtaining it. If all members of the community are similarly rational, then collective action never occurs. Only if group members receive selective incentives or are coerced into participating will protest materialize. Therefore, even the most aggrieved people will not protest if they cannot cooperate to pursue their shared objectives.

Other theories of collective action center on communication dilemmas (Kielbowicz and Scherer, 1998; Tarrow, 1998). Here, the problem is not cooperation but coordination. For people to work together toward a common goal, they must agree on a course of action – where to meet, which message to convey, and what tactics to use. It can be especially difficult to coordinate in developing countries where the mail system is slow, Internet service is limited, and cellular phone reception is unreliable.[5] Repressive governments compound communication problems by restricting the media (Bueno de Mesquita and Downs, 2005). Under heavy censorship, people might not even know whom to target with their demands, let alone how to coordinate the logistics of a demonstration. Low levels of formal labor force participation further limit the sharing of information and collective action (Ross, 2008, 108). Protest efforts can therefore fail even if all members of a group want to speak up.

In Africa, rural people are theoretically more likely than urbanites to face collective action problems. They are geographically dispersed and historically excluded from technological and employment-based information networks (Bates, 1981). The countryside is also geographically farther from the government, which is the usual target of protests (Hendrix and Salehyan, 2015). Indeed, Bratton and van de Walle (1992) found no cases of rural uprisings in their sample of protests from sixteen African countries between 1989 and 1991.

Hypothesis 7: Rural people are less likely to protest than urban people.

Addressing cooperation problems, Scacco (2008) estimated that Nigerians who attended community meetings were more likely to have rioted against members of another religion. This is because community meetings expose people to social networks that "pull" rioters to the front lines, not because rioters are already more likely to socialize or because community meetings drum up grievances. Community meetings could similarly encourage participation in non-violent protests (as opposed to violent riots) by exerting social pressure that discourages free-riding, hence solving cooperation problems, and by facilitating the

---

[5] Cell phone coverage in Africa is improving, with consequences for collective action. Pierskalla and Hollenbach (2013) use data on cell phone coverage and the location of organized violence in Africa to show a correlation between access to coverage and the probability of conflict.

exchange of information, hence solving coordination problems. Attendance at community meetings is one way of operationalizing social capital, which other scholars cite as a catalyst of political participation in general (Putnam, 1993; Krishna, 2002).

Hypothesis 8:   People who attend community meetings are more likely to protest than people who do not attend community meetings.

Data and Methods

I test the above hypotheses with survey data from Afrobarometer. Enumerators conducted six rounds of surveys in thirty-six African countries from 1999 to 2015, although not every country was surveyed every year. Samples were nationally representative. Survey rounds two through six featured standard questions about respondents' grievances and protest involvement, permitting analysis of nearly 200,000 observations. Such a large sample offers several advantages. First, it allows me to estimate a thoroughly specified regression model with adequate statistical power, and thus to detect complex nonlinear relationships and interaction terms. I can also exploit numerous observations to estimate separate models on subsamples of the data. A large sample does pose some estimation problems (Lin, Lucas Jr. and Shmueli, 2013), which I address in the discussion of results.

Social desirability bias is the principal disadvantage of Afrobarometer data, especially with respect to questions about protest participation. Beissinger (2013, 5) cautions, "there are obvious issues with using a retrospective survey of revolutionary participation. Attitudes and beliefs may themselves be affected by the experience of revolution, and bandwagoning and preference falsification are inherent parts of the revolutionary process." We might expect respondents to over-report protest participation when social pressure to protest is high. Conversely, subjects might under-report participation when they sense a stigma against protesting. Enumerators' identities could further bias responses. Adida et al. (2013) studied more than 40,000 Afrobarometer interviews in fifteen countries and observed that respondents' answers varied according to the ethnic match between respondent and enumerator.

Still, Afrobarometer data are arguably the best available source of systematic information about Africans' grievances and protest participation. They offer a large number of observations across many countries and years, and the design and implementation of the surveys mitigate social desirability bias in several ways. First, enumerators interviewed respondents in private or semi-private settings to help respondents feel comfortable about sharing sensitive information. Second, surveys inquire about recent protest participation (occurring in the previous twelve months), thereby lowering the risk of selective memory that might result from asking about behavior that occurred in the more distant past. Social desirability bias from the ethnic identities of enumerators and respondents should be minimal, because the survey questions that provide data for most of my key variables are not ethnically sensitive.

Variables

Table 5.1 displays summary statistics for the variables used to test the hypotheses. The dependent variable is *Protest Participation*, which is measured using respondents' answers to the following Afrobarometer survey question:

Here is a list of actions that people sometimes take as citizens. For each of these, please tell me whether you, personally, have done any of these things during the past year. If not, would you do this if you had the chance: attended a demonstration or protest march?

Response options included the following:

- No, would never do this.
- No, but would do if had the chance.
- Yes, once or twice.
- Yes, several times.
- Yes, often.
- Don't know.

I recoded responses into a dichotomous variable taking a value of "1" if a respondent said she or he had participated in a demonstration or protest march, and "0" otherwise. I coded intent to protest as "0." Although one could argue that the intent to protest is qualitatively different from the resolve never to protest, bias resulting from dichotomization should be in the direction of a null finding. About 11 percent of respondents in the sample of 182,838 said they had protested in the

Table 5.1 *Summary Statistics*

Variable	N	Min.	Max.	Mean	Std. Dev.
Protested	182838	0	1	0.109	0.312
Absolute deprivation	182712	0	1	0.480	0.500
Relative deprivation (egoistic)	182677	0	1	0.358	0.480
Relative deprivation (temporal)	181634	0	1	0.361	0.480
Ethnic group treated unfairly	156738	0	1	0.194	0.395
Low expectations of upward mobility	182777	0	1	0.199	0.400
Gone without income	182774	0	1	0.756	0.430
Employed	182788	0	1	0.230	0.421
Urban	182933	0	1	0.390	0.488
Attended community meeting	182859	0	1	0.596	0.491
Religious group member	181746	0	1	0.574	0.494
State legitimacy	169915	3	15	11.376	2.761
Female	182932	0	1	0.501	0.500
Age	180926	18	100	36.883	14.612
Education	182021	1	4	2.407	0.942

Data are from Afrobarometer, covering 31 countries over 2002–2015.

past year (Table 5.1). Protest participation rates vary within a plausible range across countries, from 4 percent in Burundi to 18 percent in South Africa; most countries fall within one standard deviation of the 10 percent average. I account for country-level variation by including country fixed effects in the main regression models and by omitting outliers in robustness tests.

Afrobarometer surveys also provide data for the following dichotomous independent variables:

- *Absolute Deprivation*: Takes a value of "1" if a respondent considers her or his present living conditions to be either "bad" or "very bad"; "0" otherwise.
- *Relative Deprivation (Egoistic)*: Takes a value of "1" if a respondent thinks her or his living conditions are worse than those of co-nationals; "0" otherwise.

- *Relative Deprivation (Temporal)*: Takes a value of "1" if a respondent considers her or his living conditions to be worse now than they were 12 months ago; "0" otherwise.[6]
- *Ethnic Group Treated Unfairly*: Takes a value of "1" if a respondent feels that her or his ethnic group has been treated unfairly by the government; "0" otherwise.[7]
- *Low Expectations of Upward Mobility*: Takes a value of "1" if a respondent expects her or his living conditions to be worse in the next 12 months; "0" otherwise.[8]
- *State Legitimacy*: Following Kirwin and Cho's coding rules, I measure state legitimacy with a composite score ranging from 3 to 15 based on how strongly respondents agree with the following statements:
  - The courts have the right to make decisions that people always have to abide by.
  - The police always have the right to make people obey the law.
  - The tax department always has the right to make people pay taxes.
- *Urban*: Takes a value of "1" if a respondent lives in an urban area; "0" if a respondent lives in a rural area.
- *Attendance at Community Meetings*: Takes a value of "1" if a respondent has attended a community meeting in the past 12 months; "0" otherwise.

The statistical analysis also includes the following control variables:

- *Member of a Religious Group*: Religion and social insurance help people cope with adversity and can substitute for protest (Scheve and

[6] Round 6 used slightly different wording: "Looking back, how do you rate economic conditions in this country compared to twelve months ago?" Results are robust to omitting round 6.

[7] The Fraternal Relative Deprivation Hypothesis (Hypothesis 3) refers to peer rather than government treatment: "People who feel that their ethnic group is disadvantaged relative to other ethnic groups are more likely to protest than people who do not perceive such injustice." Afrobarometer did ask how respondents perceive their living conditions relative to those of other ethnic groups, but this question was not available for round 6. I therefore use a similar question that is available for all countries in rounds 2 through 6, except for Sudan.

[8] Round 6 used slightly different wording: "Looking ahead, do you expect economic conditions in this country to be better or worse in twelve months time?" Results are robust to omitting round 6.

Stasavage, 2006). I control for whether respondents have recently contacted a religious leader "about some important problem" or to share their views. Although I expect this variable to exhibit a negative relationship with protest participation, membership in religious organizations might promote protest if religious leaders provide mobilization goods.

- *Female*: In general across sub-Saharan Africa, men are more visible in political life than women and may therefore be more likely to join protests. I include a dummy variable that takes a value of "1" if a respondent is female and "0" if a respondent is male (according to Afrobarometer coding).

- *Age*: Students and other young people were often the most active protesters in Africa's independence and pro-democracy movements (Nkinyangi, 1991). Youth tend to be free from family and occupational obligations that ordinarily deter people from protesting. Scholars have attributed the American civil rights movement and the collapse of the Soviet Union to demographic shifts and "life-course processes" producing large populations of frustrated young people (Goldstone and McAdam, 2002, 195). Similar processes could explain recent uprisings in Africa, although Resnick and Casale (2011) raise the possibility that African societies follow different patterns.

- *Education*: Sears and McConahay (1970) observed higher education levels among American rioters as compared to non-rioters, whereas Schussman and Soule (2005) found no influence of education on protest participation in the United States. Studying Africa, Kirwin, and Cho (2009) found that education has a significant and positive effect on protest participation, which they suspect is because better educated people are more politically aware. There is a historical relationship between university attendance and participation in African protests (Nkinyangi, 1991). I include a categorical variable measuring the highest level of education a respondent has completed, on a scale of one to four: no formal schooling, primary school, secondary school, or post-secondary school.

- Measures of objective well-being: I include two variables to test the theory that perceived well-being, and not objective well-being, motivates protest participation. *Gone without Income* takes a value of "1" if a respondent's family has foregone a cash income in the past twelve months, and "0" otherwise. *Employed* takes a value of "1" if a respondent has a job that pays a cash income, and "0" otherwise.

Explaining Protest Participation

Before examining the main regression analyses, consider Figure 5.1, which breaks down summary statistics by protesters and non-protesters. The two groups are demographically alike and about equally aggrieved on most issues. The continuous variables *Age* and *Legitimacy*, which are not included in the figure, also have similar values across groups: the average age is thirty-five among protesters and thirty-seven among non-protesters; the average rating of state legitimacy is eleven (on a scale of three to fifteen) in both groups. Subtle differences between the protester and non-protester categories are mostly in the expected directions. Protesters are more likely than non-protesters to be male, urban, and highly educated. The most obvious difference between groups is attendance at community meetings: 79 percent of protesters said they had attended a meeting in the past twelve months, whereas only 57 percent of non-protesters said so.

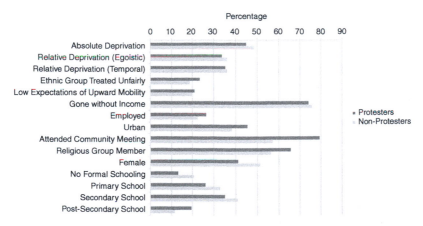

Figure 5.1: Protesters and Non-Protesters Compared
Numbers denote percentage of protesters or non-protesters with a value of "1" for a given dichotomous explanatory variable. Data are from Afrobarometer, covering 31 countries over 2002–2015. Sample is approximately 180,000 respondents, depending on the variable.

Some information in Figure 5.1 contradicts common assumptions about African protests. Nearly three-quarters of all protesters in the sample said they had gone without a cash income in the past year. Yet, there were slightly more respondents who said the same among non-protesters. The perception of deprivation (*Absolute Deprivation*) is also higher among non-protesters than among protesters. This challenges portrayals of African protests as insurrections by the poorest of society (Bush, 2009; Walton and Seddon, 1994). Patterns in Figure 5.1 also contradict descriptions of African protests as revolts by the labor aristocracy, meaning workers who are "part of the privileged exploitative group within society" (Wiseman, 1986, 511). Only about a quarter of protesters reported being employed in cash-paying jobs, indicating that most protesters are not labor aristocrats.

There is further evidence that African protesters are more vocationally diverse than master narratives imply. Rounds 2, 3, and 6 of the Afrobarometer surveys included an open-ended question asking respondents to state their main occupations. The summary of protesters' jobs in Table 5.2 shows that salaried workers are well represented among protesters, but so are informal sector workers. Farming/herding[9] is the most common occupation among protesters, despite the fact that nearly half of all protesters live in urban areas. This could reflect the growth of urban and periurban agriculture across Africa in response to inadequate public services in rapidly expanding cities (Cissé, Gueye, and Sy, 2005; Mbiba, 2001). The main takeaway from Figure 5.1 and Table 5.2 is that teachers, students, miners, and government workers do not comprise the bulk of rank-and-file protesters, even if they were historically the leaders of first-wave and second-wave protests in Africa (Wiseman, 1986; Nkinyangi, 1991; Diseko, 1992).

Multivariate regression analysis complements the descriptive information in Figure 5.1 and Table 5.2 by including statistical controls to estimate net relationships between each explanatory variable and the likelihood of protest participation. Table 5.4 displays estimates from three regression models, all with country and round fixed effects (I conduct separate country-level analyses in the robustness checks). The dependent variable is whether a respondent reported having

---

[9] Some Afrobarometer surveys combine these categories, although it bears noting that conflict between farmers and herders is becoming more common as climate change reduces the availability of farmland and pastures, especially in the semi-arid Sahel.

Table 5.2 *Protesters' Occupations*

Occupation	% of Protesters
Farmer/Herder	24
Informal Sector Worker	19
Formal Sector Worker	15
Student	13
Domestic Worker	8
Artisan (Informal Sector)	7
Businessperson	4
Civil Servant	4
Teacher	3
Other	2
Miner	1

Data are from responses to the open-ended question, "What is your main occupation?" Only rounds 2, 3, and 6 of the Afrobarometer surveys included this question, providing a total of 10,647 observations. Original responses included more than 50 categories, many of which were redundant (e.g., "farm worker" and "farmer"); responses are re-coded into 11 general categories.

participated in a demonstration or protest march in the past year. Each successive model introduces additional variables to demonstrate the stability of coefficient estimates.

Model 1 includes measures of community involvement and demographic controls, but omits measures of objective and subjective deprivation. All coefficients in Model 1 are statistically significant and in the expected directions, supporting the hypotheses that people are more likely to protest, ceteris paribus, if they are urban, involved with their communities, or educated; people are less likely to protest if they are female or older. Consistent with findings by Scacco (2008), attendance at community meetings has a strong net relationship with protest participation. Attending a community meeting in the past year is associated with an increase of 1.196 in the log-odds of protesting, all else equal. Afrobarometer data do not provide information about the content of community meetings that respondents attend, so I cannot rule out the possibility that protest-prone people select into community meetings. However, Scacco (2008) explores the content of community meetings in Nigeria and does not observe self-selection. She also finds that meeting attendees seldom discuss their grievances, which suggests that community meetings mobilize people by helping them coordinate and cooperate, not by making them more upset.

Model 2 adds two measures of objective deprivation: whether a respondent is employed in a cash-paying job and whether a respondent's household has foregone cash income in the past year. Neither variable has a statistically significant relationship with protest participation, supporting the theory that it is subjective and not objective well-being that influences political behavior (Langer and Smedts, 2013; Graham and Pettinato, 2002; Ravallion and Lokshin, 2000). Further evidence of the difference between subjective and objective well-being lies in the weak correlation between income or employment status and whether a respondent feels her or his living conditions are bad.[10] The regression estimates for other variables remain stable across the first and second models.

Model 3 is a fully specified model, incorporating measures of subjective well-being to test hypotheses about the relationship between different grievances and protest participation. To allay concerns about multicollinearity, I confirmed that grievances do not highly correlate with one another (Table 5.3). Perhaps surprisingly, perceived inequality across individuals (*Relative Deprivation [Egoistic]*) has no statistically significant link with protest participation, despite the increased objective inequality documented in Chapter 3. This implies that inequality matters because it creates an environment where *other* material concerns become inflamed. The economic grievance with the largest net relationship to protest participation is *Low Expectations of Upward Mobility*: respondents who expect their living conditions to be worse in the next year are significantly more likely to protest than more optimistic respondents, controlling for covariates. The size of the coefficient is modest, but it could potentially grow if future improvements in well-being do not meet Africans' expectations: Hirschman and Rothschild (1973) predict that people become more likely to protest as their patience wears thin and the "tunnel effect" expires

---

[10] The correlation between *Employed* and *Absolute Deprivation* is –0.1; the correlation between *Gone without Income* and *Absolute Deprivation* is 0.2. A rule of thumb for a weak correlation is a correlation coefficient less than |0.3|.

Table 5.3 *Correlations between Grievances*

	Absolute Deprivation	RD (Egoistic)	RD (Temporal)	Ethnic Grievance	Low EOUM
Absolute Deprivation	1.0000				
RD (Egoistic)	0.4003	1.0000			
RD (Temporal)	0.2821	0.2720	1.0000		
Ethnic Grievance	0.0749	0.0746	0.0642	1.0000	
Low EOUM	0.2192	0.2098	0.2806	0.0747	1.0000

"RD" = Relative Deprivation; "EOUM" = Expectations of Upward Mobility; "Ethnic Grievance" = Respondent believes that the government has treated her or his ethnic group unfairly.

(Hirschman and Rothschild, 1973). *Absolute Deprivation* has a *negative* relationship with protest participation, possibly reflecting the high perceived risk of protesting for people who see themselves as very poor. Respondents are more intolerant of *Temporal Relative Deprivation*: those who feel that their living conditions have declined over the past year are more likely to protest than people who perceive no declines in their living conditions. The likelihood of protest participation also increases when respondents feel that their ethnic group has been treated unfairly. This finding implies that scholars of social conflict in Africa are not wrong to highlight the salience of ethnicity. However, my results show that perceived ethnic injustice is only one of several grievances motivating people to join protests. African protesters also care about various dimensions of economic well-being, in contrast with many protesters in industrial and post-industrial societies who are principally motivated by post-materialist values such as identity and ideology (Johnston, Laraña, and Gusfield, 2010; Inglehart and Abramson, 1999; Benson and Rochon, 2004). For ease of interpretation, the graph in Figure 5.2 plots coefficient point estimates and 95 percent confidence intervals for all grievances in Model 3. The sum of evidence supports Bayart's intuition that "in Africa ethnicity is almost never absent from politics, yet at the same time it does not provide its basic fabric" (Bayart, 1993, 55).

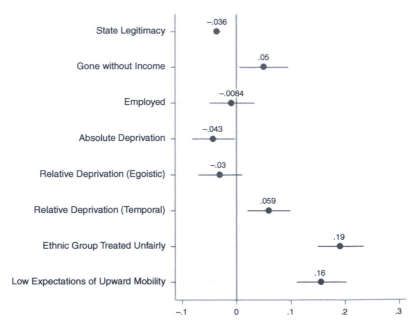

Figure 5.2: Estimated Effects of Grievances on Protest Participation
  Points denote coefficients from full logit model (controls not shown). Bars denote 95% confidence intervals.

Robustness and Model Sensitivity

I tested several variants of my main regression model (Model 3 in Table 5.4) to demonstrate robustness. Full results from robustness tests are in Appendix A. I first re-estimated the model while omitting the most protest-prone country, South Africa. Eighteen percent of all 11,989 South African survey respondents said they had participated in a demonstration or protest march in the previous twelve months. This is almost two standard deviations above the mean protest participation rate of 10.4 percent, making South Africa an outlier. Regression estimates remained virtually unchanged after removing South African respondents from the sample.

Next, I tested whether low expectations of upward mobility have different relationships with protest across different demographic groups. Some scholars theorize that highly educated or salaried people will feel entitled to upward mobility and blame the government if they see their economic opportunities as constricting (Bernstein and Crosby,

Table 5.4 *Individual-Level Analysis of Protest Participation*

	(1)	(2)	(3)
Urban	0.176***	0.178***	0.164***
	(0.0181)	(0.0182)	(0.0194)
Attended Community	1.196***	1.193***	1.205***
Meeting	(0.0212)	(0.0213)	(0.0229)
Religious Group Member	0.181***	0.179***	0.181***
	(0.0190)	(0.0190)	(0.0203)
State Legitimacy	−0.0408***	−0.0406***	−0.0357***
	(0.00296)	(0.00296)	(0.00314)
Female	−0.287***	−0.288***	−0.287***
	(0.0170)	(0.0171)	(0.0181)
Age	−0.0123***	−0.0122***	−0.0124***
	(0.000669)	(0.000672)	(0.000715)
Primary School	0.170***	0.172***	0.192***
	(0.0301)	(0.0302)	(0.0316)
Secondary School	0.422***	0.426***	0.424***
	(0.0303)	(0.0305)	(0.0320)
Post-Secondary School	0.764***	0.776***	0.750***
	(0.0343)	(0.0350)	(0.0373)
Gone without Income		0.0379	0.0504*
		(0.0209)	(0.0229)
Employed		−0.0105	−0.00838
		(0.0201)	(0.0214)
Absolute Deprivation			−0.0427*
			(0.0203)
Relative Deprivation			−0.0300
(Egoistic)			(0.0209)
Relative Deprivation			0.0592**
(Temporal)			(0.0201)
Ethnic Group Treated			0.191***
Unfairly			(0.0217)
Low Expectations of			0.156***
Upward Mobility			(0.0235)
Observations	157588	157349	140631
Pseudo R^2	0.085	0.085	0.087

Logit estimates with round and country fixed effects and standard errors in parentheses. Dependent variable is *Protest Participation*. Reference education category is "No Formal Schooling." Data are from Afrobarometer, covering 31 countries over 2002–2015.
* $p < 0.05$, ** $p < 0.01$, *** $p < 0.001$.

1980; Major, 1994; Olson and Ross, 1984). In contrast, poorer or less educated people might blame bad luck or a lack of personal effort for their perceived lack of mobility (Shapiro, 2002). One could therefore hypothesize that low expectations of upward mobility have a greater positive relationship with protest participation if a respondent is highly educated or salaried. To test this hypothesis, I estimated versions of the main regression model while including two interaction terms: *Employed * Low Expectations of Upward Mobility*; and *Graduate * Low Expectations of Upward Mobility* (where *Graduate* is a dummy variable indicating whether a respondent has a post-graduate education). Neither of these interaction terms was statistically significant, suggesting that low expectations of upward mobility are equally likely to motivate protest participation regardless of how entitled to gainful employment a respondent is.

I also tested the sensitivity of regression estimates to reducing the overall sample size. One downside of a very large sample is the risk of making a type one error. This risk arises because standard errors of consistent estimators become extremely small as the sample size increases (Lin, Lucas Jr. and Shmueli, 2013). I re-ran the main model using a randomly selected sub-sample of 90,000 observations (roughly half of the original sample size), and results were robust.

An advantage of a large sample size is the ability to estimate models on sub-samples of the population. Running separate regression models for each country revealed cross-national variation in the salience of low expectations of upward mobility. Anticipating declines in one's living conditions motivates protest participation in only fourteen out of thirty-one countries (Table 5.5). This does not invalidate the original finding that low expectations of upward mobility motivate protest participation on average across individuals, and these fourteen countries contain a sizable part of Africa's population (Nigeria is the most populous country on the continent at 193,392,500 people). It does, though, present interesting puzzles about the reasons for cross-national variation that country experts could explore in the future. For instance, low expectations of upward mobility appear to *discourage* protesting in Côte d'Ivoire. Another anomaly in Table 5.5 is Niger, where low expectations of upward mobility are substantially more salient than in any other country. I take a closer look at Niger in the next chapter.

Table 5.5 *Salience of Low Expectations of Upward Mobility: Estimates by Country*

Country	Logit Estimate, Net Controls
Benin	.070
Botswana	.216*
Burkina Faso	−.054
Burundi	.877*
Cameroon	.182
Cape Verde	−.044
Côte d'Ivoire	−.498*
Gabon	.191
Ghana	.047
Guinea	.175
Kenya	−.044
Lesotho	.367***
Liberia	.496***
Madagascar	.172
Malawi	−.023
Mali	.335**
Mauritius	.525**
Mozambique	.741***
Namibia	.038
Niger	1.003***
Nigeria	.350***
São Tomé and Príncipe	.782**
Senegal	.194*
Sierra Leone	.547**
South Africa	−.128
Tanzania	.141*
Togo	.117
Uganda	.134*
Zambia	−.210
Zimbabwe	.287

Coefficients estimated using country sub-samples and Model 3 in Table 5.4.
* $p < 0.10$, ** $p < 0.05$, *** $p < 0.01$.

Explaining Pessimism and Its Salience

A billboard in front of a large commercial bank in Dakar, Senegal depicts a sparkling modern city. Luxury cars circle glistening skyscrapers under a clear blue sky. A caption reassures passersby that investment – using the bank's products – will one day produce this Dakar of the future. The implicit advertising strategy is to cultivate hope in a better tomorrow so as to influence people's financial decisions today. The preceding statistical analyses showed that hope (or the lack thereof) can also influence people's short-term political behavior: Africans are more likely to protest, on average and other variables equal, if they have low expectations of upward mobility. These results raise an additional question: why are some people pessimistic about their economic opportunities, whereas others are more optimistic?

Observed correlations between grievances and protest participation might reflect reverse causality: protests are "passionate political processes" (Gould, 2003), so perhaps protesting causes low expectations of upward mobility and not the reverse. Ethnographers and clinical psychologists who work with activists note that "[s]ome emotions exist or arise in individuals before they join protest groups; others are formed or reinforced in collective action itself" (Jasper, 1998, 397). Drawing inferences about the causal effects of grievances on protest participation is difficult because experimental methods are inappropriate. Using randomized cues to stoke people's anger and see if they join protests would endanger human subjects, especially in authoritarian and semi-authoritarian regimes. Randomizing protest participation to see if the causal arrow runs from behavior to grievances would also be ethically dubious. Simulating protest participation in a laboratory might be safer, but it would tell researchers little about the causes of protest behavior in riskier real-world situations.[11]

In all likelihood, grievances and protest participation contribute to each other. The inferential challenge is not to demonstrate that protest participation has *no* effect on grievances, but rather to make a reasonable case that grievances have sources *beside* protest participation. Below, I draw on social psychology theories to identify where grievances come from. Some of those theories I am able to test empirically.

---

[11] Young (2016b) conducts a rare lab-in-the-field experiment on protest participation in Zimbabwe.

Why Do Some People Have Low Expectations of Upward Mobility?

Social psychologists advance two general arguments about why people come to anticipate declines in their living conditions. One states that low expectations of upward mobility are cultural: people become pessimistic by experiencing rigid class systems, media influence or propaganda, and other "framing effects" (Benford and Snow, 2000). A second argument states that low expectations of upward mobility arise from objective economic conditions: people who seldom experience or witness prosperity and social mobility have no basis on which to develop high expectations for their own economic advancement.

Cultural Roots of Low Expectations of Upward Mobility

Culture, meaning one's values, beliefs, and assumptions about social life (della Porta and Diani, 2006, 66), may condition people's expectations of higher incomes, job promotions, and other improvements in well-being. Cultural influences include "social mythologies that enshroud the mobility process" and "the norms in the popular culture of each nation that tell citizens in different groups how they are doing and how they should be doing in relation to other groups" (Turner, 1992, 5). While interviewing youths in post-war Rwanda and Burundi, Sommers and Uvin (2011) detected a culturally ingrained "capitalist ethos" and hope of social mobility among Burundians that Rwandans seemed to lack. De Tocqueville (1835/1961) proposed that rags-to-riches myths ("The American Dream") and a firm belief in meritocracy explain divergent attitudes toward redistribution in Europe and the United States. Tales of upward mobility can affect expectations of upward mobility by serving as "anecdotal distractions" from the true chances of advancement (Shapiro, 2002). As Decalo (1985) documents, rags-to-riches themes were common in the political rhetoric of African personalistic dictators including Idi Amin and Jean-Bédel Bokassa.

Conversely, cultural assumptions about the abilities of different identity groups can *dampen* expectations of upward mobility. Kelley and Kelley (2009) show with cross-national surveys that women are more likely than men to under-estimate their actual occupational mobility. Marx and Friedman (2009) find that African-American school children are more likely than children of other races to under-estimate their ability to score high on standardized tests.

Culture shapes individual repertoires of psychological responses to objective conditions by making some thoughts more accessible than others. Zaller (1992) argues that political attitudes do not come from deep reasoning about social injustice or right and wrong, but instead from the considerations and assumptions that are freshest in one's mind at a given moment. Lieberman, Schreiber, and Oschsner (2001, 684) explain: "Thinking takes effort; hence, individuals usually make judgments on the basis of the information that comes easily to mind, without conducting an exhaustive search of memory for all relevant knowledge and beliefs." Thus, if people receive steady cues indicating that social mobility is imminent (or impossible), then their expectations will tend to reflect those messages.

Elites strategically modify cultural cues to condition high expecta-tions of upward mobility and stave off popular revolt. Elites – meaning politicians, employers, and other "influential minorities" (Keller, 1991b) – inspire the poor with anecdotal distractions and populist promises, thereby "maintaining the morale and motivation of their members without significantly and concretely improving either their social ranking or rewards" (Tumin, 1967, 37). For example, South African President Jacob Zuma campaigned in 2014 on a platform of expanding business opportunities and land ownership for traditionally disadvantaged non-white citizens (Laing, 2014). Elites employ euphe-misms to make the economically disadvantaged perceive or anticipate improvements in their well-being and social status even in the absence of objective mobility: janitors become "maintenance engineers"; sales clerks become "customer service associates"; instructors become "assistant professors." These devices generate optimism that Tumin terms "fictitious mobility," which in turn makes people more likely to tolerate the extant system of distribution and rewards.

The above theories imply that low expectations of upward mobility emerge when elites fail to alter people's basic assumptions about eco-nomic security and entitlement by framing chronic deprivation as temporary.[12] However, social scientists struggle to explain variations

---

[12] Elites are not solely responsible for constructing culture to enhance impressions of economic mobility. "One 'nondeliberate' source for this construction stems from the familiar 'truncation bias' created by the media, which will report

in elites' strategies because "those at the top rarely reveal the inner workings of their worlds," except in occasional eyewitness accounts or leaked diaries and letters (Keller, 1991b). Cultural explanations for low expectations of upward mobility are plausible, but it is difficult to validate them empirically.

Material Roots of Low Expectations of Upward Mobility

Researchers studying the roots of pessimism and optimism therefore tend to focus on material well-being as an explanation, which is easier to observe and to measure. Individual-level studies show that people have higher expectations of upward mobility when they have experienced or witnessed actual mobility in the past. Expectations of upward mobility are pronounced in Cape Town, a South African city known for its economic opportunities and large upper and middle classes (Telzak, 2012, 12). Cape Town youths, including those who are objectively disadvantaged, commonly overestimate their educational potential. Surveys from the University of Cape Town's National Income Dynamics Study revealed that over two-thirds of people in the lowest income quintile expect their income will rise more than that of the average South African (Burns, 2009). Kelley and Kelley (2009) measured subjective mobility with ISSP Inequality-III surveys from thirty countries in 1999 and 2000, which asked respondents to compare the status of their most recent job with the status of their father's job. Subjective mobility correlated positively with actual generational mobility. Studying surveys of 16,234 Poles from 1992 to 2008, Sokolowska (2013) estimated that various dimensions of objective well-being – including education and occupation and those of one's father – made people feel like their incomes were improving.

Country-level variables also seem to influence subjective mobility. The percentage of South Africans who expect to experience upward mobility within two years fell from 75 percent to 50 percent between 2008 and 2010, during a significant economic downturn (Telzak, 2012, 13). Kelley and Kelley (2009) observed in a sample of thirty diverse countries that "people who have experienced GDP growth, independent of their actual occupational mobility and other individual characteristics, believe that they have risen a little more from their

newsworthy 'successes' (lottery winners, basketball superstars) but not mundane 'failures'" (Ray, 2006, 414).

fathers than do comparable individuals who experienced no GDP growth." Analyzing survey data from six Latin American countries, Fletcher (2013) found that economic growth correlates with higher perceived control over one's life. Bárcena et al. (2010) used household surveys to demonstrate that optimism in Latin American countries began to fall in 2007, just as the growth of national economies began to rapidly decelerate. In sum, witnessing aggregate economic improvements primes people to expect improvements in their individual lot, whereas witnessing economic setbacks depresses expectations.

The above evidence supports the theory that experiencing economic gain is necessary to imagine the possibility of further gains and to bridge the "empathy gulf" between rich and poor (Shapiro, 2002). Fletcher (2013, 5) explains, "people cannot aspire to what they do not know, and they are less likely to know the next steps on the ladder of living conditions when the step is large." Pickett and Wilkinson (2010, 40) echo, "in general the further up the social ladder you are, the more help the world seems to give you in keeping the self-doubts at bay ... "

Data availability prevents me from testing the relationship between individual objective mobility and expectations of upward mobility in a large sample of African countries. Afrobarometer enumerators did not record changes over time in respondents' objective income levels or the incomes and occupations of respondents' parents. Existing studies on socioeconomic mobility in Africa are mostly anthropological case studies (usually of South Africa) or small-sample statistical analyses covering just a few countries.[13]

But data do exist to test the relationship between a country's economy and individual expectations of upward mobility. The graph in Figure 5.3 plots economic growth against the percent of a country's Afrobarometer respondents who said that they expected their economic conditions to be worse in the next year. Data are from the 2014–2015 round of surveys, which covered the largest sample of countries (thirty-one). The scatterplot offers preliminary evidence that pessimism and economic growth negatively correlate, ever so slightly, in sub-Saharan Africa as they do in non-African countries (Kelley and Kelley, 2009; Fletcher, 2013; Barcena et al., 2010).

---

[13] See, for example, Hertz (2001); Collinson et al. (2003); Woolard and Klasen (2007); Baulch and Hoddinott (2000); Bledsoe (1990); Porter (2002); Little (1974).

Table 5.6 *Cross-Country, Time-Series Analysis of Low Expectations of Upward Mobility*

	(1)	(2)	(3)
GDP per Capita Growth	−0.867	−0.862	−0.822
(Annual%)	(0.543)	(0.527)	(0.543)
Log GDP per Capita		−0.306	0.439
(PPP, Current Int'l $)		(1.023)	(1.574)
Unemployment			−0.162
(% of Labor Force, ILO Estimates)			(0.169)
R^2	0.0597	0.0602	0.0695
Observations	116	116	116

Ordinary Least Squares estimates with panel-corrected standard errors in parentheses. The dependent variable is the percentage of Afrobarometer survey respondents in a given country-year who said that they expect their economic conditions to get worse in the next twelve months. Measures of explanatory variables are from the World Bank. * $p < 0.05$, ** $p < 0.01$, *** $p < 0.001$.

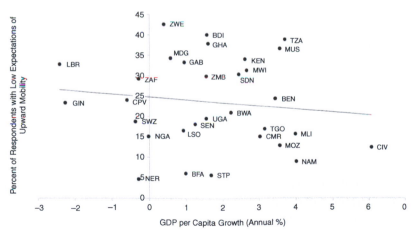

Figure 5.3: Growth and Low Expectations of Upward Mobility

Low Expectations of Upward Mobility data are from round 6 of the Afrobarometer surveys (2014–2015). Growth data are from the World Bank in each country's corresponding survey year. Sierra Leone omitted for readability, due to extremely low growth rate of –22%.

The regression analysis in Table 5.6 complements Figure 5.3 with modest evidence that Africans have lower expectations of upward mobility, on average, when they live in poorer countries or countries with more slowly growing economies. The dependent variable is the percentage of Afrobarometer survey respondents in a given country-year who said they expect their economic conditions to get worse in the next twelve months, and the main independent variable is the economic growth of the respondent's country in the survey year. Models 1 through 3 show a negative (though not statistically significant) relationship between growth in GDP per capita and low expectations of upward mobility, even after controlling for other country-level variables that plausibly affect how people see the future. These results offer a partial answer to the question of why some Africans have low expectations of upward mobility whereas others are more optimistic: people become hopeful about their personal well-being when they witness aggregate economic development.

Conclusion

This chapter explored why some people in Africa protest and others do not. Analyzing Afrobarometer survey data from thirty-one African countries over the period 2002 to 2015, I tested hypotheses about grievances and resource mobilization, estimating that people are more likely to protest, on average, if they anticipate declines in their living standards. Other grievances motivating protest participation include the feeling that one's ethnic group has been treated unfairly and the feeling that one's economic conditions have worsened in the past. Objective measures of well-being, including poverty and employment status, have no measurable relationship with protest propensity. Attitudes about the legitimacy of the incumbent regime matter very little, in contrast with the motivating grievances of protest leaders. Corroborating other scholars' findings, I also found that people are more likely to protest when they are embedded in community networks.

If policymakers want to identify the triggers of social unrest in Africa, it is not enough to track variables such as economic growth, poverty, life expectancy, and income inequality. They must also pay attention to "the moral consequences of economic growth," meaning "how the citizens of any country think about economic growth, and what actions they take in consequence" (Friedman, 2006, 16). This will involve supplementing objective measures of well-being with subjective measures. Investing in the collection and analysis of public opinion surveys similar to Afrobarometer could help policymakers understand popular grievances and thus the scale of protests.

6 | Not-So-Great Expectations: Pessimism and Protest in Niger

Nouhou Mahamadou Arzika has been organizing protests in Niger for most of his life. "I grew up a militant," he says. "Even when I was very young I had a taste for helping the weak. I was born this way. My father fought for national independence from France."[1] Arzika is best known in Niger for helping to spearhead the Movement Against the High Cost of Living, which brought more than a hundred thousand people out onto the dusty avenues of Niamey after lawmakers introduced a 19 percent tax on primary commodities in 2005 (Bonnecase, 2013, 100). His more recent organization, the Movement for the Promotion of Responsible Citizenship, promotes both economic justice and democracy. Arzika spells out his strategy of espousing multiple goals at the same time: "You can't mobilize anyone without appealing to their particular interests and convictions. We have a specific language that we use for different groups – students, merchants – to tell them that they can win. To make them feel like they must mobilize."

Knowing the most salient grievances in a protesting crowd is difficult when protest leaders send mixed messages about their objectives. This chapter highlights one such case, the 2009–2010 uprisings in Niger, which precipitated a military coup against President Mamadou Tandja.[2] Protest spokespeople and the international media framed the uprisings, alternately, as a defense of constitutional democracy and an expression of anger with the high cost of living. Employing regression analysis of original survey data, and using protest participation as the dependent variable, I reinforce my finding that economic grievances – especially, low expectations of upward mobility – had a stronger relationship with Nigeriens' decisions to protest than dissatisfaction with Tandja's attempt to circumvent presidential term limits. This is consistent with the cross-national results of the previous

---

[1] Interview on May 24, 2016.
[2] Parts of this analysis appeared in Mueller (2013).

chapter. Poor people were also more likely to protest at the urging of middle-class organizers, which suggests that protest participation stems from a combination of latent grievances and leaders who compel people to bear the individual costs of collective action.

My dataset, based on a quasi-random sample of over 300 Nigerien protesters and non-protesters, allows me to mitigate several limitations of the Afrobarometer data. Namely, Afrobarometer questions focus on attitudes about ongoing economic and political conditions, such as, "in general, how would you describe your own present living conditions?" Questions do not ask about respondents' attitudes toward the abrupt actions of incumbents that ostensibly trigger democratic revolutions. This hinders an understanding of the extent to which specific grievances motivate participation in corresponding events. I overcome this limitation by including questions in my surveys explicitly about Tandja's bid for an extra-constitutional third term in office.

My observation that many Nigeriens actually supported extending Tandja's tenure contradicts international perceptions of the 2009–2010 uprisings as a public outcry for democracy. Indeed, self-proclaimed people's champion Nouhou Arzika ultimately sided with Tandja, claiming that Tandja's opponents had no concrete plan for reform.[3] Members of the opposition accused him of flip-flopping from fighting against government tax hikes to eating out of the government's hand (Planète Afrique, 2009).[4] In the following analysis, I cast doubt on the motivations behind supposedly pro-democracy movements, especially those unfolding in contexts where autocracy and poverty coincide. Although political and economic grievances are not mutually exclusive, economic grievances are sometimes more politically salient than dissatisfaction with autocracy, even in repressive regimes.

The analysis begins with background on the 2009–2010 uprisings. This historical overview raises several possibilities for why Nigeriens decided to join protests "against Tandja," including political, economic, and social grievances. Next, I analyze which grievances motivated participation in the uprisings. According to survey data,

---

[3] Interview on May 24, 2016.

[4] In 2017, Arzika announced his own intent to run for president in 2021, purportedly with behind-the-scenes support from Tandja. Rumor had it that Tandja was using Arzika as a proxy to launch a new political career. Niamey journalists reported seeing Arzika entering Tandja's home for late-night consultations.

Nigerien society at the time was ambivalent toward the president, and more critical citizens were no more likely to rise up than less critical ones. Instead, a pessimistic economic outlook distinguished protesters from non-protesters. The chapter concludes with the advice to take headlines about "democratic revolutions" with a grain of salt.

The Uprisings of 2009–2010

Former army colonel Mamadou Tandja became Niger's president in late 1999 through elections that international observers widely deemed to be free and fair, raising hopes that he would finally reverse decades of economic and political turmoil. During his early years in power, Niger returned to civilian rule after a string of military regimes and held its first-ever municipal elections. Tandja was freely elected to a second term in 2004 while pledging to revitalize an economy in the grip of a dire food shortage.

He belied this promise by failing to alleviate hunger that peaked with a locust infestation and severe drought in 2005. Under his watch, thousands of children died and malnutrition reached 13.4 percent in some regions. USAID's Famine Early Warning Systems Network estimated that 2.7 million Nigeriens were highly to extremely food insecure, with an additional 5.1 million people at risk for moderate food insecurity (Tsai, 2010). Tandja forbade public debate on the emergency and accused journalists covering the topic of being anti-patriotic. Nevertheless, foreign media criticized him for ignoring Niger's urgent needs and for refusing to distribute grain from state warehouses (Nossiter, 2009).

Flouting his critics, Tandja announced in 2008 that he would seek a third term in order to, as he put it, "satisfy the popular will" and "finish some projects" (Baudais and Chauzal, 2011). In 2009, he launched a public relations campaign to raise support for a referendum on revising the constitution's two-term limit. This attempt, known as *tazartché* ("continuity" in Hausa), prompted lawmakers and judges to invoke Article 49 of the constitution prohibiting referenda on constitutional amendments. Tandja then dissolved the National Assembly and began ruling by decree, effectively dismantling the democratic institutions established at the National Conference of 1991. He held and won an allegedly fraudulent referendum. Opposition groups boycotted elections, denying legitimacy to the ruling party's sweep of local and parliamentary races and the 92.5 percent of ballots cast in favor of the constitutional revision (Miller, 2011, 45).

After the referendum, an estimated ten thousand protesters turned out in the capital and labor unions declared a 48-hour nationwide strike (BBC, 2010b). The government dispersed crowds with tear gas and declared strikes illegal, drawing censure from diplomats and regional organizations like the Economic Community of West African States. While reprimanding Tandja, foreign governments were also quick to praise the protesters and striking workers as guardians of democracy. A former U.S. ambassador to South Africa and Nigeria implored the international community "to commend the Nigeriens for continuing in this fight to sustain and return democracy to Niger" (RFI, 2010). Painting Nigeriens as democratic revolutionaries, foreign journalists published quotes from opposition members admonishing Tandja and denouncing *tazartché*. "This isn't good at all for democracy," reported a Nigerien street vendor to *The New York Times*. "We don't want a president for life here. Yes, democracy is in serious, serious trouble." Another vendor hinted at the multiplicity of grievances driving the protests: "*tazartché* is no good. The country doesn't agree with it. There's nothing to eat, and there are loads of problems" (Nossiter, 2009).

On February 18, 2010, an army faction calling itself the Supreme Council for the Restoration of Democracy stormed the presidential palace during a cabinet meeting, seized Tandja, and dissolved the government. The faction consisted of four colonels, including coup leader Salou Djibo, who appeared on television that night and announced their intention to "make Niger an example of democracy and good governance" and "save Niger and its population from poverty, deception and corruption" (Perry, 2010). They promised to address food insecurity and to hold free and fair elections, using rhetoric that was "eminently well adapted to international democratic standards" (Baudais and Chauzal, 2011, 299). "What we did was in the best interest of Niger," military spokesperson Harouna Djibrilla Amadou reassured citizens. "We ask you to stay calm, we're here for you, we're listening and we assure you that we will never let you down" (BBC, 2010b).

True to their word, the junta held elections nine months later and ceded power to the winners. Niger's military had some high-profile detractors, including United Nations Secretary-General Ban Ki-moon

(UN News Centre, 2010), but the international community by and large regarded Tandja's ousting as a "corrective coup" (Baudais and Chauzal, 2011; Barnett, 2010).[5] Thousands of Nigeriens once more poured into the streets of Niamey, seemingly in celebration (*The Economist*, 2013). Ali Idrissa, the president of a coalition of Nigerien NGOs, alluded to democratic values in his cautious praise of the coup: "As democratic people, we can't cheer a military coup d'état. But in reality, deep down, we are cheering it. For us, it's a good coup d'état" (Armstrong, 2010). Opposition spokesman Bazoum Mohamed was more candid: "We say thank you to the junta for their intervention. We are for the restoration of democracy and we are committed to joining the army in this mission" (BBC, *2010b*). The public reaction to the coup reinforced an image of Nigeriens as committed democrats and of Niger as "a compelling test case for the viability of meaningful democracy in the poorest countries" (Davis and Kossomi, 2001, 87). But the uprisings have more ambiguous roots when viewed in the broader context of Niger's political, economic, and social landscape.

The Political Context

History was repeating itself in 2009. Since national independence from France in 1960, the Republic of Niger has had seven constitutions, two long periods of rule by decree, and four military coups. Tandja mirrored the country's first president Hamani Diori, as much as he tried to distinguish himself from his Gallophile counterpart by displacing French nuclear power companies with Chinese-operated uranium mines (Burgis, 2010). Diori succumbed to a welcomed putsch in 1974, in part because of his closeness with Niger's former colonial rulers, and in part because of his autocratic leanings and inattention to near-famine conditions during a three-year drought. Niger's first constitution gave him virtually absolute power, which he wielded for almost every purpose except to address misery in the countryside (Raynal, 1993). Historical accounts of Diori's downfall are interchangeable with accounts of Tandja's final days in office: "Obvious as the drought problem in general was as a factor for instability for

---

[5]   For a counter-argument, see Miller (2011) on "Debunking the Myth of the 'Good' Coup d'Etat in Africa."

Diori's régime, of greater political damage was the not only incompetent, but blatantly corrupt handling of the relief aid by members of the [ruling party]" (Higgott and Fuglestad, 1975, 390). Inspectors uncovered 3,000 tons of grain that the president had been hoarding in warehouses while waiting for prices to rise (Higgott and Fuglestad, 1975, 390). This history bears resemblance to reports of Tandja refusing to distribute grain stores at the most critical point of Niger's 2005 hunger crisis (Nossiter, 2009).

Diori's successors were each ineffective in their own ways. The general who deposed him, Seyni Kountché, increased the state's presence in the countryside with the Supreme Military Council, the Development Society, and a rural youth movement called *Samariya* ("youth" in Hausa). Nigeriens harbor some nostalgia for Kountché, whom they remember as a man of integrity and a model nationalist. However, time has softened the edges of a regime that used military brutality to promote development programs that left many citizens still in poverty. After Kountché's death from a brain tumor in 1987, Colonel Ali Saibou seized power but proved a weak president. His most significant legacy was founding the National Movement for a Developing Society (Mouvement National pour la Société du Développement, or MNSD) as the country's sole legal political party, which survived the switch to multi-party democracy in 1991. Under the eventual helm of Mamadou Tandja, the MNSD would outlast several coups, constitutional revisions, and the proliferation of new parties.

On February 9, 1990, students in Niamey boycotted classes, apparently to protest structural adjustment measures that threatened school budgets and a long-standing system of automatic public-sector employment for graduates (Gervais, 1995). Civil disobedience reached a turning point when state troops opened fire on a crowd of students marching toward the John F. Kennedy Bridge spanning the Niger River, which the United States financed during the Cold War to foster support for Western liberalism (Bloise, 2001). The Saibou regime showed its willingness to repress civil liberties despite paying lip service to democracy with theatrical elections in 1989.

The massacre that would become known as Black Friday was the symbolic start of the second wave of protest in Niger (Ibrahim, 1999b, 194). Niger's first independent newspaper, *Haske*, launched four months later and shattered the regime's veneer of popularity. The Union of Workers' Trade Unions of Niger (Union des Syndicats des Travailleurs du Niger, or

USTN) awoke from three decades of government co-optation and "responsible participation" to stage a general strike and the largest public demonstration since anti-colonial protests of the 1950s (Ibrahim, 1999b, 194). Openly challenging the ruling party for the first time, the USTN recruited an estimated 100,000 protesters to file through Niamey chanting, "Down with the IMF," "Down with the Second Republic," and "Down with Whiskey" (referring to Saibou's drinking habit) (Ibrahim, 1994).

Saibou finally acquiesced to civil society's demands for reform. A national conference convened on July 29, 1991, lasting almost 100 days and involving 1,200 representatives from the incumbent government, nascent opposition parties, labor unions, student groups, and civil society (Moestrup, 1999). Delegates adopted semi-presidential government and a proportional representation electoral system accommodating a unicameral National Assembly of nine parties, six of which formed a majority coalition. The MNSD emerged with 29 seats as the largest opposition party, although its disgraced founder Ali Saibou surrendered leadership (Moestrup, 1999).

The transformation of the MNSD "from an authoritarian sole party to an effective player in the democratic game" and back again paralleled Mamadou Tandja's political transformation (Ibrahim and Souley, 1998, 152). A former colonel in Kountché's military, Tandja climbed party ranks as a well-connected businessman and an alternative to the party's other heir apparent, Adamou Djermakoye. Djermakoye had also served in the Kountché administration, but in a very different capacity from Tandja, as a member of the Zarma ethnic group's reigning oligarchy. Tandja won the biggest endorsement in MNSD succession deliberations because he was from neither of Niger's dominant Zarma and Hausa groups. This positioned him to broker ethnic cooperation within a fracturing party.

In the post-Saibou era, Tandja restored not only party cohesion, but also the party's active role in politics. He ran for president in elections following the National Conference, winning the initial round of votes but not the run-off. Initially playing by the rules of Niger's fledgling democracy, he congratulated Mahamane Ousmane on the victory, ignoring pressure from his own party to contest the results. This earned Tandja international kudos and allowed the MNSD to remain a viable opposition player in the Alliance of the Forces of Change (Alliance des Forces du Changement, or AFC) coalition. Tandja cast himself as the savior of the MNSD, in one instance even using his military prowess to fight back an armed attack on the party's campaign caravan (Ibrahim and Souley, 1998, 151).

Tandja took advantage of a split in the government to advance his party's political position and his own. In September 1994, President Ousmane stripped nearly all powers from Prime Minister Mahamadou Issoufou amid personal disagreements, violating a constitutional provision for power sharing. Issoufou resigned and retaliated by withdrawing from the AFC coalition and defecting to the MNSD despite having battled the opposition for years. This was a boon to Tandja both as MNSD chief and as a presidential hopeful, because it loosened the AFC's hold on the parliamentary majority and eroded Ousmane's legitimacy. Foreseeing a political opening, Tandja redoubled his efforts to remain prominent in a party on the rise.

As a minority president, Ousmane faced a vote of no confidence and desperately called parliamentary elections. The MNSD won a plurality of seats in the National Assembly and assumed its long-awaited position in the majority coalition, with Secretary-General Hama Amadou assuming the prime ministry in a tenuous co-habitation with Ousmane. Wishing to completely purge the government of Ousmane's supporters, Colonel Ibrahim Baré Mainassara staged a coup d'état on January 27, 1996 and placed Ousmane under house arrest. This reinstated military rule and marked a "rebirth of authoritarianism" in Niger (Ibrahim, 1999a), a mere six years after the National Conference inaugurated Nigerien democracy. Mainassara won allegedly fraudulent elections and overturned elements of the constitution that he blamed for the outgoing regime's failures. The Constitution of the Fourth Republic instituted a presidential system and first-past-the-post electoral rules that concentrated executive power and facilitated majority party dominance.

Public enthusiasm for Mainassara's reforms did not last long. Opposition leaders, including Tandja, organized demonstrations outside the National Assembly on January 11, 1997. The protesters braved tear gas and beatings at the hands of government troops (Amnesty International, 1997). Tandja again became a hero of the pro-democracy movement when Mainassara jailed him and several other adversaries for two weeks, notwithstanding an order from the Niamey Appeal Court for the prisoners' release (Amnesty International, 1996). After snubbing legal and popular resistance, Mainassara died in an "unfortunate accident" on April 9, 1999 (Amnesty International,

2000). A referendum the next July reversed most of his amendments to the constitution, and five months later interim leaders held parliamentary and presidential elections. Tandja at last set his hand on the Koran to take the oath of presidential office on December 22, 1999. This sealed the dominance of the MNSD, which the month before had already swept most of the legislative seats and elected Tandja to the National Assembly – a post that Tandja happily declined so he could serve as president.

The new power configuration brought citizens little relief from natural disasters and the negative side effects of structural adjustment. Tandja had once led students in dissent against Mainassara but became the target of violent protests in 2001 following funding cuts at the University of Niamey (Francis, 2007, 148). He withstood student anger and a ten-day mutiny of underpaid soldiers by dispensing a new influx of foreign aid to pacify his critics (BBC, 2002). Ironically, the aid that donors sent as a reward for clean elections allowed Tandja to pay forty thousand civil servants without reforming the economy (Elischer, 2013, 15). Tandja won a second term in 2004, which he served until the coup of 2010. By that point, Nigeriens had plenty of reasons to protest political conditions, but the economic context was arguably grimmer.

The Economic Context

Landlocked Niger is one of the least developed countries in the world. Its first commercial uranium mine opened in 1971, interrupting a downward spiral of economic mismanagement. However, a collapse in uranium prices in the early 1980s made GDP plummet once again (Graybeal and Picard, 1991, 286). The graph of per capita incomes in Figure 6.1 shows that the economy never came close to recovering. Niger's Human Development Index (HDI) – a composite measure of income, life expectancy, and education – consistently ranks last, even among other African countries. Life expectancy is sixty years, the literacy rate is 15.5 percent (8.9 percent for women), and almost half of the population lives below the international poverty line of $1.99 per day, according to World Bank estimates. Population growth offset an improvement in the aggregate poverty rate from 64.4 percent in 2005 to 60.8 percent in 2007. The absolute number of poor

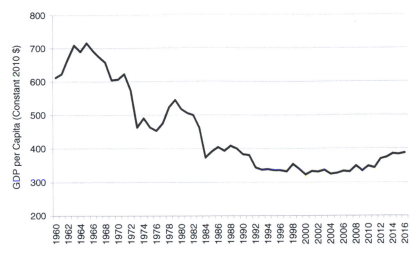

Figure 6.1: GDP per Capita in Niger, 1960–2016
Data are from the World Bank's World Development Indicators.

Nigeriens actually increased during that same period, to 8.2 million (Dabalen et al., 2012).

Desperation and persistent international pressure compelled President Kountché to cooperate with IMF and World Bank structural adjustment programs (Gervais, 1995). Aid was conditional on public sector reforms that never fulfilled their purpose of reducing government debt and stimulating investment. Nigeriens rose up en masse in the early 1990s after leaders privatized public enterprises and shrank the civil service by 38 percent (Graybeal and Picard, 1991, 293). The government lacked revenues to counterbalance these pains of austerity. Ninety percent of Niger's population works in the informal agricultural sector, which is largely untaxed and accounts for only 40 percent of GDP (Dabalen et al., 2012). Falling uranium prices reduced tax revenues to as low as 9 percent of GNP in some years (Barlow and Snyder, 1993).

Greater reliance on borrowing triggered a debt crisis (Gazibo, 2005). Figure 6.2 reveals a significant rise in external debt during structural adjustment of the 1970s and 1980s. A momentary drop between 2000 and 2008 resulted more from IMF debt relief than from better economic planning by incumbents (Sacerdoti and Callier, 2008). Loans rebounded under Tandja and continued climbing after the World Bank

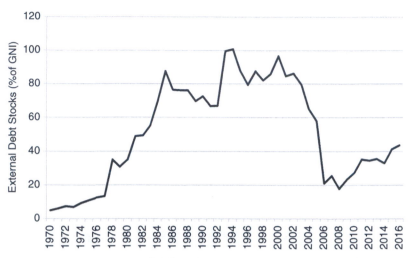

Figure 6.2: Niger's External Debt, 1970–2016
Total external debt stock is the sum of debt owed to non-residents, including
IMF credit, public debt, and private non-guaranteed long-term debt. Data are
from the World Bank's World Development Indicators.

showed its support for the 2010 coup by lending to the new military
regime (World Bank, 2012). Before the fall of Muammar Gaddafi in
2011, Niger's leaders supplemented loans with aid from Libya
(Gazibo, 2007, 32). The loss of those funds became a sore spot for
many elite and ordinary Nigeriens.[6]

Even in relatively bountiful years, Nigerien farmers struggle with
volatile markets and weather events that grow more extreme with
climate change. Supplies are often imported over long distances from
coastal ports and more fertile regions, making the little food that is
available extremely expensive for the average citizen. Niger has experienced successive food shortages as a result of droughts and locust
invasions (*The Economist*, 2005; Tsai, 2010). Although the 2005 crisis
was not officially a famine according to the Howe and Devereux famine
scale, it approached famine proportions: Malnutrition accounted for

---

[6] Nostalgia for Gaddafi is pronounced in the Agadez region of Niger. When
Gaddafi's regime dissolved, so did policies facilitating the safe seasonal migration
of laborers from Agadez to Libya. Thereafter, migrants from Niger and other
sub-Saharan countries faced exploitation, kidnapping, and worse. Migration to
Libya continued regardless, as the local tourist economy in Agadez took a hit
during the Tuareg rebellion of 2007.

an estimated 52 percent of deaths among children under five years old, and 22 percent of children's caregivers lacked strategies for coping with food shortfalls (Reza et al., 2008). International food aid was unable to compensate for government inaction, a fact that Niger's leaders tried unsuccessfully to conceal (BBC, 2005). There is an empirical link between food scarcity and political unrest, both across and within countries (Barrett, 2013; Smith, 2013; Bellemare, 2011; Arezki and Brückner, 2011). The food crisis is thus a plausible source of economic grievances in the 2009–2010 uprisings. A second drought occurred just before the protests began (Dabalen et al., 2012, 27).

Inequality, and not just poverty, is severe in Niger. In 2005, the wealthiest 30 percent of the population accounted for 63.3 percent of total household consumption, while the poorest 30 percent accounted for only 9.3 percent (Dabalen et al., 2012, 11). Weather shocks disproportionately affect rural communities. In 2007, half of rural households ranked weather as their top concern, compared to less than 15 percent of urban households (people in urban households tend to be more concerned about price shocks) (Dabalen et al., 2012, 29). There is also inequality across sectors. The government has tended to tax formal-sector incomes more heavily than informal-sector incomes of the same size, burdening urban business owners and discouraging merchants from applying for licenses (Barlow and Snyder, 1993, 1184).

In light of these economic problems, some observers of the 2009–2010 uprisings interpreted the events as bread riots. Bonnecase (2013) theorized that commodity prices and the high cost of living constituted "local repertoires of anger" spurring people to action. He underlined hunger as a theme common to all three waves of protest in Niger. It is uncertain, though, whether chronic hunger and gradual increases in the cost of living can explain the onset of protests in 2009, a year when some macroeconomic indicators such as GDP per capita were slightly better than they were a few years before.

The Social Context

On the surface, Niger has all the ingredients for ethnic strife. Approximately 56 percent of Nigeriens are Hausa. The Hausa thus constitute a dominant group, defined as making up 45 to 90 percent of a country's population; ethnic dominance correlates with a higher risk of civil conflict (Collier and Hoeffler, 2004). Hausa people live mainly in south-central and eastern Niger along the border with Nigeria, which splits a region once known as Hausaland. Niger's next largest group is the Zarma, at 22 percent of the population, followed by at least thirty smaller distinct groups. During colonial times, French occupiers favored the Zarma, whom they considered easier to subdue given the group's internal divisions and lack of strong state structures compared to the Hausa (Charlick, 1991, 9). We might therefore expect the Hausa to harbor grievances from their historic marginalization, and to exclude other groups from power when given the chance.

But surprisingly, "Niger has been spared the levels of ethnic hostility seen in many other countries" (Davis and Kossomi, 2001, 81). Geographic and cultural boundaries between the Hausa and Zarma are fluid. Members of both groups sometimes change their ethnicities by adopting each other's languages and practices (Charlick, 1991, 8). Intermarriage across all of Niger's ethnicities is widespread, even including the periodically separatist Tuaregs (Turshen, 2010; Gosselain, 2008). Cross-cutting identities are strong, especially Islam and nationality (Miles and Rochefort, 1991). Niger retains a pre-colonial tradition of *cousinage*, or "joking kinship," whereby families of different ethnic identities form deep social ties (Aboubacar Yenikoye, 2007; de Sardan, 1984).

Niger maintained a "culture of peace" (Aboubacar Yenikoye, 2007) partly by political engineering. The country's first presidents discouraged research on ethnicity in order to prevent divisions during a long period of Zarma dominance (Charlick, 1991, 8). Later, delegates at the National Conference adopted proportional representation and semi-presidential systems to open the government to multiple ethnic groups. In many African countries, the switch to multi-party democracy ignited ethnic conflict by increasing electoral competition and creating incentives for politicians to make ethnic appeals.[7] But ethnicity does not define politics in Niger. The Democratic and Social Convention (Convention Démocratique et Sociale, or CDS) party, for example, began as a civic association in Zinder, the seat of Hausa resistance to the Zarma oligarchy. "Yet, although the party was built to have a strong Hausa nationalist orientation, many of its top

[7] Eifert, Miguel, and Posner (2010) find that survey respondents across ten African countries are 1.8 percentage points more likely to identify in ethnic terms for every month closer their country is to a competitive presidential election.

leadership are not 'ethnically' Hausa" (Ibrahim and Souley, 1998, 152). The party's leaders have been diverse – Hausa, Kanuri, and Tuareg. The MNSD, a rival of the CDS, hand-picked Mamadou Tandja as the face of the party because he was "the most 'de-tribalised' frontline politician in the country" (Ibrahim and Souley, 1998, 151). Tandja was of mixed Kanuri and Fulani ancestry, helping protect the MNSD from becoming dominated by either the Zarma or the Hausa. Tandja thus strengthened his party, but he made strategic errors that undermined his personal hold on power.

Political Society and the Capacity for Collective Action

Tandja invested extensively in mobile communications infrastructure, which contributed to his downfall by allowing the opposition to coordinate. Only half of Niger had Global System for Mobile Communications (GSM) signal coverage when Tandja left office in 2010, but coverage was almost nonexistent as late as 2000. Mobile phone subscribers increased from 2.4 per 100 people in 2005 to 12.8 in 2008, and phones are now as common a sight in Niamey as in any African capital (Dominguez-Torres and Foster, 2011, 31). Protesters in 2009 and 2010 also used Niger's still-limited Internet service to share logistical information (Azizou, 2010).

Conventional technologies remained an important tool of political society. Since the launch of Niger's first independent newspaper in 1990, many more papers started circulating and openly criticizing the government, including several dedicated to political cartoons and satire, like *Le Canard Déchaîné* (*The Wild Duck*). Newspaper sellers who line the streets of Niamey each morning will often ask whether the buyer prefers a government paper or an opposition paper. This choice indicates the lasting effects of political liberalization. Candid debate carried on even as the administration of Mahamadou Issoufou, Tandja's successor, started arresting journalists for inciting anti-government plots.

Advances in communication technology injected new life into organizations that predated the 1991 National Conference. Although some, like the anti-colonial Sawaba movement, are no longer active (van Walraven, 2013), others evolved to shape contemporary politics. For example, the Nigerien Progressive Party-African Democratic Rally (Parti Progressiste Nigérien-Rassemblement Démocratique Africain, or PPN-RDA) takes part of its name from a pre-independence organization, the RDA, which was a syndicalist alliance between colonies in French West Africa. Nigerien trade unions formed an influential wing of the RDA, and still pursue the joint struggle for labor rights and self-determination (Charlick, 2007). Niger's early dictators were unable to completely stifle the labor movement despite a thirty-year ban on union organizing. There have been two major union "awakenings," involving strikes and protests. The first occurred in the 1980s, when President Saibou violated workers' trust by slashing civil service jobs. Another followed in the 1990s, when new democratic institutions gave unions the freedom to openly engage in political dialogue (Gazibo, 2007; Adji, 2000; Elischer, 2013). Workers have been major players in many third-wave protests, including those in 2009–2010. It is unclear, though, whether labor activists are committed to democratic values or care more about traditional workplace issues like wages. According to some accounts, the USTN attempted to join forces with non-union democracy activists (Adji, 2000, 11). But according to others, labor never championed inclusive participation; instead, "economic motives were truly at the heart of union agitation" (Elischer, 2013).

A few organizations formed in 2009 and 2010 expressly to challenge the Tandja regime. The Coordination of Democratic Forces for the Republic appeared six months before protests erupted, rallying various citizen groups, political opposition parties, and defectors from Tandja's camp (Azizou, 2010, 125). Reinforcing the mobilizational efforts of preexisting student and labor unions, this coalition claimed to be "a new type of actor capable of animating political life in the long term" (Azizou, 2010, 127). It was analogous to Y'en a Marre in Senegal, which around the same time began rallying protesters against President Abdoulaye Wade and promoting the ideal of "a new type of Senegalese."

We cannot read the goals of individual protesters from the names of organizations or the statements of protest leaders. It is important to avoid the common pitfall of construing large numbers of citizens as "the people" and interpreting their motivations "through the lens of the master narratives that oppositions articulate to mobilize them" (Beissinger, 2013, 2). Protest leaders usually proclaim their objectives and ideologies, but it is not obvious whether the rank-and-file protesters who answer their calls to action are sincere devotees or "contingent democrats" (Bellin, 2000).

Democratic Revolutionaries or Pocketbook Protesters?

To estimate the salience of different grievances among protesters and non-protesters, I analyze survey data that I collected in the early aftermath of the 2009–2010 uprisings. I reprise hypotheses from the previous chapter, but add a context-specific one: People who oppose *tazartché* are more likely to protest than people who support it. Survey questions focused on citizens' attitudes toward *tazartché* and economic conditions. To facilitate comparisons with earlier research, some questions resembled those from Afrobarometer surveys. I restricted my sample to the capital city because the protests of 2009–2010 were concentrated there. This allowed me to maximize variation on the dependent variable of protest participation. The urban milieu is representative of mobilization contexts in most developing countries, where urbanites are more likely than rural dwellers to protest; people in the countryside face heightened coordination problems associated with being geographically dispersed and excluded from technological or vocational information networks (Bates, 1981).[8]

In Niger, as in many developing countries, it is difficult to achieve a representative sample of the population given the lack of reliable demographic data and neighborhood maps. I therefore constructed an informal sampling frame by consulting social scientists at the Laboratory for the Study and Research of Social Dynamics and Local Development in Niamey. Colleagues' research experience and knowledge of local patterns of ethnicity, religion, education, and other demographic variables made it possible to select neighborhoods so as to approximate a representative sample (see Table 6.1).

Local enumerators used this sampling frame to administer questionnaires to over 300 men and women in forty of Niamey's ninety-nine neighborhoods. Neighborhoods were dispersed throughout Niamey,

---

[8] In addition to coordination effects, Rule (1988, 94) proposed that physical proximity affects protest propensity through emotional mechanisms:
"The shared experience of reacting to a single source of stimulation, or sharing a strong emotion, almost irresistibly draws the exposed individual into the crowd state."

Table 6.1 *Summary Statistics*

Protest participation	30%
Opposition to *tazartché*	42%
Absolute deprivation	19%
Relative deprivation (egoistic)	10%
Relative deprivation (fraternal)	7%
Relative deprivation (temporal)	18%
Low expectations of upward mobility	47%
Organization member	18%
Female	30%
Age 18–29	37%
Age 30–39	32%
Age 40 and over	31%
Primary education or less	22%
Koranic school	21%
Secondary education	23%
Post-secondary education	34%
Very religious	31%
Religious	37%
Somewhat religious	13%
Not religious	19%

covering both sides of the river that divides the city. On each day of the ten-day survey period, enumerators began at local meeting points (usually a taxi stop) and walked in opposite directions. They selected houses at intervals determined by randomly drawing a number from one to five (e.g., drawing a "3" would mean knocking on the door of every third house). Although enumerators typically surveyed the first person to answer the door, they were instructed to sample approximately the same number of men as women each day, which sometimes required asking members of a household whether a woman was available for an interview.[9] Exact employment statistics are unavailable, but Niamey's generally high unemployment rate (Brilleau,

---

[9] Women did not usually answer the door and were sometimes discouraged by their male relatives from participating in the survey. According to focus group participants, this tendency stemmed from religious customs (most Nigeriens are observant Muslims). Enumerators gently inquired about the availability of women, resulting in a sample that was about 30 percent female.

Roubaud, and Torelli, 2005) reduced the bias that sometimes results from collecting surveys at residences during the day. Since many people in Niamey are unemployed or work near their homes in the informal sector, the sample probably over-represents unemployed individuals, but not by as much as it would in other countries. Surveys were conducted in the respondent's language of choice – usually Hausa, Zarma, or French.

Although asking politically sensitive questions creates the potential for enumerator bias and respondent dishonesty, several precautions were taken to avoid these pitfalls. First, I conducted focus groups prior to administering the survey in order to gauge the political openness of Niamey society. It was common for focus group participants to respond to questions such as "what does *tazartché* mean to you?" with animated and prolonged debates. The candor with which local citizens volunteered their political opinions both for and against the outgoing regime suggested that survey respondents would likewise be sincere. Second, enumerators were all Niamey residents whose fluency in local languages and sensitivity to subtle cultural cues helped reduce bias in both recruiting subjects and eliciting responses to survey questions. Using local enumerators was doubly important given some people's suspicions that international plots were behind the anti-Tandja movement (*Jeune Afrique*, 2009). Third, a rigorous enumerator training, including repeated role-plays, prepared enumerators to maximize respondents' comfort and honesty during interviews. For instance, the training encouraged enumerators to appear politically neutral and to interview respondents in settings where they could not be overheard.

Variables

The dichotomous dependent variable is *Protest Participation*, derived from a question asking respondents whether they participated in a protest during the previous year. Independent variables include the following:

- *Opposition to Tazartché*: Whether a respondent opposes Tandja's attempt to change the constitution and seek a third term in office.

This variable was coded from responses to the open-ended question, "What is your opinion on *tazartché*?"[10]

- *Absolute Deprivation*: Whether a respondent considers her or his present living conditions to be either "bad" or "very bad."
- *Relative Deprivation (Egoistic)*: Whether a respondent considers her or his living conditions to be worse than those of other Nigeriens.
- *Relative Deprivation (Fraternal)*: Whether a respondent considers the living conditions of her or his ethnic group to be worse than those of other ethnic groups in the country. A respondent's specific ethnicity (mainly Hausa, Zarma, or Tuareg) is not expected to be related to the likelihood of participating in a protest against the president, because Tandja is of mixed parentage and does not hail not from one of Niger's major politically salient ethnic groups (he was the first Nigerien president who was not Hausa or Zarma). Tuaregs are a minority in Niamey, and numbered very few among protesters and survey respondents. The vast majority of protesters and respondents were therefore undifferentiated, in that they all were from a different ethnic group than the president. As ethnicity was not found to be a significant factor in respondent's answers, it is not included in the regression models.
- *Relative Deprivation (Temporal)*: Whether a respondent considers her or his living conditions to be worse now than they were a year ago.
- *Low Expectations of Upward Mobility*: Whether a respondent expects her or his living conditions to be no better in the next five years.
- *Organization Member*: Whether a respondent is a member of an organization such as a student group, a labor union, or a neighborhood association.

Regressions also include the following control variables that often correlate with protest participation:

- *Female*: Takes a value of "1" if the respondent is female and "0" if the respondent is male. In Niger, men are considerably more visible than women in political life and are thus expected to be more likely to protest.

---

[10] See Appendix B for the complete survey instrument.

- *Age*: Younger people can be expected to protest more, because they are more likely to be students and free from family or work obligations that raise the opportunity costs of protesting. I follow common practice by breaking age into brackets (18–29, 30–39, and 40 and over).

- *Education*: A categorical variable indicating the respondent's highest level of education: primary school or less, Koranic (religious) school, secondary school, or post-secondary school. Kirwin and Cho (2009) found a significant and positive effect of education on protest participation in Africa, proposing that better educated people are more politically aware than less educated people.

- *Religiosity*: A variable indicating whether a respondent is "very religious," "religious," "somewhat religious," or "not religious." In focus groups and open-ended survey questions, many Nigeriens attributed their economic conditions to God's will, suggesting that people who are more religious may be less likely to protest.

Some scholars have argued that social movements are "ecology-dependent," meaning that physical spaces organize people into networks that facilitate or impede protest mobilization (Fantasia, 1988; Zhao, 1996). In addition to exposing people to grievances and affecting their ability to coordinate, location might simply make it more or less convenient to protest. All of these considerations are salient in Niamey, which is divided into two sections by the Niger River, with businesses and government buildings concentrated on one side and residences and university facilities concentrated on the other. Examining the data revealed that protesters indeed lived mainly on one side of the river and in downtown neighborhoods. Some of the forty neighborhoods surveyed had protest participation rates as low as 7 percent, whereas others had rates as high as 60 percent. To account for this spatial variation, the models include neighborhood fixed effects.

Results

Table 6.1 displays summary statistics for all variables. Considering Niger's levels of poverty and hunger, surprisingly few respondents expressed grievances of any kind. The most common economic grievance was absolute deprivation, although less than one fifth of respondents said that their current economic situations were bad or very bad.

Respondents were also very hopeful for the future: most expected their economic situations to improve in the next year. During visits to Niger in 2011, 2014, 2016, and 2017, I was routinely struck by the degree of hope that people displayed amid objectively dire circumstances. "As long as there is life, there is hope," said one woman. Another focus group participant insisted that the common perception of Niger's downward trajectory "is all media spin."

At first glance, Nigeriens appear more politically than economically aggrieved. Forty-two percent of respondents opposed Tandja's attempt to stay in power, although international observers might be surprised that opposition to *tazartché* was not higher. While some respondents said *tazartché* led to famine and anarchy, many felt it was good for the country. Twelve percent of respondents even associated *tazartché* with democracy, echoing Tandja's claim that changing the constitution was in line with popular wishes.

However, grievances do not necessarily drive people to protest. To investigate the relationship between grievances and protest participation, I estimate the logistic regression model summarized in Table 6.2. Having low expectations of upward mobility is the only economic grievance with a statistically and substantively significant coefficient. Expecting that one's economic situation will not improve over the next five years is associated with a 0.8 net increase in the log-odds of protesting.

Social networks, too, seem to influence the likelihood that a respondent protested in the past year. Table 6.2 shows that being a member of an organization correlates with higher protest propensity, consistent with earlier research and theoretical predictions. A preliminary analysis of the data confirmed that virtually all protest participants had been asked to participate, whereas virtually all respondents who did not protest had not been asked. Indeed, being asked to protest almost perfectly determines protest participation. The fact that respondents have been asked to protest by student groups and labor unions (Figure 6.3) points to a mobilizational mechanism and not simply a self-selection mechanism (whereby people who join civic organizations are already more likely to protest). Students and wage earners are better off than most Nigeriens, so their prominence in the 2009–2010 uprisings exemplifies the cross-class alliances driving Africa's third wave of protest. It furthermore distinguishes the Niger

Table 6.2 *Logit Model of Protest Participation*

Opposition to *tazartché*	0.198
	(0.363)
Absolute deprivation	−0.081
	(0.567)
Relative deprivation (egoistic)	−0.090
	(0.664)
Relative deprivation (fraternal)	−0.485
	(0.795)
Relative deprivation (temporal)	0.713
	(0.512)
Low expectations of upward mobility	0.801**
	(0.415)
Organization member	1.442***
	(0.408)
Female	−0.467
	(0.406)
Age	−0.011
	(0.017)
Koranic school (vs. primary education or less)	−2.400***
	(0.722)
Secondary education (vs. primary education or less)	−0.427
	(0.514)
Post-secondary education (vs. primary education or less)	0.570
	(0.475)
Religious (vs. very religious)	−0.355
	(0.431)
Somewhat religious (vs. very religious)	−0.433
	(0.674)
Not religious (vs. very religious)	−0.257
	(0.687)
R^2	0.249
N	311

Logit estimates using neighborhood fixed effects, with standard errors in parentheses.
* $p < 0.05$, ** $p < 0.01$, *** $p < 0.001$.

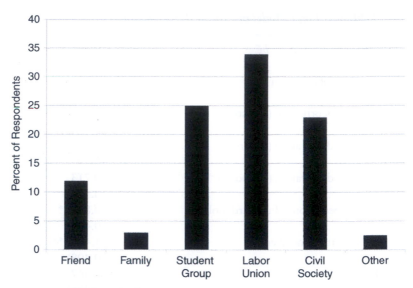

Figure 6.3: "Who Asked You to Protest?"

protests from those in other countries, such as Senegal, where many citizens suspect unions of being politically co-opted.

It is also interesting to examine what impedes protest participation. Attending Koranic school has a negative relationship with taking to the streets, although religiosity in general does not. This suggests that membership in a religious network, and not faith per se, deters protesting. The result squares with previous research showing that "social ties may constrain as well as encourage activism" (McAdam and Paulsen, 1993) and that being engaged in religious organizations has a negative and significant effect in some African settings (Pilati, 2011). People in Nairobi may heed Pentecostal church leaders' calls to political action (McClendon and Riedl, 2015), but Koranic school teachers were not a similar organizing force in Niamey during 2009 and 2010. Although the Niger Islamic Council publicly denounced Tandja's constitutional referendum, it advocated dialogue over direct confrontation. Therefore, even if Tandja failed to co-opt religious organizations, Muslim leaders' limited support for the protests could have discouraged the involvement of Koranic school communities. There is a precedent for this non-confrontational stance: religious conservatives in Niger did not mobilize

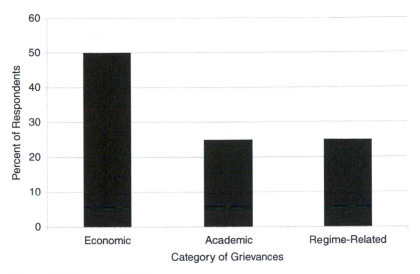

Figure 6.4: Protesters' Grievances

in 1999–2001, even though many opposed the gender quota law that women's rights activists were demanding at the time (Kang, 2015).[11]

In sum, attitudes toward *tazartché* have no apparent ties to protest participation. The primacy of economic (as opposed to regime-related) grievances is also evident in responses to the open-ended question, "what were you protesting against?" Figure 6.4 shows that a minority of protesters had concerns about the regime, whereas most said they were protesting "*la vie chère*" (the high cost of living). The most politically salient economic grievance is low expectations of upward mobility, shedding light on why present economic conditions do not necessarily correlate with demands for redistribution.

In addition to asking whether respondents expect their economic situations to be worse in the next five years, enumerators asked about respondents' expectations for the next year alone. To check the robustness my results, I re-estimated the model using this alternative measure of expectations of upward mobility. Shorter-term expectations of upward mobility do not have a significant influence on protest

[11] Kang (2015) notes that conservative activists did mobilize against other women's rights reforms, including the Convention on the Elimination of All forms of Discrimination against Women in 1994–1999 and the Maputo Protocol in 2002–2011.

propensity, suggesting that people who joined the protests in 2009 and 2010 had long time horizons and were targeting a president that they expected to remain in power for a third term.

It is plausible that older people are not as anxious about future economic conditions as younger people. I therefore re-estimated the model while including an interaction term between age and expectations of upward mobility. The term was negative and statistically significant, suggesting that, indeed, the older one is, the weaker the relationship between low expectations of upward mobility and one's likelihood of protesting. This substantiates the literature portraying African adolescents as restless "change agents" (Gavin, 2007) and vindicates NGOs that urge African governments to invest in education and employment programs to keep youth out of "socially subversive activities or political protest" (Abbink, 2005, 9). Including the interaction term did not, however, change the significance of the main effect. People with low expectations of upward mobility were still more likely to protest, other variables held constant.

The fact that low expectations of upward mobility were the most salient grievance in Niger's recent protests raises the question of why this is so. Did civil society groups rhetorically frame events to make people believe that the economic future was bleak and warranted protesting? Did Tandja manage to paint *tazartché* as democratic, thereby allaying concerns about his attempt to stay in power? Although it is beyond the scope of this study to explain individuals' psychological responses to political and economic shocks, existing data permit a general analysis of the sources of grievances in the uprisings.

Numerous studies have underlined the role of social contacts in conditioning grievances (Christopoulos, 1978; Morris and Staggenborg, 2005; Popkin, 1988; Robnett, 1996). Political entrepreneurs such as labor union leaders can strategically frame current events and convince people a) that they have low expectations of upward mobility; and b) that they should protest about it. Hence, being a member of an organization might encourage protest participation not only through coordination effects (i.e., by facilitating communication about protest logistics) and cooperation effects (i.e., by facilitating social sanctioning and the transfer of selective incentives), but also through framing effects.

Simple cross-tabulation suggests that group membership is not the reason why people have low expectations of upward mobility.

In reality, group members are relatively optimistic: 35 percent of them have low expectations of upward mobility, versus half of non-members. To test whether group membership encourages people with low expectations of upward mobility to protest, I re-estimated the main model while including an interaction term between low expectations of upward mobility and group membership. This term was statistically significant and negative, implying that group membership attenuates the relationship between expectations of upward mobility and protest participation (possibly because civic organizations provide a forum outside of the streets for voicing grievances). In short, framing effects do not seem to explain the relative salience of low expectations of upward mobility in the 2009–2010 protests. To the extent that group membership relates to protest participation, it is more likely because of coordination and cooperation effects. Scholars have observed these mechanisms at play in a variety of contexts, citing that organizations like church and student groups coordinate protests and incentivize collective action through social pressure (Robinson and White, 1997).

Despite the coup that eventually removed him from power, there are signs that Tandja was rather successful at managing popular dissatisfaction. Having helped to overthrow President Hamani Diori in 1974, Tandja likely foresaw the risks of appearing to defy the will of citizens. He launched an aggressive pro-*tazartché* public relations campaign, benefiting from a strong democratic mandate acquired by winning two runs for office in elections that observers judged free and fair. Based on the evidence I have presented, these efforts convinced a sizeable portion of the population that revising the constitution was both democratic and necessary for completing development projects such as a uranium mine and a dam on the Niger River. For example, 38 percent of survey respondents who protested also supported *tazartché*; some lauded the president's projects when answering the open-ended question, "what do you think about *tazartché*?" Notwithstanding the international media's focus on "opposition demonstrations," some Nigeriens marched in support of Tandja, carrying portraits of the leader and shouting, "Long live *tazartché*!" According to news reports and original interviews conducted in Niamey during the summer of 2011, Tandja supplemented his populist rhetoric by distributing patronage and censoring the media (BBC, 2010a; FIDH, 2012). His more extreme tactics, like detaining journalists and shutting down the constitutional court, were a last resort after public relations failed. Although the anti-*tazartché* movement ultimately succeeded, the president's strategic use of soft and hard power helps explain the relatively low level of political grievances during the protests of 2009–2010 – despite outspoken opposition from prominent figures like coup leader Salou Djibo.

Conclusion

Analyses in this chapter suggest that harboring grievances does not necessarily lead to political action. Only specific grievances correlate with protest participation, which are not necessarily those that seem most salient in the rhetoric of protest leaders or the media. Although the 2009–2010 uprisings in Niger appeared to international audiences as expressions of discontent with President Tandja's antidemocratic tendencies, opposition to *tazartché* had no measurable influence on the likelihood of protesting. It appears that the international press misreported events on the ground, especially compared to Nigerien newspapers that tended to cover the constitutional debate in the broader context of an economic crisis. In fact, many of those surveyed actually supported revising the constitution to allow Tandja to remain in power, and some even considered *tazartché* to be democratic. Together, these observations shed doubt on whether supposed prodemocracy movements necessarily reflect popular preferences for Western-style democracy. Instead, people's expectations for their future economic conditions might be a more important influence on whether they are willing to bear the considerable costs and risks of challenging entrenched autocratic regimes. This chapter also highlighted the importance of mobilization mechanisms, specifically membership in civil society organizations and middle-class outreach to the poor. Grievances alone are not enough to bring people to the streets; foot soldiers of the revolution must have both the will and the way to overcome coordination and cooperation problems.

7 | Conclusion

The Protester was *Time* magazine's Person of the Year in 2011, joining a list of past honorees including heads of state, popes, and Facebook founder Mark Zuckerberg. *Time* had the widest circulation of any weekly news magazine in the world, signaling considerable interest in why "the protester once again became a maker of history" after decades of relative apathy (Andersen, 2011). Occupy Wall Street and the Arab Spring dominated the media in 2011, but since then events suggest that it is time to turn attention to sub-Saharan Africa.

Starting around 2011, sub-Saharan Africa experienced a crescendo of popular uprisings reminiscent of two periods from the past: the "first wave" of African protests, which helped unravel colonial rule in the 1940s to 1960s, and the "second wave" of African protests during democratic transitions of the 1990s. As of 2017, the latest wave was still developing. Students in South Africa agitated to reduce school fees and decolonize the university system. At least 500 Ethiopian protesters died in 2016 amid drought, ethnic exclusion, and draconian limits on civil freedoms; the year before, state troops killed more than 100 protesters in Ethiopia's Oromia region. Supporters of Zambia's United Party for National Development held a naked rally in May 2017 after state forces arrested party chief Hakainde Hichilema on treason charges. Thousands of Malians turned out in Bamako in the summer of 2017 after the government announced a constitutional reform that would allow the president to appoint a third of future senators, ostensibly to increase the representation of marginal northern regions. Even countries whose populations have long exhibited restraint in the face of poverty and autocracy show signs that political society is reawakening despite state repression. In Niger, activist Abdourahmane Insar persisted in organizing a movement for democratic renewal after being arrested and sentenced to six months in prison for allegedly inciting violence on social media in 2017.

The third wave of protests came as a surprise to many economists and political scientists who had watched African countries achieve historic levels of economic growth and move toward democratic consolidation at the turn of the twenty-first century (e.g., Radelet, 2010; Rotberg, 2013; Ncube and Lufumpa, 2015). Journalists, too, had gradually traded "Afro-pessimism" for "Afro-optimism" and struggled to make sense of mounting turmoil (e.g., Gettleman, 2016). Why were people in Africa radiating discontent at the very juncture when their opportunities seemed to be expanding? This book addressed that puzzle by systematically analyzing the timing and scale of contemporary African protests. It also tackled broader questions that have long puzzled scholars across disciplines: Why do the poor and politically disenfranchised sometimes speak out and other times stay quiet? What allows aggrieved individuals to overcome collective action problems? Why do some movements last and others fade?

Recap of the Argument and Findings

In October 2016, hundreds of people marched on Wits University in South Africa after administrators proposed a 10.5 percent fee hike. The increase would have disproportionately burdened black enrollees, who make up more than 60 percent of the student body and tend to be poorer than their classmates from other racial groups. Students also seethed over the university's treatment of predominantly black low-wage staff. Janitors laid down their brooms and started marching alongside students in gratitude and solidarity; sympathetic faculty and other white-collar employees eventually joined the front lines of the demonstration. Protesters chanted and stomped their feet in a performance of the *toyi-toyi*, an improvisational dance that was a weapon against authorities of the apartheid regime in the 1970s and 1980s. Police and private security guards arrived in riot gear to control the crowd. They fired rubber bullets, stun grenades, and tear gas as demonstrators threw stones and set a bus on fire. Officials canceled classes in response to the pandemonium, calling international attention to racial and economic injustices that still festered more than twenty years after South Africa's nominal transition to majority rule (Sibeko, 2016).

Protests are dramatic; people experience and witness them on a psychological, visceral level. Just as cyclists struggle to explain exactly how they pedal down the road without falling over, protesters struggle to understand or articulate why they take to the streets (Lieberman, Schreiber, and Oschsner, 2001; Wilson and Dunn, 2004). Rising up can feel like a reflexive decision stemming from, say, an episodic memory of discrimination or deprivation. Though most scholars no longer pathologize protests as "moments of madness" (Zolberg, 1972), some view joining risky collective action as an essentially emotional reaction, not a choice born of deliberate cost-benefit calculation (e.g., Rule, 1988; Wood, 2003; Van Zomeren et al., 2009; Cloninger and Leibo, 2017). Observers of protests typically suppose that protesters act out of anger, and infer about the nature of that anger from available cues such as marchers' signs, protest leaders' public statements, and newspaper headlines. Consider, for example, a newspaper article on South Africa entitled, "In One Country, Anger over Soaring College Costs Has Led to Violent Protest" and accompanied by a photo of demonstrators holding signs reading, "Fees must fall" (Marcus, 2017). Because scholarly accounts of recent uprisings in Johannesburg, Ouagadougou, and other African cities rely so heavily on news reports, they tend to portray those events in one of two ways: as economic riots by the poor (e.g., Smith, 2013; Berazneva and Lee, 2013; Macatory, Oumarou, and Poncelet, 2010; Adam, 2008) or as democratic revolutions by the disenfranchised middle class, akin to the Arab Spring or the "color revolutions" in former Soviet republics (e.g., Harsch, 2012; Dibba, 2013; Sowore, 2013). When analysts interpret protesting by others based on their own affective experiences of activism, they naturally presume a causal link between anger and protest – even if they would be hard-pressed to explain their personal protesting behavior.

Our intuitions can mislead us. Distrust of vaccines reflects intuitive theories of illness that are grounded in behavior (what we should do to avoid getting sick) and not microbes (Shtulman, 2017, 3). Intuitive theories of geology assume that the earth is a static object, which is why some people cannot fathom how humans are shaping the earth through carbon emissions (Shtulman, 2017, 3). The intuitive theory of protest is that protest arises from anger about problems we can read on signs. Emotions might have real causal – even biological – effects on protest participation (Cloninger and Leibo, 2017; Young, 2016b). However, additional factors allow or constrain people from raising their voices against the status quo (Klandermans, 2015).

In African countries, the majority of citizens remain extremely poor regardless of aggregate economic growth. As a result, the practical requirements of protest are in short supply – buses to transport participants, electricity to charge phones, literacy to read flyers, money to offset foregone income, and lawyers to defend political prisoners. Incumbents can use censorship and reduce public spending to further restrict the opposition's access to "coordination goods" (Bueno de Mesquita and Downs, 2005). This happens not just in the most repressive countries like Ethiopia, but also in titular democracies like Niger where political competition takes place on an "uneven playing field" (Levitsky and Way, 2010). Anger about democracy, poverty, inequality, or other issues might motivate subjects to speak out in the relative safety of laboratory experiments (Stürmer and Simon, 2009; Young, 2016b), but that does not mean the same subjects would be willing or able to speak out in the real world.

Besides studying the mobilizational power of anger, studying the content of anger is also complicated. It would be reasonable to draw inferences about popular grievances from posters, speeches, and headlines if all protesters waved signs and held press conferences. But such cues are in fact unreliable because the average protester fades into a throng of anonymous faces and voices. Reporting bias is a distinct pitfall when studying protests; journalists, activists, and incumbents all have an interest in spotlighting non-representative elements of demonstrations that favor their side (McCarthy, McPhail, and Smith, 1996). Leaders throughout history have doctored images or statistics from rallies to overstate supporter turnout or understate opposition turnout. U.S. President Donald Trump famously inflated attendance figures from his 2017 inauguration ceremony without bothering to manipulate aerial photos that showed only modest crowds. Sociologists have started using drones to estimate crowd sizes in an attempt to overcome strategic deception (Choi-Fitzpatrick and Juskauskas, 2017). But while scholars routinely call out propaganda and overt lies, they often overlook subtler reporting bias and rarely peer beneath the surface of the crowd.[1]

Another shortcoming of existing research is the presumption that objective problems such as autocracy or economic inequality are the same as protesters' subjective concerns. One tends to think, "Niger's president meddled with the constitution, so the protests

---

[1] An exception is The Protest Project by sociologist Dana R. Fisher, who deploys research teams to survey participants in large-scale protests.

must be about that." There is a pronounced risk of misinterpreting local realities when non-African observers project meanings onto African protests (Smith, 2012; Emerson, Fretz, and Shaw, 2011). That risk grows as political science and sociology departments deemphasize immersive fieldwork in graduate training (Agarwala and Teitelbaum, 2010).

Reporting bias and empathy gulfs are impossible to avoid entirely, but I mitigated them in two ways. First, I drew on diverse data sources to examine protests from multiple vantage points: interviews of protest leaders and incumbents, surveys of ordinary protesters and nonprotesters, and content analysis of media reports. I chose interlocutors and inspected data with an eye toward learning the following: Who animates protests? What defines the roles of various protest actors? Whose voices – leaders or joiners – do protest narratives privilege? Second, my face-to-face interviews with activists allowed local actors to interpret events for themselves. First-person accounts complement the abundance of second-hand information in previous studies.

The sum of evidence supported my argument that the motivations and profiles of rank-and-file demonstrators diverge from those of protest leaders. Members of Africa's rising middle class, who are increasingly autonomous from clientelist networks, launch protests in response to incumbent ploys to retain power. They wield their entrepreneurial skills and resources to mobilize protesters who are disproportionately poor and harbor economic grievances. Thus, the third wave of protests in sub-Saharan Africa stands out from recent unrest in other parts of the world where many protesters are relatively well-off. The present wave also differs from earlier waves of African protests, which were largely elite-driven and ended with radicals being co-opted into the state. Today's middle-class protest leaders – which I term "generals of the revolution" – brand themselves as alternatives to the parties, unions, and religious organizations comprising traditional civil society. And their outspoken political independence makes them credible allies to ordinary protesters, the "foot soldiers of the revolution." Cross-class coalitions drive African protests of the early twenty-first century, though they might fray in the future as the middle class continues to grow and the poor become less essential for filling the streets.

Contributions

Focusing a Telescope on Social Movements

Scholars and journalists instinctively label uprisings as "pro-democracy marches," "bread riots," or "ethnic conflicts," despite the mixed motivations of people in the streets. Their bird's-eye perspective creates an impression of the crowd as having a single mind, impeding valid interpretation of what protests are "about." By the same token, the micro-level methods preferred by some social scientists (e.g., Scacco, 2008) shed light on the psychology of individual protesters but tend to overlook differences between protest leaders and joiners. Most studies of protest behavior focus exclusively on participation, ignoring that protests involve both leadership (relating to timing) and participation (relating to protest size).

I examined protests through a telescopic lens, starting by zooming out on the long course of African history to document how macroeconomic trends shape protests over time. Two trends are especially noteworthy. First, sub-Saharan Africa as a whole has experienced twenty years of impressive economic growth combined with severe economic inequality. This allowed a small middle class to emerge while most Africans remained poor. Second, the liberalization of capital under international pressures changed the nature of the middle class from one made almost exclusively of state cronies to one that derives more of its wealth from private sources and is thus freer to organize opposition movements. After examining these big-picture developments, I zoomed in on individual members of the crowd to explain why they instigate protests or answer the call to action. I dissected activist biographies, public statements, and tactics while drawing on data from thirty-one African countries and fieldwork in Niger, Senegal, Burkina Faso, and Malawi. Breaking with convention, I did not assume that people's subjective concerns match their objective conditions. I used interviews and surveys to reveal which grievances most closely correlate with involvement in contentious politics. Although I concentrated on Africa, this telescopic and interpretive approach is adaptable to the study of protest anywhere.

Take, for example, the deadly uprisings that paralyzed Venezuela for months in 2017. The dominant narrative about these events held that hundreds of thousands of protesters were weary of food shortages, economic decline, and the government of President Nicolás Maduro, which had shut down the opposition-led National Assembly (McCarthy, 2017). However, images in the global media gave a distorted view of protesters' identities and motivations. A video went viral during the spring of 2017 in which an activist named Mariel narrated a montage of violent confrontations between protesters and police. She described the crowds as youth who were mainly upset about the collapsing national economy. Viewers later noticed that the video was from protests three years before, and that many other old videos and photos were circulating on the web and misrepresenting Venezuelans' grievances.[2] Experts took a closer look at the 2017 protests in Venezuela, observing that many participants were actually middle-aged or elderly, not student-aged like in Mariel's documentary. They found, moreover, that "despite years of extreme economic deprivation, protesters [were] focusing their current demands on protecting basic political and civic rights" (Onuch and Sagarzazu, 2017). These analysts discovered the reverse of what I found, which is that African protests are often less about constitutional democracy and more about material concerns than they appear.

Close inspection of grievances can be worthwhile even when the mobilizing issues seem obvious. American protesters clashed with counter-protesters for two days in August 2017 at the "Unite the Right" rally in Charlottesville, Virginia. Rally spokespeople claimed their goal was to oppose the removal of a statue of Robert E. Lee, a commander of the Confederate Army in the U.S. Civil War and, for many Americans, a symbol of slavery and racism. A protester plowed his car into the crowd, killing a woman. In the following days, President Trump chided offenses "on both sides," implying an equivalence between white nationalists and civil rights activists. Democratic Party organizer Tom Perriello objected in an article entitled, "There Is Only One Side to the Story of Charlottesville":

First, this was unequivocally about race, about white tribalism. For the hundreds who rallied, many of them heavily armed, race was the defining issue. No one I talked to mentioned economic anxiety or trade policy. "You will not replace us" was the leading chant, and I was told multiple times that I was clearly a "Jew banker," "faggot," or "sellout to my people." Their

---

[2] A similar mistake happened when photos from Ukraine's 2004 Orange Revolution appeared in coverage of the 2014 Euromaidan protests.

signs read 'White Lives Matter' and said that Charlottesville's black vice-mayor 'Wes Bellamy is a Nigger.' I have met Trump voters who were not primarily motivated by race – these were not them (Perriello, 2017).

Perriello's insistence on a single story might remind readers of a contrasting view by Nigerian novelist Chimamanda Ngozi Adichie: "When we reject the single story, when we realize that there is never a single story about any place, we regain a kind of paradise" (Adichie, 2009). In other words, we validate our humanity by refusing to reduce complex individuals and circumstances to a dominant narrative – like we do by rejecting stereotypes of all Africans as starving and miserable. Conservative *New York Times* columnist David Brooks applied Adichie's philosophy to politics in the United States, lamenting how people on both the right and left of the ideological spectrum "must embrace the approved story to show you are not complicit in a system of oppression" (Brooks, 2016). Relating this debate to the Charlottesville protest, one can ask what is more oppressive: insinuating that the story of Charlottesville had one side or that it had two? Or is each interpretation oppressive in its own way? This book does not set out to resolve normative conundrums, but it makes a relevant case for using hard evidence to uncover what the salient grievances of a protest empirically are. Interviewing protesters in addition to reading their posters is a good start. Perriello took such an approach, albeit without specifying how many people he interviewed or how he chose respondents. If enumerators could gather more fine-grained data on the motivations behind protest leadership and participation, it would be easier to ascertain what protests in Charlottesville, Caracas, or Nairobi are "about."

The above examples underscore a need to interpret protests in their temporal and geographic contexts. Video footage of a Venezuelan protest in 2014 might seem like it could be from 2017, but the two episodes have different underlying dynamics. Demonstrators might have marched on Charlottesville for various reasons. The third wave of protests in sub-Saharan Africa might look like the Arab Spring, but the demographics and salient grievances in each instance are unique.

This book brought sub-Saharan Africa front and center in the study of social movements. My emphasis on waves of protest recalls *Making Waves* (2014) in which Weyland attributes the ebb of African democracy movements in the 1990s to a dearth of visionary political party leaders to negotiate democratic bargains. However, I revealed the opposite: political parties had plenty of charismatic leaders in the 1990s, but they did not drive democracy movements; it was instead a new crop of activists from outside the party system who emerged as the staunchest defenders of democracy.

Books on revolution "from below" often focus on Europe, Latin America, and the "Arab world" while relegating sub-Saharan Africa to an afterthought or omitting it altogether. Examples include classics by Moore (1978), Skocpol (1979), Rueschemeyer, Huber Stephens, and Stephens (1992), and Acemoglu and Robinson (2006). Wood (2000) considers South Africa alongside a case study of El Salvador, but South Africa is an outlier with respect to colonial history, social cleavages, and development trajectories and tells us only so much about protest in sub-Saharan Africa as a whole.

Rethinking "Classless Africa"

This book's major contribution to the African politics literature is to "bring class back in."[3] Apart from a brief, unpredictable time following independence, Africanists have maintained that class is irrelevant in their subfield despite being pivotal in general political science (Englebert and Dunn, 2013, 109). The main pillar of Marxist theory, the ownership of the means of production, seemed of little consequence in African societies with low levels of industrialization and wage labor. The conventional thinking was that identity cleavages (especially ethnicity, religion, and language) determine everything from elections to war to the distribution of goods.[4] Nothing could be farther from the Marxist credo that class is the only "true" division between people. A few studies proposed that class pertains to Africa insofar as it designates relations of power and not production (Sklar, 1979; Boone, 1998). This idea provided my theoretical foundation for studying the role of middle-class Africans in contemporary protests. I defined

---

[3] I join a growing community of scholars with that goal, including contributors to edited volumes by Melber (2016) and Darbon and Toulabor (2014).

[4] Zeilig (2009) and Dwyer and Zeilig (2012) are exceptions, but their rare class-based reading of African protests does not address the questions about temporal and cross-sectional variation that I answer. I further depart from their classical Marxist framework by tailoring a class-based model to reflect the realities of present-day Africa.

the middle class as a "diminished subtype" (Collier and Levitsky, 1997) of the root concept – as a stratum of Africans who meet their basic material needs with income from sources outside the state. I thus avoided "stretching" the concept of middle class that scholars normally use (the class between the ruling elite and the proletariat, i.e., the bourgeoisie or petite bourgeoisie).

The middle class currently emerging in Africa may not be a class "in itself and for itself" in the Marxist sense, but it has considerable social and political influence from several sources. First, it has the power to challenge incumbent regimes in ways that well-to-do Africans have not traditionally had, thanks to expanding professional links with private business and NGOs as opposed to the state. The African middle class also has the power of consumption, which it uses to distinguish itself from the rest of society, sometimes in ostentatious ways (*NewAfrican*, 2012). Most importantly, middle-class status comes with the power to mobilize crowds. Launching a protest involves start-up costs that few ordinary Africans can afford; and once a protest starts, getting thousands of people to turn out requires additional resources for overcoming coordination and cooperation dilemmas. Granted, many middle-class Africans lack the degree of economic autonomy that Marx envisioned the middle class to have; they occupy a precarious "floating middle class" that owns little formal property and depends on unreliable income sources (Ncube and Lufumpa, 2015). All the same, the African middle class enjoys multiple privileges vis-à-vis the masses. This disparity conditions the overall "landscape of dissent" (Mitchell and Staeheli, 2005) in the region.

Middle-class generals and lower-income foot soldiers form ad-hoc coalitions that were not possible in previous generations when middle-class Africans usually preferred joining the state to challenging it. The relationship between generals and foot soldiers is increasingly symbiotic. The poor can better overcome barriers to collective action when they have professional leaders who are capable of wooing powerful allies, providing transportation to protests, and keeping the lights on at social movement headquarters. Middle-class protest leaders, on their part, must recruit from beyond the still-small middle class if they hope to assemble crowds big enough to grab headlines and topple regimes. This is not to say that all protest leaders are equally effective coalition builders. Some, particularly older ones who forged civil service careers before market liberalization, succumb to the lingering pull of patronage and seek the favor of political elites instead of ordinary citizens. They subsequently lose their mass following and fail to achieve their objectives. Third-wave protest generals start protests in response to political shocks; once in progress, protests grow larger and last longer when generals acknowledge foot soldiers' primary economic grievance – low expectations of upward mobility.

Africanists can integrate class into their research by asking themselves these questions: what does class mean in the setting I am studying? How does neglecting class potentially bias my conclusions about the determinants of phenomena like collective action, elections, and development? How do class relations shape coalitions not just in social movements, but also in political parties and other groups?

Scholars of South Asia have undertaken such conceptual updating. In India, economists realized that patterns of latrine use – and therefore health outcomes – correlate with caste status: rural people associate pit maintenance with degrading types of work historically assigned to the lowest castes (Coffey and Spears, 2017). Like socioeconomic categories in Africa, caste systems in India do not perfectly map onto canonical definitions of class; there are differences between Marxist classes and Indian castes in terms of secularism and mobility, for instance (Sharma, 1984). Still, the assumption that class, broadly defined, was irrelevant in rural India led to specious explanations of latrine use centered on poverty and low education. An adapted class framework corrected those inferences. Rethinking class in less restrictive, less Marxist terms can also be fruitful for scholars of Western regions who wrestle with grafting Marxist thought onto societies where shuttered factories, labor surpluses, and bitter clashes between identity groups are more and more common (e.g., Srnicek and Williams, 2015; Hardt and Negri, 2017).

This book makes several other contributions to the African politics literature. One is updating knowledge with recent data. An influential study by Bratton and van de Walle (1997) attributed democratic transitions to "economic protests" in the 1990s but did not dissect the different motivations of leaders and participants or extend to twenty-first-century protests. Tripp et al. (2009), too, ended their analysis before Africa's third wave of protests began in earnest. Branch and Mampilly (2015) underscored continuities across waves of African protests and illustrated them with a handful of prominent cases. I expanded on that research by considering different cases, notably

encompassing Francophone countries that the English-language literature neglects. LeBas (2011) related the strength of social movements in
Kenya, Zambia, and Zimbabwe to the subsequent cohesion of political
parties. Her thesis echoed the "protest cycles" theory from sociology
whereby protesters enter formal politics after fulfilling their activist
agendas (Hipsher, 1998). In contrast, I stressed that the current wave of
African protests is noteworthy because many activists are disillusioned
with party politics as a way of effecting political change. Chapter 4 of
this book acknowledged social movements like Y'en a Marre in Senegal
and the Ufungamano Initiative in Kenya, which arose expressly to
counterbalance political parties that citizens perceived as conservative
and corrupt. I also built on work by Arriola (2013a) showing how the
spread of liberal capital allowed private businesses to finance opposition parties. Middle-class beneficiaries of liberalization have a second
option: investing in social movements. Contentious politics in Africa
have historically played out in the street, not just in the legislature.

Avenues for Future Research

This book explained the timing and scale of African protests, but not
the aftermath. A next step is to ask: do uprisings catalyze government
reforms even if, as I have shown, participants do not necessarily prioritize them? On the one hand, protests of any makeup might generate
a "democratic culture" (Diamond, 1993) and enable citizens to credibly threaten politicians who renege on their political bargains
(Acemoglu and Robinson, 2006). Lindberg (2006) argued that elections improve civil liberties in Africa even when they are not free and
fair, by raising awareness about citizens' rights, creating new roles for
the media, and improving the organizing capacity of civil society.
Future studies can investigate whether a similar logic applies to protest,
and thereby balance the bias in political science toward electoral forms
of political participation. Elections are blunt tools for enacting the
people's will in authoritarian or semi-authoritarian settings (Gandhi
and Lust-Okar, 2009; Wiseman, 1986). In such environments, protests
may return "disruptive leverage" (Piven and Cloward, 1977) to the
people.

On the other hand, united and committed crowds might be more
effective than divided and ambivalent ones at communicating consistent preferences and holding incumbents accountable for good

governance (Mistry et al., 2015). Shared interests help demonstrators coordinate around a message and a course of action even in the absence of selective incentives (Wood, 2003; Fireman and Gamson, 1979). Social network analysis indicates that people who are devoted to a cause are less likely to abandon their struggle and are more ambitious in recruiting other participants (McAdam, 1986). In one longitudinal study, peace activists who identified less with their comrades had less confidence in their ability to influence government decision makers, which in turn correlated with a greater chance of movement failure (Blackwood and Louis, 2012). Thus, the effectiveness of protests may depend on the motivations of protesters.

Scholars can adjudicate between among the above hypotheses using a combination of statistical methods – to explore the average determinants of post-protest reforms – and long-form interviews – to explore protesters' detailed priorities and incumbents' reasons for enacting reforms or not. Analyzing both macro-level protest outcomes and the motivations of individual actors would fill a gap in the extant literature, which tends to address only one or the other variable. A state is not a unitary actor controlling public policy within a territory, but rather an assemblage of elected leaders and appointed bureaucrats whose decisions reflect their interactions with people outside the state (Migdal, 2001). Variations in protesters' grievances plausibly condition state responses to protests, including policies on democracy, economic development, and national security.

A voluminous literature examines protest outcomes outside of Africa,[5] but it remains difficult to apply earlier findings to African contexts given that "social movements can achieve political change via different causal processes" and "we can also expect different independent variables ... to be influential for different social movements" or at different moments in time (Kolb, 2007, 43). Africanists could test the generalizability of research about the American civil rights movement, British miners' strikes, and other non-African protests. Studies on such events show several variables to shape protest outcomes: political institutional structure (including a state's autonomy to meet protesters' demands), partisanship of government, elite conflict,

---

[5] See, for example, Bosi, Giugni, and Uba (2016), Kolb (2007), and the December 2009 special issue of *Mobilization* on protest outcomes (Volume 14, Issue 4).

instability of political alignments, public opinion, mass media, windows for reform, and strength of counter-mobilization (Bosi, Giugni, and Uba, 2016; Kolb, 2007).

Kang (2015) provides one excellent example of cross-validating non-African findings using African data. She evaluates four policy proposals that women's rights activists in Niger pursued with different levels of success between 1960 and 2011: the family law (rejected by the National Assembly), the gender quota law (adopted with amendments), the Convention on the Elimination of All Forms of Discrimination against Women (ratified with reservations), and the Maputo Protocol (ratification rejected). Analyzing interviews with key actors, Kang concludes that the adoption of women's rights policies is more likely when: 1) women's activists mobilize; 2) conservative activists fail to mobilize; and 3) the legislature does not exercise its autonomy to amend or reject women's proposals. Kang's results are consistent with research on Europe and the United States showing that the strength of counter-mobilization matters for movement success. Most other theories about protest outcomes have not yet been tested in (or across) Africa.

Another avenue for future research is to explain cross-national variation in the salience of low expectations of upward mobility (see Chapter 5, Table 5.5). What national myths, norms, shared experiences, or other variables lead certain grievances to arouse protest in some countries but not in others? How do specific grievances become focal points that serve as clues for coordinating collective action? In a study of thirty-one countries, Singer (2011) found that the economy is more likely to dominate other concerns under conditions of economic recession, volatility, and economic underdevelopment. He further showed that the individual-level salience of economic performance increases with unemployment and economic vulnerability. However, Singer (2011) looked at the salience of grievances only with respect to elections, not protest, and used data from the Comparative Study of Electoral Systems surveys, which do not cover Africa.

Scholars could also investigate how grievances fuel protest over time. How long do high expectations of upward mobility avert social unrest? In a classic paper, Hirschman and Rothschild (1973) proposed that ethnically homogenous societies tolerate inequality between elites and the masses longer than more diverse societies, because people in homogenous societies feel hopeful rather than resentful when they see others "like them" becoming rich and powerful. Social scientists could bring current data and methods to bear on testing this and other hypotheses about temporal variation in the salience of grievances.

Finally, a long-term research agenda might inquire how new communication technologies influence the balance of power between incumbents, generals of the revolution, and foot soldiers of the revolution. This book highlighted illiteracy as one reason why the poor in Africa rely so much on middle-class comrades for help mounting social movements. WhatsApp could change that. Users of the social media platform, which Facebook purchased for $19 billion in 2014, numbered one billion as of February 1, 2016 (Statt, 2016). WhatsApp lets people share not just text and images, but also short audio files in local languages, giving rise to what one Nigerien described as the "revenge of the illiterate." WhatsApp is becoming de rigueur for political organizing across Africa. In 2016, Burundians used it to circulate photos of police brutality during protests surrounding President Pierre Nkurunziza's attempt to stay in office for a third term. For the time being, end-to-end encryption makes it practically impossible for incumbents to track who shares what.[6] Thus, people continued sending messages in Burundi even after a state-enforced blackout of traditional media like radio (Vircoulon, 2016). Habeb Elebed, an activist in Sudan's "sharing revolution," praised WhatsApp's privacy features: "I use it because the security services announced that they are watching Facebook and other means of communication, so WhatsApp is safer in that respect" (Albaih, 2015). In July 2016, Zimbabweans used WhatsApp to coordinate a nationwide shutdown of schools and businesses for two days after the government failed to pay civil servant salaries (*BBC*, 2016b). There is ample research on mobile phones as "liberation technology" in Africa (e.g., Diamond, 2010; Ekine, 2010; Chiumbu, 2012; Wasserman, 2011) but less on newer technologies.

---

[6] Not even WhatsApp employees can read the data moving across its network. British Home Secretary Amber Rudd called for WhatsApp and similar companies using end-to-end encryption to make messaging accessible to authorities and security agencies. Consumer advocate groups like The Open Rights Group condemned her statements on the grounds that stopping end-to-end encryption would violate users' privacy (Sparrow, 2017).

Protesters: Troublemakers or Heroes?

Social science teaches us that protest can affect a host of phenomena such as democracy, development, and human rights (Brancati, 2016; Beaulieu, 2014; Stephan and Chenoweth, 2008; Wood, 2000; Bratton and van de Walle, 1997). The stakes of social unrest are exceptionally high in sub-Saharan Africa, an area marked by chronic poverty, weak governance, extreme weather, and attacks from fundamentalist groups like Boko Haram and al-Qaeda in the Islamic Maghreb. These crises do not afflict all of Africa with the same severity, but virtually no corner of the region is immune. Some outside observers have responded to African protests with fear that they will destabilize governments, amplify economic uncertainty, and derail counterterrorism campaigns (e.g., Kllegman, 2015). Others see potential for Africans to advance democracy, development, and peace by pressuring incumbents for reforms. The staff director for the U.S. House of Representatives Subcommittee on Africa, Health, Human Rights, and International Organizations affirmed, "There is cause for hope from below ... as opposition leaders, civil society activists, and ordinary citizens increasingly are demanding responsive and accountable government. Moreover, the massive protests sparked by attempts at constitutional manipulation indicate that Africans want democracy and favor limits on presidential terms" (Yarwood, 2016).[7] *The Economist* extolled the democratizing potential of the middle class: "one big hope lies in the continuing rise of an educated, wealthier middle class. As Africa in general gets richer and the younger generation turns against the bribery and corruption of the old order, the demand for decent governance will get louder" (*The Economist*, 2016). Gauging by my interactions over the years with U.S. government agencies and NGOs,[8] policymakers are eager to understand the consequences of African protests so they can forestall crises and support local agents of positive change.

This book examined protests mainly at the level of individual actors, but it has implications at the event level. The findings offer guidance for donors and foreign officials who wish to identify

---

[7] At the time of publication, Yarwood was chair of the Sub-Saharan Africa Area Studies Program at the U.S. Foreign Service Institute.

[8] Including the State Department, USAID, the intelligence community, and the National Endowment for Democracy.

protest hot spots. They indicate that ordinary citizens' expectations of upward mobility and middle-class activists' leadership partially explain the onset and size of protests. Policymakers can therefore anticipate where and when major unrest will break out by monitoring the convergence of economic pessimism and middle-class growth. The map in Figure 7.1 provides a rough illustration. It summarizes the economic expectations of respondents in African countries from the sixth round of Afrobarometer surveys (2014–2015), which asked, "looking ahead, do you expect economic conditions in this country to be better or worse in twelve months' time?"[9] Afrobarometer coders translated answers into an index, ranging from 0 to 100, where lower numbers denote more pessimism ("much worse; worse") and higher numbers denote more optimism ("better; much better").[10] Niger, for example, is one of the most hopeful countries in Africa, despite a chronically depressed economy,[11] and has one of the smallest middle classes.[12] This

---

[9] Survey rounds 2 through 5 used slightly differing wording, asking about respondents' *personal* economic prospects as opposed to the future of their country as a whole. Results of statistical analyses in Chapter 5 were robust to omitting round 6. I use round 6 data here because they are the most recent.

[10] See the Appendix C for indices by country.

[11] See Chapter 6 for an analysis of Niger's economy. The reason for Nigeriens' hopefulness may be cultural. The phrase "inshallah" ("God willing"), while ubiquitous in Muslim West Africa, seems to have deeper meaning in Niger. Nigeriens mention that their faith in God allows them to tolerate political and economic situations that might spark revolutions elsewhere. The country is approximately 98 percent Muslim, with three quarters of citizens actively practicing their religion (praying, reading religious texts, or participating in religious services) more than once per day. In contrast, only a quarter of respondents across all thirty-seven countries in round 6 of the Afrobarometer surveys practice religion with such frequency.

[12] The African Development Bank (2011) codes just 14 percent of Nigeriens as "middle class," even using the conservative benchmark of $2.20 of income per day. By comparison, Senegal's middle class comprises around 36 percent of the population; in the Sahel, only Burkina Faso has a smaller middle class than Niger, at 13 percent. Looking beyond income, Nigeriens also rely more on the state for their well-being and are more easily co-opted into the ruling party compared with citizens of high growth-countries in "Emerging Africa" (Radelet, 2010). There are scarce remunerative opportunities in formal private business; domestic credit to the private sector makes up only 13.7 percent of GDP, compared to a world median of 45.6 (The World Bank, 2017). Consequently, almost all wage-paying jobs are in the civil service, and many would-be protest leaders have neither the political autonomy nor the discretionary finances to mount viable opposition parties or social movements.

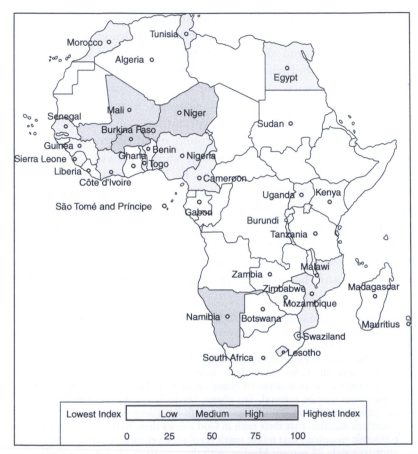

Figure 7.1: Low Expectations of Upward Mobility in Africa, 2014–2015

Note: Data are from Afrobarometer surveys (round 6), which asked, "Looking ahead, do you expect economic conditions in this country to be better or worse in twelve months' time?" Afrobarometer coded answers into an index, ranging from 0 to 100 where lower numbers denote more pessimism ("much worse; worse") and higher numbers denote more optimism ("better; much better"). See Appendix C for indices by country. Map was produced using Afrobarometer's online analysis tool.

combination of optimism and class structure is a clue as to why Niger was less protest-prone than other African countries during the concurrent Afrobarometer enumeration period (see Figure 7.2) and is likely to remain so unless economic expectations or the size of the middle class changes in coming years. In contrast, South

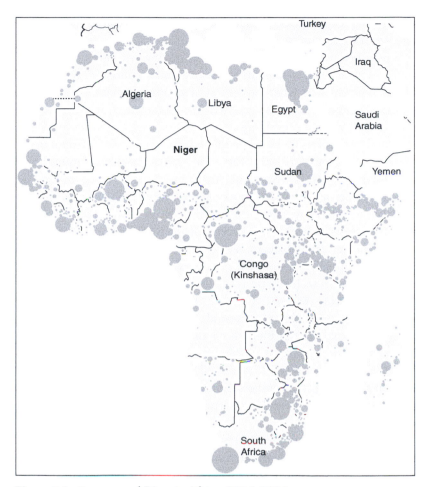

Figure 7.2: Protests and Riots in Africa, 2014–2015

Note: Data are from ACLED (2014–2015). Location and size of circles denote location and frequency of events, respectively. Map was produced using ACLED's online analysis tool.

Africa is much more pessimistic and has a thriving middle class,[13] which may account for its high rate of protest activity, as apparent in Figure 7.2. More refined studies, including regressions to control for confounding variables like population size, are necessary to reliably identify protest hot spots. Policymakers can enhance their

---

[13] Forty-three percent of the population is middle-class according to the African Development Bank (2011).

monitoring capabilities by allocating resources for the collection and analysis of quality data.

Where people have low expectations of upward mobility but lack well-endowed leaders to help them overcome collective action problems, policymakers have the option of stepping in with financial and logistical support. There is precedent for this strategy. In South Africa during the 1980s, a crumbling national economy and strict legal and informal restrictions on black people's access to domestic capital made outside funding critical for the anti-apartheid movement. The International Defence and Aid Fund began wiring money to South African organizations to pay for lawyers to represent protesters who got arrested. By 1988, the South African Council of Churches (SACC) received nearly 95 percent of its R15 million ($6 million) annual budget from foreign donors, which it distributed to allied groups and families of political prisoners. SACC was instrumental in mobilizing multi-sector actions, such as a strike in response to anti-union legislation (Battersby, 1988). The South African government severed activists' lines of external funding by passing the 1988 Orderly Internal Politics Bill, which also terminated U.S. assistance to the victims of apartheid under the 1986 Comprehensive Anti-Apartheid Act (Gerhart and Glaser, 2010, 166). Protesters were resourceful in procuring clandestine sources of money, but it is possible that the apartheid regime would have crumbled sooner without this setback to public organizing.

More recently, Ethiopia's 2009 Charities and Societies Proclamation curbed foreign and anonymous funding for organizations working on human rights and good governance. Other countries are less restrictive. For example, the U.S. National Endowment for Democracy awarded a Reagan-Fascell Democracy Fellowship in 2014 to an organizer of the Senegalese social movement Y'en a Marre for his work promoting government accountability and civic engagement. In 2017, Amnesty International gave its prestigious Ambassador of Conscience Award to Y'en a Marre and two other African social movements, Le Balai Citoyen from Burkina Faso and La Lutte Pour Le Changement from the Democratic Republic of Congo. The award carried significant political capital if not financial reward, helping to level the playing field between governments and the people.

Outside intervention is almost always controversial, but it may be necessary for African societies break free from the self-perpetuating traps of bad governance and poverty (Collier, 2007). When incumbents manage to repress or co-opt most of their challengers, citizens tend to "recycle" elites instead of booting them out of office (Chabal and Daloz, 1999, 31). Policymakers have been willing to intervene in these situations before, although they are usually reluctant to fund non-state actors (Mampilly, 2011). As a general rule, directors of democracy-building and development initiatives prefer working through states rather than against them, often in the form of capacity-building workshops and "sensitization" programs. For instance, training is a central component of USAID's Democracy, Rights, and Governance strategy for nurturing "democratic values and practices" in Southern Africa. Coaching public officials on how to be good democrats and economic planners can seem a safer bet than aiding anti-establishment activists who tout revolutionary agendas. At the same time, the United States, France, and other Western powers pour billions of dollars into military counterterrorism campaigns in Africa. This risks perverse effects, like allowing African leaders to channel aid into "domestic security" that amounts to crackdowns on the opposition.

On April 10, 2017, Nigerien authorities killed fifty-seven Boko Haram fighters in Diffa near the border with Nigeria, and the same day fired tear gas on students who had gathered at the University of Niamey to voice grievances about study conditions and other issues. One protester died and a hundred were injured.[14] Niger's democracy, which the Issoufou government helped to restore after a coup in 2010, began regressing just as foreign military aid ramped up. The United States raised its pledge one-hundred fold in 2016 (Brown and O'Donnell, 2016), and in 2014, France launched Operation Barkhane, a comprehensive counterterrorism mission that also received British contributions. Niger's 2016 national elections were rife with irregularities, among them fraudulent voter registration lists, arrests of journalists, and the months-long imprisonment of the main opposition candidate on charges of baby trafficking (Mueller and Matthews, 2016). In October 2017, coordinators of the movement Tournons La Page, representing seven African countries including Niger, issued an open letter to French President Emmanuel Macron: "... we denounce the frequent collusion between political and multi-national powers who enrich each other to the detriment of a population

---

[14] Three police officers later received one-year prison sentences for the violence.

deprived of basic social services … France must suspend military cooperation with all African states whose armies rape, kill, and oppress their people." How should policymakers manage the tension between security and democracy?

Case studies in this book suggested that protests can improve democracy even when protesters do not all seek democratic reforms. Policymakers can try to harbor people-power more intentionally to deter governments from violating democratic rules and to compensate for state weakness. An autonomous political society is critical when official government agencies succumb to conflicts of interest. In August 2017, Niger's president abruptly fired the top official at the state-affiliated High Authority for the Fight against Corruption and Assimilated Offenses (Haute Autorité de Lutte contre la Corruption et les Infractions Assimilées, or HALCIA) without naming a replacement.[15] Editorialists speculated about the death of the organization, which President Issoufou established only in 2011 (Gambo, 2017). With the HALCIA in shambles, there might have been hope for transparency in the grassroots Network of Organizations for Transparency and Budget Analysis (Réseau des Organisations pour la Transparence et l'Analyse Budgétaire, or ROTAB). The group occasionally holds protests surrounding the misuse of public funds, but ROTAB is a lean operation. It has neither office space nor adequate legal funds to assist members who have been arrested, and external support is elusive.

Since the democratic transitions of the 1990s, most African regimes do not stipulate outright bans on foreign aid for domestic activists. However, policymakers have erected their own barriers to sending aid, in the form of policies for preventing rebellions and coups d'état. International organizations and the mostly Western countries that control them have a longstanding practice of "naming and shaming" rebels by placing them on terrorist lists or working with governments to actively combat insurgencies (Mampilly, 2011). Yet it is unclear who exactly constitutes a rebel; to some incumbents, a rebel is any critic, and definitely anyone who denounces the regime at a rally. Mampilly (2011) warns that assuming the worst about "rebels" can have adverse impacts on citizens who rely on non-state actors for basic goods such as protection, education, and political representation.

[15] He eventually appointed Gousmane Abdourahamane, a veteran of the state's judicial machine.

Policymakers also withhold assistance to activists out of fear that protests will embolden the military to seize control by force. Protests and coups are not the same thing, but the former often precede the latter because crowds aggregate information about public opinion and provide soldiers with a signal that helps them coordinate around the strategy of staging a putsch (Casper, 2014). The U.S. Congress created the Millennium Challenge Corporation (MCC) in 2004 to implement an innovative system of foreign aid based on a scorecard of seventeen criteria including rule of law, civil liberties, and control of corruption. A country's scores and commensurate aid level often fluctuate gradually, but the MCC has a blanket policy of stripping a country's eligibility in the event of a coup. When a group of generals unseated the Mauritanian president in 2008, the U.S. State Department froze most aid within the month (Main and Johnston, 2009). In 2009, a coup in Madagascar prompted a hold on the country's $110 million five-year poverty reduction program (Main and Johnston, 2009). Niger lost a $23 million MCC commitment after a military faction removed Mamadou Tandja in 2010; Niger was also suspended from the Economic Community of West African States (Aker, 2010). The MCC's emphasis on democratic governance is not inherently bad, and the strict enforcement of rules gives the organization its "teeth." Coups can indeed be detrimental when they turn violent or replace bad leaders with worse ones (Singh, 2014).

Nevertheless, a zero-tolerance policy on coups is problematic for several reasons. First, a coup might replace a bad leader not with a worse one but with a better one, which is why analysts initially referred to Tandja's ousting as a "corrective coup" (Baudais and Chauzal, 2011). Second, automatically withdrawing aid after a coup might discourage activists from speaking out against injustices by sending the message that organizing protests will result in economic sanctions. Third, a full-blown civil war could be the price for coup-proofing a country. Unpopular African rulers who have clung to presidential power have occasionally provoked excluded groups to commit large-scale violence. This notably occurred in South Sudan in 2013 and is called the "coup-civil war trap" (Roessler, 2016). The MCC officially espouses "country-led solutions" and "country-led implementation," but aggressive anti-coup and anti-rebellion policies preclude donors from supporting citizens who might improve conditions for their countries from the bottom up.

It is admittedly difficult to predict the long-term consequences of intervening in conflict processes, but perhaps donors are too risk averse. If they became more open to carefully working with protesters instead of automatically obstructing them, then social unrest could be a window of opportunity for aid to disrupt development traps. A coup or a revolution shifts, however briefly, the balance of power between elites and the masses (Acemoglu and Robinson, 2006). The shock lets citizens claim "transitory power," meaning they have influence on politics today but might lose it again tomorrow. In such moments, a boost of external support in the form of training and information is critical for new norms and rules to take root; once a crisis settles, people become less willing to take a chance on reforms (Guiso, Sapienza, and Zingales, 2013). Aid should be delivered more like venture capital than like a steady pipeline of projects with no regard for political opportunities (Collier, 2007).

This book is not the first study to advocate for less state-centric policies toward Africa. Jackson and Rosberg (1982) argued that weak African states persist because the international community granted colonies juridical statehood at independence, guaranteeing states a legal existence despite their artificial borders and empirical weakness. Juridical statehood also hindered self-determination movements, as there was no hope for secessionists to earn international recognition (Jackson and Rosberg, 1982). Englebert (2009) added that the exogenous nature of sovereignty engenders political acquiescence, because affiliating with the state provides a symbolic currency of legal command that people use to dominate others for personal profit. Echoing Herbst (1990), he endorsed the "rational policy fantasy" of de-recognizing Africa's feeble states to incentivize better performance. I agree with these authors' basic critique of the double standard in development policy whereby states get the benefit of the doubt while the challengers of states do not.

But the development community needs realistic advice, not fantasies. Protesters have shown throughout history their ability to reform weak states from within (Brancati, 2016; Beaulieu, 2014; Stephan and Chenoweth, 2008; Wood, 2000; Bratton and van de Walle, 1997). Thus, rather than de-recognizing states for bad performance, policymakers could use appropriate vetting to recognize certain protesters as legitimate political actors eligible for assistance. This is more politically feasible than proposals to recognize rebel groups (Mampilly, 2011) or secessionist movements (Englebert, 2009), although these are not mutually exclusive solutions. I recommend a shift to the mindset that "sovereignty does not define the entire field of politics, and nonsovereign forms of organization and institution can be powerful and lasting" (Hardt and Negri, 2017, 14).

In concrete terms, policymakers ought to treat social movements more like NGOs than reckless troublemakers. Certainly, not all NGOs have pristine track records; it does not take much cynicism to realize that some are corrupt and fall short of accomplishing their stated missions. Still, many do good work and receive generous foreign aid to finance it (Delville, 2015). A notorious flaw of NGOs is their tendency to be elite organizations that fail to represent popular needs. Especially in larger jurisdictions, NGOs cannot effectively help the poor overcome collective action problems and end up delivering services for which incumbents claim credit (Boulding and Gibson, 2009). Plus, NGOs often engage in demonstrations, marches, and riots (Boulding, 2014), making the distinction between them and self-described activist networks an arbitrary one. African social movements should have a fair chance to realize their potential as agents of positive change, particularly considering their capacity to mobilize collective action among masses of non-elites. It is time for the development community to back up its rhetoric of empowering the people.

Appendix A Robustness Tests for Chapter 5

Table A.1 *Individual-Level Analysis of Protest Participation, South Africa Omitted*

	(1)	(2)	(3)
Urban	0.191***	0.190***	0.176***
	(0.0191)	(0.0192)	(0.0205)
Attended Community Meeting	1.083***	1.081***	1.090***
	(0.0223)	(0.0224)	(0.0241)
Religious Group Member	0.192***	0.190***	0.191***
	(0.0201)	(0.0202)	(0.0202)
State Legitimacy	−0.0432***	−0.0432***	−0.0380***
	(0.00309)	(0.00310)	(0.00329)
Female	−0.292***	−0.293***	−0.291***
	(0.0180)	(0.0181)	(0.0192)
Age	−0.0116***	−0.0115***	−0.0117***
	(0.000710)	(0.000714)	(0.000763)
Primary School	0.175***	0.176***	0.197***
	(0.0308)	(0.0308)	(0.0323)
Secondary School	0.435***	0.436***	0.434***
	(0.0311)	(0.0313)	(0.0329)
Post-Secondary School	0.795***	0.797***	0.767***
	(0.0354)	(0.0362)	(0.0386)
Gone without Income		−0.00411	0.00136
		(0.0225)	(0.0248)
Employed		−0.00467	−0.00362
		(0.0214)	(0.0229)
Absolute Deprivation			−0.0553**
			(0.0214)
Relative Deprivation (Egoistic)			−0.0305
			(0.0219)

Table A.1 (*cont.*)

	(1)	(2)	(3)
Relative Deprivation (Temporal)			0.0641**
			(0.0211)
Ethnic Group Treated Unfairly			0.231***
			(0.0230)
Low Expectations of Upward Mobility			0.194***
			(0.0248)
Pseudo R^2	0.0769	0.0768	0.0785
Observations	146810	146571	130718

Logit estimates with round and country fixed effects and standard errors in parentheses. Dependent variable is Protest Participation. Reference education category is "No Formal Schooling." Data are from Afrobarometer, covering 31 countries over 2002–2015.
* $p < 0.05$, ** $p < 0.01$, *** $p < 0.001$.

Table A.2 *Individual-Level Analysis of Protest Participation with Interaction Terms*

	(1)	(2)
Urban	0.164***	0.164***
	(0.0194)	(0.0194)
Attended Community Meeting	1.205***	1.205***
	(0.0229)	(0.0229)
Religious Group Member	0.181***	0.181***
	(0.0203)	(0.0203)
State Legitimacy	−0.0357***	−0.0357***
	(0.00314)	(0.00314)
Female	−0.287***	−0.287***
	(0.0181)	(0.0181)
Age	−0.0125***	−0.0125***
	(0.000715)	(0.000715)
Primary School	0.192***	0.192***
	(0.0316)	(0.0316)
Secondary School	0.424***	0.424***
	(0.0320)	(0.0320)

Table A.2 (*cont.*)

	(1)	(2)
Post-Secondary School	0.749***	0.759***
	(0.0373)	(0.0390)
Gone without Income	0.0506*	0.0506*
	(0.0229)	(0.0229)
Employed	0.00566	−0.00839
	(0.0237)	(0.0214)
Absolute Deprivation	−0.0427*	−0.0427*
	(0.0203)	(0.0203)
Relative Deprivation (Egoistic)	−0.0301	−0.0302
	(0.0209)	(0.0209)
Relative Deprivation (Temporal)	0.0595**	0.0595**
	(0.0201)	(0.0201)
Ethnic Group Treated Unfairly	0.192***	0.192***
	(0.0217)	(0.0217)
Low Expectations of Upward Mobility	0.173***	0.164***
	(0.0266)	(0.0253)
Employed * Low Expectations of Upward Mobility	−0.0692	
	(0.0505)	
Graduate * Low Expectations of Upward Mobility		−0.0474
		(0.0598)
Pseudo R^2	0.0867	0.0867
Observations	140631	140631

Logit estimates with round and country fixed effects and standard errors in parentheses. Dependent variable is *Protest Participation*. Reference education category is "No Formal Schooling." Data are from Afrobarometer, covering 31 countries over 2002–2015.
* $p < 0.05$, ** $p < 0.01$, *** $p < 0.001$.

Table A.3 *Individual-Level Analysis of Protest Participation, Reduced Sample*

	(1)	(2)	(3)
Urban	0.185***	0.186***	0.173***
	(0.0257)	(0.0258)	(0.0275)
Attended Community Meeting	1.222***	1.220***	1.232***
	(0.0302)	(0.0303)	(0.0326)
Religious Group Member	0.209***	0.208***	0.203***
	(0.0270)	(0.0270)	(0.0288)

Table A.3 (*cont.*)

	(1)	(2)	(3)
State Legitimacy	−0.0475***	−0.0471***	−0.0407***
	(0.00416)	(0.00417)	(0.00444)
Female	−0.282***	−0.282***	−0.281***
	(0.0241)	(0.0242)	(0.0257)
Age	−0.0140***	−0.0139***	−0.0138***
	(0.000958)	(0.000964)	(0.00103)
Primary School	0.137**	0.141**	0.173***
	(0.0428)	(0.0429)	(0.0451)
Secondary School	0.405***	0.409***	0.421***
	(0.0430)	(0.0433)	(0.0456)
Post-Secondary School	0.733***	0.740***	0.717***
	(0.0486)	(0.0497)	(0.0530)
Gone without Income		0.0196	0.0333
		(0.0296)	(0.0324)
Employed		−0.000841	0.00364
		(0.0286)	(0.0304)
Absolute Deprivation			−0.0632*
			(0.0288)
Relative Deprivation (Egoistic)			−0.0114
			(0.0296)
Relative Deprivation (Temporal)			0.0699*
			(0.0285)
Ethnic Group Treated Unfairly			0.200***
			(0.0309)
Low Expectations of Upward Mobility			0.133***
			(0.0334)
Observations	77604	77489	69280
Pseudo R^2	0.0886	0.0885	0.0892

Logit estimates with round and country fixed effects and standard errors in parentheses. Dependent variable is Protest Participation. Reference education category is "No Formal Schooling." Data are from Afrobarometer, covering 31 countries over 2002–2015.
* $p < 0.05$, ** $p < 0.01$, *** $p < 0.001$.

Appendix B Survey Instrument for Chapter 6

The following questions are translated from original surveys in French, Hausa, and Zarma.

Table B.1 *Survey Questions and Coding*

Variable	Question	Scale	Coding
Protest participation	Over the last 12 months, have you participated in a protest or a strike?	Binary response (Yes/No).	Participation=1, no participation=0.
Asked to protest	Did anyone ask you to protest? If so, who?	Open-ended question.	Coded into Friend/Family/Student Group/Labour Union/Civil Society/Other/None.
Opposition to tazartché	What do you think about tazartché	Open-ended question.	Collapsed into a binary variable where "support tazartché"=1, "opposed to tazartche"=0.
Absolute deprivation	In general, how do you consider your economic situation?	Very bad/Quite bad/ Neither good nor bad/ Quite good/Very good/ Don't know.	Collapsed into a binary variable where "very bad and rather bad"=1, and other responses (excluding "don't know")=0.
Relative deprivation (egoistic)	In general, how do you consider your economic situation relative to the economic situation of other Nigeriens?	Better/The same/Worse/ Don't know.	Collapsed into a binary variable where "worse"=1, and other responses (besides "don't know")=0.
Relative deprivation (fraternal)	In general, how do you consider the economic situation of [respondent's identity group] relative to the economic situation of other [identity groups]?	Better/The same/Worse/ Don't know.	Collapsed into a binary variable where "worse"=1, and other responses (besides "don't know")=0.

Table B.1 (*cont.*)

Variable	Question	Scale	Coding
Relative deprivation (temporal)	Thinking about the past, how do you consider your economic situation relative to your economic situation 12 months ago?	Better/The same/Worse/ Don't know.	Collapsed into a binary variable where "worse" =1, and other responses (besides "don't know") =0.
Low expectations of upward mobility	In the next 12 months (five years), do you expect your economic situation to be better, the same, or worse than it is right now?	Better/The same/Worse/ Don't know.	Collapsed into a binary variable where "worse" =1, and other responses (besides "don't know") =0.
Organization member	Are you a member of a union, rural association, student association, or some other organization?	Union/Rural association/ Student association/Other organization/None.	Collapsed into a binary variable where "member of an organization" =1 and "not a member of any organization" =0.
Education	What is the highest level of education that you have completed?	None/Koranic school/ Primary school/Secondary school/Lycée/University.	Used to create a series of binary variables, where "Koranic school"/ "Secondary education"/"Post-secondary education" =1 and "primary education or less" =0
Religiosity	Do you consider yourself . . . ?	Very religious/ Religious/ Somewhat religious/Not very religious.	Used to create a series of binary variables, where "religious"/ "religious"/"not religious" =1 and "very religious" =0.

Appendix C Economic Expectations: Indices by Country (Afrobarometer 2014–2015)

Table C.1 *Economic Expectations: Indices by Country (Afrobarometer 2014/2015)*

Country	Value
Algeria	11
Botswana	25
Burundi	−1
Cameroon	43
Cape Verde	35
Benin	30
Gabon	9
Ghana	−8
Guinea	31
Côte d'Ivoire	54
Kenya	8
Lesotho	46
Liberia	3
Madagascar	−4
Malawi	5
Mali	62
Mauritius	−15
Morocco	42
Mozambique	46
Namibia	63

Table C.1 (*cont.*)

Country	Value
Niger	72
Nigeria	49
São Tomé and Príncipe	67
Senegal	44
Sierra Leon	26
South Africa	13
Zimbabwe	−17
Sudan	22
Swaziland	37
Togo	45
Tunisia	48
Uganda	31
Egypt	49
Tanzania	−20
Burkina Faso	79
Zambia	8

Afrobarometer (2014/2015) data are from responses to the question, "Looking ahead, do you expect economic conditions in this country to be better or worse in twelve months time?" Higher numbers denote "better; much better," and lower numbers denote "much worse; worse." N = 53935.

Bibliography

Abbink, Jon. 2005. Being Young in Africa: The Politics of Despair and Renewal. In *Vanguard or Vandals: Youth, Politics and Conflict in Africa*, ed. Jon Abbink and Ineke van Kessel. Leiden: Brill pp. 1–33.

Abdul-Raheem, Tajudeen, ed. 1996. *Pan Africanism: Politics, Economy and Social Change in the Twenty-First Century*. London: Pluto Press.

Aboubacar Yenikoye, Ismaël. 2007. *Ethnicité, Citoyenneté et Culture de la Paix en Afrique: L'Example du Niger*. Paris: L'Harmattan.

Acemoglu, Daron and James A. Robinson. 2006. *Economic Origins of Dictatorship and Democracy*. Cambridge: Cambridge University Press.

Acquaah-Gaisie, Gerald Anselm. 2005. "Curbing Financial Crime among Third World Elites." *Journal of Money Laundering Control* 8 (4):371–381.

ActuNiger. 2017. "M. Maikoul Zodi, Coordonnateur pays de la Campagne 'Tournons la Page'." September 27. www.actuniger.com.

Adam, David. 2008. "Food Prices Threaten Global Security." *The Guardian*. April 9. www.guardian.co.uk/environment/2008/apr/09/food.unitednations.

Adichie, Chimamanda Ngozi. 2009. "The Danger of a Single Story." Speech delivered at TEDGlobal.

Adida, Claire L., Karen Ferree, Daniel N. Posner, and Amanda L. Robinson. 2013. "Social Desirability Bias in African Survey Data." Working Paper Presented at the Comparative Politics Workshop, UCLA, May 3.

Adji, Souley. 2000. "Globalization and Union Strategies in Niger." Discussion Paper, International Institute for Labour Studies, Geneva.

African Development Bank. 2011. "The Middle of the Pyramid: Dynamics of the Middle Class in Africa." African Development Bank Report.

African Development Bank. 2014. "Tracking Africa's Progress in Figures." African Development Bank Report.

Agarwala, Rina and Emmanuel Teitelbaum. 2010. "Trends in Funding for Dissertation Field Research: Why Do Political Science and Sociology Students Win So Few Awards?" *PS: Political Science and Politics* 43 (2):283–293.

213

Ahougnon, Servan. 2016. "Awadi, la révolution par la rime." June 3. https://ecceafrica.com/awadi-revolution-rime/.V4F vpOAN Bc.

Aizenman, Joshua and Nancy P. Marion. 1993. "Policy Uncertainty, Persistence and Growth." *Review of International Economics* 1 (2):145–163.

Aker, Jenny. 2010. "Despite Coup in Niger, Wrong Time to Yank Humanitarian Assistance." www.cgdev.org/blog/despite-coup-niger -wrong-time-yank-humanitarian-assistance.

Albaih, Khalid. 2015. "How WhatsApp Is Fueling a 'Sharing Revolution' in Sudan." *The Guardian*. October 15. www.theguardian.com/world/2015/oct/15/sudan-whatsapp-sharing-revolution.

Alesina, Alberto and Eliana La Ferrara. 2004. "Preferences for Redistribution in the Land of Opportunities." *Journal of Public Economics* 89:897–931.

Alesina, Alberto, Sule Özler, Nouriel Roubini, and Phillip Swagel. 1996. "Political Instability and Economic Growth." *Journal of Economic Growth* 1(2):189–211.

Al Jazeera. 2012. "Nigeria Protests on Hold as Oil Strike Looms." January 13. www.aljazeera.com/news/africa/2012/01/2012113132530230380.html.

Allison, Simon. 2012. "Ethiopia Rocked by Massive Muslim Protests." *Daily Maverick*. July 17. www.dailymaverick.co.za/article/2012-07-17 -ethiopia-rocked-by-massive-muslim-protests.VpuRhqAOko.

Almeida, Paul D. 2010. Social Movement Partyism: Collective Action and Oppositional Political Parties. In *Strategic Alliances: Coalition Building and Social Movements*, ed. Nella Van Dyke and Holly J. McCammon. Minneapolis, MN: University of Minnesota Press pp. 170–196.

Almeida, Paul D. 2003. "Opportunity Organizations and Threat-Induced Contention: Protest Waves in Authoritarian Settings." *American Journal of Sociology* 109(2):345–400.

Amadala, Ben and Kennedy Lumwamu. 2000. "NCEC Retreats on Mass Action." *Daily Nation*. June 5. www.nation.co.ke/news/1056-367526-l8 hmd6z/index.html.

Amamoo, Joseph G. 1958. *The New Ghana: The Birth of a Nation*. London: Pan Books.

Amare, Tighisti. 2014. "Africa's High Youth Unemployment: Is Population to Blame?" *The Guardian*. July 11. www.theguardian.com/global -development-professionals-network/2014/jul/11/africa-youth-unemploy ment-population-growth.

Amin, Samir. 1969. "La bourgeosie d'affaires sénégalaise." *L'Homme et la société* 12(12):29–41.

Amnesty International. 1996. "Niger: A Major Step Backwards." Amnesty International Press Release, October 16.

Amnesty International. 1997. "Harassment of Government Opponents Has Become Systematic." Amnesty International Press Release, May 1.

Amnesty International. 2000. "The People of Niger Have the Right to Truth and Justice." Amnesty International Press Release, April 4.

Andersen, Kurt. 2011. "The Protester." *Time*. December 14. http://content.time .com/time/specials/packages/article/0,28804,21017452102132,00.html.

Ansell, Ben W. and David J. Samuels. 2014. *Inequality and Democratization: An Elite- Competition Approach*. Cambridge: Cambridge University Press.

Antoine, Philippe and Abdou Salame Fall. 2004. "Crise, passage à l'âge adulte et devenir de la famille dans les classes moyennes et pauvres à Dakar." Codesria Working Paper 8-COD-3.

Antwi-Boateng, Osman. 2015. "No Spring in Africa: How Sub-Saharan Africa Has Avoided the Arab Spring Phenomenon." *Politics and Policy* 43(5):754–784.

Appadurai, Arjun. 2004. The Capacity to Aspire: Culture and the Terms. In *Culture and Public Action*, ed. Vijayendra Rao and Michael Walton. Washington, D.C.: Oxford University Press pp. 59–84.

Arezki, Rabah and Markus Brückner. 2011. "Food Prices and Political Instability." IMF Working Paper.

Ariyo, Ademola and Afeikhena Jerome. 1999. "Privatization in Africa: An Appraisal." *World Development* 27(1):201–213.

Armstrong, Hannah. 2010. "Niger Coup: Can Africa Use Military Power for Good?" *The Christian Science Monitor*. March 25. https://www .csmonitor.com/World/Africa/2010/0325/Niger-coup-Can-Africa-use-mi litary-power-for-good.

Arriola, Leonardo R. 2013a. *Multi-Ethnic Coalitions in Africa: Business Financing of Opposition Election Campaigns*. Cambridge: Cambridge University Press.

Arriola, Leonardo R. 2013b. "Protesting and Policing in a Multiethnic Authoritarian State: Evidence from Ethiopia." *Comparative Politics* 45 (2):147–168.

Artadi, Elsa V. and Xavier Sala-i-Martin. 2003. "The Economic Tragedy of the XXth Century: Growth in Africa." NBER Working Paper 9865.

Asuncion-Reed, Redante. 2010. Fahamu: Using Cell Phones in an Activist Campaign. In *SMS Uprising: Mobile Activism in Africa*, ed. Sokari Ekine. Cape Town: Pambazuka Press pp. 56–70.

Auyero, Javier. 2003. *Contentious Lives: Two Argentine Women, Two Protests, and the Quest for Recognition*. Durham, NC: Duke University Press.

Avineri, Shlomo. 1967. "Marx and the Intellectuals." *Journal of the History of Ideas* 28(2):269–278.

Awenengo-Dalberto, Séverine. 2012. "Sénégal: les nouvelles formes de mobilisations de la jeunesse." Les Carnets du CAP Working Paper.

Ayittey, George. 2006. *Africa Unchained: The Blueprint for Africa's Future.* New York, NY: Palgrave Macmillan.

Azizou, Garba Abdoul. 2010. "Niger: La Société Civile Face au '*Tazartché*'." *Alternatives Sud* 17:119–127.

Bagguley, Paul. 1995. Middle-Class Radicalism Revisited. In *Social Change and the Middle Classes*, ed. Tim Butler and Mike Savage. London: Routledge pp. 293–312.

Balandier, Georges. 1970. *Sociologie actuelle de l'Afrique noire*. Paris: Presses Universitaires de France.

Baldez, Lisa. 2002. *Why Women Protest: Women's Movements in Chile.* Cambridge: Cambridge University Press.

Baloyi, Basani and Gilad Isaacs. 2015. "South Africa's 'fees must fall' protests are about more than tuition costs." www.cnn.com/2015/10/27/ africa/fees-must-fall-student-protest-south-africa-explainer/.

Banerjee, Abhijit V. and Esther Duflo. 2008. "What Is Middle Class about the Middle Classes around the World?" *Journal of Economic Perspectives* 22(2):3–28.

Banks, Arthur S. and Kenneth A. Wilson. 2015. "Cross-National Time-Series Data Archive." www.databanksinternational.com.

Barcena, Alicia, Antonio Prado, Luis Beccaria and Susana Malchik. 2010. "Latin America in the Mirror: Objective and Subjective Dimensions of Social Inequity and Well-Being in the Region." United Nations Working Paper.

Barker, Colin, Alan Johnson and Michael Lavalette. 2001. Leadership Matters: An Introduction. In *Leadership and Social Movements*, ed. Colin Barker, Alan Johnson and Michael Lavalette. Manchester: Manchester University Press pp. 1–23.

Barlow, Robin and Wayne Snyder. 1993. "Taxation in Niger: Problems and Proposals." *World Development* 21(7):1179–1189.

Barnett, David. 2010. "Niger and the Benevolent Military Coup." *The Oxonian Globalist.* http://toglobalist.org/2010/11/niger-and-the -benevolent-military-coup/.

Barrett, Christopher B., ed. 2013. *Food Security and Sociopolitical Stability.* Oxford: Oxford University Press.

Bates, Robert H. 1981. *Markets and States in Tropical Africa*. Berkeley, CA: University of California Press.

Bates, Robert H. and Steven A. Block. 2013. "Revisiting African Agriculture: Institutional Change and Productivity Growth." *The Journal of Politics* 75 (2):372–384.

Battersby, John D. 1988. "South Africa Clerics Back Protest Strikes." *New York Times.* June 1. www.nytimes.com/1988/06/01/world/south -africa-clerics-back-protest-strikes.html?mcubz=0.

Baudais, Virginie and Grégory Chauzal. 2011. "The 2010 Coup d'Etat in Niger: A Praetorian Regulation of Politics?" *African Affairs* 112 (447):1–10.

Baulch, Bob and John Hoddinott. 2000. "Economic Mobility and Poverty Dynamics in Developing Countries." *Journal of Development Studies* 36 (6):1–24.

Bayart, Jean François. 1993. *The State in Africa: The Politics of the Belly.* London: Longman.

BBC. 2002. "Troops Put Down Niger Mutiny." August 9. http://news.bbc.co .uk/2/hi/africa/2183345.stm.

BBC. 2005. "Niger's President in Famine Zone." July 21. http://news.bbc.co .uk/2/hi/africa/4698943.stm.

BBC. 2010a. "Profile: Mamadou Tandja." February 18. http://news.bbc.co .uk/2/hi/africa/8181537.stm.

BBC. 2010b. "Thousands Rally in Support of Niger Coup." February 20. http://news.bbc.co.uk/2/hi/africa/8526072.stm.

BBC. 2011. "Tanzania Police Kill Two in Arusha at Chadema Protest." January 6. www.bbc.com/news/world-africa-12126861.

BBC. 2016a. "What Is behind Ethiopia's Wave of Protests?" August 22. www.bbc.com/news/world-africa-36940906.

BBC. 2016b. "Zimbabwe Shutdown: What Is behind the Protests?" July 13. www.bbc.com/news/world-africa-36776401.

Beaulieu, Emily. 2014. *Electoral Protest and Democracy in the Developing World.* New York, NY: Cambridge University Press.

Beck, Linda J. 2008. *Brokering Democracy in Africa: The Rise of Clientelist Democracy in Senegal.* New York, NY: Palgrave Macmillan.

Becker, Charles M., Andrew M. Hamer, and Andrew R. Morrison. 1994. *Beyond Urban Bias in Africa.* Portsmouth, NH: Heinemann.

Beissinger, Mark, Amaney Jamal and Kevin Mazur. 2012. "Who Participated in the Arab Spring? A Comparison of Egyptian and Tunisian Revolutions." Working Paper.

Beissinger, Mark R. 2013. "The Semblance of Democratic Revolution: Coalitions in Ukraine's Orange Revolution." *American Political Science Review* 107(3):20–48.

Bellemare, Marc F. 2011. "Rising Food Prices, Food Price Volatility, and Political Unrest." Working paper.

Bellin, Eva. 2000. "Contingent Democrats: Industrialists, Labor, and Democratization in Late-Developing Countries." *World Politics* 52 (2):175–205.

Bellot, Marina. 2016. "Interview de Smockey, porte-parole du Balai Citoyen." http://tournonslapage.com/753/.

Bénabou, Roland and Efe A. Ok. 2001. "Social Mobility and the Demand for Redistribution: The POUM Hypothesis." *Quarterly Journal of Economics* 116(2).

Benford, Robert D. and David A. Snow. 2000. "Framing Processes and Social Movements: An Overview and Assessment." *Annual Review of Sociology* 26:611–639.

Benson, Michelle and Thomas R. Rochon. 2004. "Interpersonal Trust and the Magnitude of Protest: A Micro and Macro Level Approach." *Comparative Political Studies* 37(4):435–457.

Berazneva, Julia and David R. Lee. 2013. "Explaining the African Food Riots of 2007–2008: An Empirical Analysis." *Food Policy* 39:28–39.

Berg-Schlosser, Dirk. 2009. Long Waves and Conjunctures of Democratization. In *Democratization*, ed. Christian W. Haerpfer, Patrick Bernhagen, Ronald F. Inglehart, and Christian Welzel. Oxford: Oxford University Press pp. 41–54.

Berkowitz, Leonard. 1972. "Frustrations, Comparisons, and Other Sources of Emotion Arousal as Contributors to Social Unrest." *Journal of Social Issues* 28(1):77–91.

Bernard, Tanguy, Stefan Dercon, and Alemayehu Seyoum Taffesse. 2011. "Beyond Fatalism. An Empirical Exploration of Self-Efficacy and Aspirations Failure in Ethiopia." IFPRI Discussion Paper 01101.

Bernstein, Ann. 2015b. "Will the Real Middle Class Please Stand Up?" *The American Interest*. October 7. https://www.the-american-interest.com/2015/10/07/will-the-real-middle-class-please-stand-up/.

Bernstein, Morty and Faye Crosby. 1980. "An Empirical Examination of Relative Deprivation Theory." *Journal of Experimental Social Psychology* 16:442–456.

Berthélemy, Jean-Claude. 1997. From Financial Repression to Liberalization: The Senegalese Experience. In *Experiences with Financial Liberalization*, ed. Kanhaya Gupta. Boston, MA: Kluwer Academic Publishers pp. 3–18.

Besley, Timothy. 2006. *Principled Agents? The Political Economy of Good Government*. Oxford: Oxford University Press.

Bjornskov, Christian, Axel Dreher, Justina A.V. Fischer, and Jan Schnellenbach. 2010. "Inequality and Happiness: When Perceived Social Mobility and Economic Reality Do Not Match." MPRA Paper 25826.

Blackwood, Leda M. and Winnifred R. Louis. 2012. "If It Matters for the Group Then It Matters to Me: Collective Action Outcomes for Seasoned Activists." *British Journal of Social Psychology* 51:72–92.

Bledsoe, Caroline. 1990. "'No Success Without Struggle': Social Mobility and Hardship for Foster Children in Sierra Leone." *Man* 25(1):70–88.

Bloise, Remo Capra, ed. 2001. *Bridge over Niger: The True Story of the J.F. Kennedy Bridge*. New York, NY: Writer's Showcase.

Blundo, Giorgio and Jean-Pierre Olivier de Sardan. 2006. *Everyday Corruption and the State: Citizens and Public Officials in Africa.* London: Zed Books.

Boisselet, Pierre and Benjamin Roger. 2015. "Les nouveaux opposants." *Jeune Afrique* 55(2830).

Boix, Carles. 2003. *Democracy and Redistribution*. Cambridge: Cambridge University Press.

Bonnecase, Vincent. 2013. "Politique des prix, vie chère et contestation sociale à Niamey: quels répertoires locaux de la colère?" *Politique Africaine* 2(130):89–111.

Boone, Catherine. 1990. "State Power and Economic Crisis in Senegal." *Comparative Politics* 22(3):341–357.

Boone, Catherine. 1992. *Merchant Capital and the Roots of State Power in Senegal, 1930–1985*. Cambridge: Cambridge University Press.

Boone, Catherine. 1998. The Making of a Rentier Class: Wealth Accumulation and Political Control in Senegal. In *Africa: Dilemmas of Development and Change*, ed. Peter Lewis. Boulder, CO: Westview Press pp. 185–212.

Bosi, Lorenzo, Marco Giugni and Katrin Uba. 2016. *The Consequences of Social Movements*. Cambridge: Cambridge University Press.

Botiveau, Raphaël. 2015. Changing Leadership Representations and Loss of Union Authority in South Africa's Mineworkers' Strikes. In *Collective Mobilisations in Africa: Enough Is Enough!* ed. Kadya Tall, Marie-Emmanuelle Pommerolle and Michel Cahen. Leiden: Brill pp. 205–223.

Boulding, Carew E. 2014. *NGOs, Political Protest, and Civil Society*. Cambridge: Cambridge University Press.

Boulding, Carew E. and Clark C. Gibson. 2009. "Supporters or Challengers? The Effects of Nongovernmental Organizations on Local Politics in Bolivia." *Comparative Political Studies* 42(4):479–500.

Bourgi, Albert and Christian Castern. 1992. *Le Printemps de l'Afrique*. Paris: Hachette.

Brancati, Dawn. 2016. *Democracy Protests: Origins, Features, and Significance*. New York, NY: Cambridge University Press.

Branch, Adam and Zachariah Mampilly. 2015. *Africa Uprising: Popular Protest and Political Change*. London: Zed Books.

Bratton, Michael. 1989. "Beyond the State: Civil Society and Associational Life in Africa." *World Politics* 41(3):407–430.

Bratton, Michael. 1998. "Second Elections in Africa." *Journal of Democracy* 9(3):51–66.

Bratton, Michael. 2002. Wide but Shallow: Popular Support for Democracy in Africa. In *Democratic Institution Performance: Research and Policy Perspectives*, ed. Edward R. McMahon and Thomas Sinclair. Westport, CT: Praeger pp. 39–63.

Bratton, Michael and Nicolas van de Walle. 1992. "Popular Protest and Political Reform in Africa." *Comparative Politics* 24(4).

Bratton, Michael and Nicolas van de Walle. 1997. *Democratic Experiments in Africa: Regime Transitions in Comparative Perspective*. Cambridge: Cambridge University Press.

Bratton, Michael and Robert Mattes. 2001. "Support for Democracy in Africa: Intrinsic or Instrumental?" *British Journal of Political Science* 31 (3):447–474.

Bratton, Michael and Robert Mattes. 2009. "Neither Consolidating Nor Fully Democratic." Afrobarometer Briefing Paper 67.

Brian, Donal and Cruise O'Brian. 1967. "Political Opposition in Senegal: 1960–1967." *Government and Opposition* 2(4):557–566.

Brilleau, Alain, François Roubaud, and Constance Torelli. 2005. "L'Emploi, le chômage et les conditions d'activité." STATECO pp. 41–63.

Brooks, David. 2016. "The Danger of a Single Story." *New York Times*. April 19. www.nytimes.com/2016/04/19/opinion/the-danger-of-a-single -story.html?mcubz=0,

Brown, Ryan Lenora and Belinda O'Donnell. 2016. "The Un-Freedom Agenda." *Foreign Policy*. April 20. http://foreignpolicy.com/2016/04/20/ the-unfreedom-agenda-niger-elections-terrorism/.

Bryson, Devin. 2014. "The Rise of a New Senegalese Cultural Philosophy?" *African Studies Quarterly* 14(3):33–56.

Bueno de Mesquita, Bruce and George Downs. 2005. "Development and Democracy." *Foreign Affairs* September/October:77–86.

Buhlungu, Sakhela. 2010. *A Paradox of Victory: COSATU and the Democratic Transition in South Africa*. Pietermaritzburg: University of KwaZulu-Natal Press.

Buijtenhuijs, Robert. 1976. "Messianisme et nationalisme en Afrique noire: Une remise en question." *African Perspectives* 1(2):25–44.

Burgis, Tom. 2010. "Uranium: Coup Alters the Balance as Nations Jostle for Position." *Financial Times*. June 13. https://www.ft.com/content/93e487 c6-74ed-11df-aed7-00144feabdc0.

Burns, Justine. 2009. "Well-Being and Social Cohesion." Input Document for Launch of NIDS Wave 1, University of Cape Town.

Bush, Barbara. 1999. *Imperialism, Race and Resistance: Africa and Britain, 1919–1945*. London: Routledge.

Bush, Ray. 2009. "Food Riots: Poverty, Power and Protest." *Journal of Agrarian Change* 10(1):119–129.

Byaruhanga, Frederick Kamuhanda. 2006. *Student Power in Africa's Higher Education: A Case of Makerere University*. New York, NY: Routledge.

Cailhol, Amandine. 2014. "Fadel Barro: Guérillero pacifique." August 25. www.liberation.fr/planete/2014/08/25/fadel-barro-guerillero-pacifique 1086754.

Casco, José Arturo Saavedra. 2006. "The Language of the Young People: Rap, Urban Culture and Protest in Tanzania." *Journal of Asian and African Studies* 41(3):226–248.

Casper, Brett Allen. 2014. "Popular Protest and Elite Coordination in a Coup d'état." *Journal of Politics* 76(2):548–564.

Castells, Manuel. 2015. *Networks of Outrage and Hope: Social Movements in the Internet Age*. Malden, MA: Polity.

Cederman, Lars-Erik, Nils B. Weidmann and Kristian Skrede Gleditsch. 2001. "Horizontal Inequalities and Ethnonationalist Civil War: A Global Comparison." *American Political Science Review* 105 (3):478–495.

Cellar, Sheldon. 1995. *Senegal: An African Nation between Islam and the West*. Bounder, CO: Westview Press.

Chabal, Patrick and Jean-Pascal Daloz. 1999. *Africa Works: Disorder as Political Instrument*. Oxford: James Currey.

Chalcraft, John. 2016. *Popular Politics in the Making of the Modern Middle East*. Cambridge: Cambridge University Press.

Chang, Yu-tzung, Yun-han Chu and Chong-Min Park. 2007. "Authoritarian Nostalgia in Asia." *Journal of Democracy* 18(3):66–81.

Chanock, M. L. 1975. "Ambiguities in the Malawian Political Tradition." *African Affairs* 74(296):326–346.

Charlick, Robert. 2007. Labor Unions and "Democratic Forces" in Niger. In *Trade Unions and the Coming of Democracy in Africa*, ed. John Kraus. New York, NY: Palgrave Macmillan pp. 61–82.

Charlick, Robert B. 1991. *Niger: Personal Rule and Survival in the Sahel*. Boulder, CO: Westview Press.

Charteris-Black, Jonathan. 2011. *Politicians and Rhetoric: The Persuasive Power of Metaphor*. Basingstoke: Palgrave Macmillan.

Chatterjee, Partha. 2006. *The Politics of the Governed: Reflections on Popular Politics in Most of the World*. New York, NY: Columbia University Press.

Chaudhuri, Maitrayee. 2014. What's "New" in the New Social Movements? Rethinking Some Old Categories. In *Social Movements: Transformative Shifts and Turning Points*, ed. Savyasaachi and Ravi Kumar. New Delhi: Routledge pp. 159–185.

Chaudhuri, Soma and Sarah Fitzgerald. 2015. "Rape Protests in India and the Birth of a New Repertoire." *Social Movement Studies: Journal of Social, Cultural and Political Protest* 14(5):622–628.

Checchi, Daniele and Antonio Filippin. 2003. "An Experimental Study of the POUM Hypothesis." IZA Discussion Paper 912.

Cheeseman, Nic. 2014. "Does the African Middle Class Defend Democracy?" Afrobarometer Working Paper 150.

Cheeseman, Nic. 2015. *Democracy in Africa: Successes, Failures, and the Struggle for Political Reform*. Cambridge: Cambridge University Press.

Cheru, Fantu. 2012. "Democracy and People Power in Africa: Still Searching for the 'Political Kingdom'." *Third World Quarterly* 33(2):265–291.

Chiumbu, Sarah. 2012. "Exploring Mobile Phone Practices in Social Movements in South Africa—The Western Cape Anti-Eviction Campaign." *African Identities* 10(2):193–206.

Choi-Fitzpatrick, Austin and Tautvydas Juskauskas. 2017. "All the Protesters Fit to Count: Using Unmanned Aerial Vehicles to Estimate Protest Event Size." Working paper.

Chouli, Lila. 2014. Les mouvements sociaux et la recherche d'alternatives au Burkina Faso. In *Les mouvements sociaux en Afrique de l'ouest*, ed. Ndongo Samba Sylla. Paris: L'Harmattan pp. 239–275.

Christiaensen, Luc, Lionel Demery and Stefano Paternostro. 2002. "Growth, Distribution and Poverty in Africa." World Bank Working Paper.

Christopoulos, Dimitrios C. 1978. "Relational Attributes of Political Entrepreneurs: A Network Perspective." *Journal of European Public Policy* 13(5):757–778.

Chuhan-Pole, Punam and Manka Angwafo, eds. 2011. *Yes Africa Can: Success Stories from a Dynamic Continent*. Washington, D.C.: The World Bank.

Chuhan-Pole, Punam and Shantayanan Devarajan. 2011. Overview. In *Yes Africa Can: Success Stories from a Dynamic Continent*, ed. Punam Chuhan-Pole and Manka Angwafo. Washington, D.C.: The World Bank pp. 1–20.

Chwe, Michael Suk-Young. 2001. *Rational Ritual: Culture, Coordination, and Common Knowledge*. Princeton, NJ: Princeton University Press.

Cissé, Oumar, Ndèye Fatou Diop Gueye, and Moussa Sy. 2005. "Institutional and Legal Aspects of Urban Agriculture in French-Speaking West Africa: from Marginalization to Legitimization." *Environment and Urbanization* 17:143–154.

Clark, Andrew F. 1999. "Imperialism, Independence, and Islam in Senegal and Mali." *Africa Today* 46(3):149–167.

Cloninger, Susan C. and Steven A. Leibo. 2017. *Understanding Angry Groups: Multidisciplinary Perspectives on Their Motivations and Effects on Society*. Santa Barbara, CA: Praeger.

Coffey, Diane and Dean Spears. 2017. *Where India Goes: Abandoned Toilets, Stunted Development and the Costs of Caste*. Noida: HarperCollins India.

Cogneau, Denis, Thomas Bossuroy, Philippe de Vreyer, Charlotte Guenard, Victor Hiller, Philippe Leite, Sandrine Mesple-Somps, Laure Pasquier-Doumer, and Constance Torelli. 2006. "Inégalités et Equité en Afrique." Working paper.

Collier, David and Steven Levitsky. 1997. "Democracy with Adjectives: Conceptual Innovation in Comparative Research." *World Politics* 49 (3):430–451.

Collier, Paul. 2007. *The Bottom Billion*. New York, NY: Oxford University Press.

Collier, Paul and Anke Hoeffler. 2004. "Greed and Grievance in Civil War." *Oxford Economic Papers* 56:563–595.

Collier, Ruth Berins. 1999. *Paths toward Democracy: The Working Class and Elites in Western Europe and South America*. Cambridge: Cambridge University Press.

Collins, Randall. 2004. *Interaction Ritual Chains*. Princeton, NJ: Princeton University Press.

Collinson, Mark, Stephen Tollman, Kathleen Kahn and Samuel Clark. 2003. "Highly Prevalent Circular Migration: Households, Mobility and Economic Status in Rural South Africa." Paper Prepared for the Conference on African Migration in Comparative Perspective, Johannesburg, June 2003.

Cooper, Frederick. 1990. "The Senegalese General Strike of 1946 and the Labor Question in Post-War French Africa." *Canadian Journal of African Studies* 24(2):165–215.

Cooper, Frederick. 1996. "'Our Strike': Equality, Anticolonial Politics and the 1947–48 Railway Strike in French West Africa." *The Journal of African History* 37(1):81–118.

Corfield, F. D. 1960. *Historical Survey of the Origins and Growth of Mau Mau*. London: Her Majesty's Stationary Office.

Corning, Alexandra F. and Daniel J. Myers. 2002. "Individual Orientation Toward Engagement in Social Action." *Political Psychology* 23 (4):703–729.

Coughlin, Peter and Gerrishon Ikiara. 1988. *Industrialization in Kenya: In Search of a Strategy*. Nairobi: East African Educational Publishers Ltd.

Coulibaly, Adama Mamadou. 2007. "Pacotille, 'le rappeur de Wade': 'Je suis contre l'émigration clandestine'." June 3. www.xibar.net/PACOTILLE -Le-rappeur-de-Wade-Je-suis-contre-lemigration-clandestinea165.html.

Coulon, Christian. 1985. Prophets of God or of History? Muslim Messianic Movements and Anti-Colonialism in Senegal. In *Theoretical Exploration in African Religion*, ed. Wim van Binsbergen and Matthew Schoffeleers. Berkeley, CA: University of California Press pp. 346–366.

Cramer, Christopher. 2003. "Does Inequality Cause Conflict?" *Journal of International Development* 15:397–412.

Creevey, Lucy, Paul Ngomo and Richard Vengroff. 2005. "Party Politics and Different Paths to Demcoratic Transitions: A Comparison of Benin and Senegal." *Party Politics* 11(4):471–493.

Cresswell, Tim. 1996. *In Place/Out of Place: Geography, Ideology, and Transgression*. Minneapolis, MN: University of Minnesota Press.

Crosby, Faye. 1976. "A Model of Egoistical Relative Deprivation." *Psychological Review* 83:85–113.

Dabalen, Andres, Janet M. Lowens, Nazmul Chaudhury, Roy Katayama, Prospere Backiny-Yetna, and John Ulimwengu. 2012. "Niger: Investing for Prosperity – A Poverty Assessment." World Bank Working Paper 61393-NE.

Dakaractu. 2012a. "Dernière minute: Comme l'avait prédit dakaractu, Moustapha Niasse se démarque du M23 pour faire cavalier seul." February 13. www.dakaractu.com/Derniere-minute-Comme-l-avait -predit-dakaractu-Moustapha-Niasse-se-demarque-du-M23-pour-faire-c avalier-seula13320.html.

Dakaractu. 2012b. "Momar Samb: 'Moustapha Niasse n'a jamais quitté le M23'." February 13. www.dakaractu.com/Momar-Samb-Moustapha- Niasse-n-a-jamais-quitte-le-M23a13389.html.

Dalberto, Séverine Awenengo. 2012. "De la rue aux urnes: La longue marche de la deuxième alternatance au Sénégal." Working paper, SciencesPo Centre de Recherches Internationales.

Daloz, Jean-Pascal. 2003. "'Big Men' in Sub-Saharan Africa: How Elites Accumulate Positions and Resources." *Comparative Sociology* 2 (1):271–285.

Daloz, Jean-Pascal. 2013. *Rethinking Social Distinction*. New York, NY: Palgrave Macmillan.

Dalton, Patricio S., Sayantan Ghosal, and Anandi Mani. 2013. "Poverty and Aspirations Failure." Netspar Discussion Paper 09/2011–098.

Darbon, Dominique. 2014. Nom de Code: "Classes Moyennes en Afrique." In *L'Invention des Classes Moyennes Africaines: Enjeux Politiques d'une Catégorie Incertaine*, ed. Dominique Darbon and Comi Toulabor. Paris: Karthala pp. 15–59.

Darbon, Dominique and Comi Toulabor. 2014. *L'Invention des Classes Moyennes Africaines: Enjeux Politiques d'une Catégorie Incertaine.* Paris: Karthala.

Davenport, Christian. 2015. *How Social Movements Die.* Cambridge: Cambridge University Press.

Davies, James C. 1962. "Toward a Theory of Revolution." *American Sociological Review* 27(1):5–19.

Davis, John Uniack and Aboubacar B. Kossomi. 2001. "Niger Gets Back on Track." *Journal of Democracy* 13(3):80–87.

Davis, Mike. 2004. *Planet of Slums.* London: Verso.

Dawson, Hannah. 2014. "Youth Politics: Waiting and Envy in a South African Informal Settlement." *Journal of Southern African Studies* 40 (4):861–882.

de Sardan, Jean-Pierre Olivier. 1984. *Les Sociétés Songhay-Zarma (Mali-Niger): Chefs, Guerriers, Esclaves, Paysans.* Paris: Editions Karthala.

de Waal, Alex and Rachel Ibreck. 2013. "Hybrid Social Movements in Africa." *Journal of Contemporary African Studies* 31(2):303–324.

Decalo, Samuel. 1985. "African Personal Dictatorships." *Journal of Modern African Studies* 23(2):209–237.

della Porta, Donatella. 2015. *Social Movements in Times of Austerity.* Malden, MA: Polity.

della Porta, Donatella and Mario Diani. 2006. *Social Movements: An Introduction.* Malden, MA: Blackwell Publishing.

Delville, Philippe Lavigne. 2015. *Aide Internationale et Sociétés Civiles au Niger.* Paris: Karthala.

Demarest, Leila. 2015. "Staging a 'Revolution': The 2011–2012 Electoral Protests in Senegal." CRPD Working Paper 20.

Demarest, Leila. 2016. "Staging a 'Revolution': The 2011–12 Electoral Protests in Senegal." *African Studies Review* 59(3):61–82.

Demery, Lionel and Lyn Squire. 1996. "Macroeconomic Adjustment and Poverty in Africa: An Emerging Picture." *The World Bank Research Observer* 11(1):39–59.

Desrosières, Alain. 1998. *The Politics of Large Numbers: A History of Statistical Reasoning.* Cambridge, MA: Harvard University Press.

Diamond, Larry. 1987. "Class Formation in the Swollen African State." *Journal of Modern African Studies* 25(4):567–596.

Diamond, Larry. 1993. *Political Culture and Democracy in Developing Countries.* Boulder, CO: Lynne Rienner.

Diamond, Larry. 2010. "Liberation Technology." *Journal of Democracy* 21 (3):69–83.

Diani, Mario. 2003. "Leaders" or "Brokers"? Positions and Influence in Social Movement Networks. In *Social Movements and Networks*, ed.

Mario Diani and Doug McAdam. Oxford: Oxford University Press pp. 105–122.

Diani, Mario. 2004. Networks and Participation. In *The Blackwell Companion to Social Movements*, ed. David A. Snow, Sarah A. Soule, and Hanspeter Kriesi. Malden, MA: Blackwell Publishing pp. 339–359.

Dibba, Velani. 2013. "Arab Spring's Impact on Sub-Saharan Africa." *International Policy Digest*.

Dieng, Moda. 2015. "La contribution des jeunes à l'alternance politique au Sénégal: Le rôle de Bul faale et de Y'en a marre." *African Sociological Review* 19(2):75–95.

Dimé, Mamadou. 2010. "'Des retraités qui entretiennent des jeunes': précarité et nouvelles dynamiques de solidarité intergénérationnelle à Dakar." Working paper.

Dimé, Mamadou. 2014. "De *bul faale* à Y'en a marre: Continuités et dissonances dans les dynamiques de contestation sociopolitique et d'affirmation citoyenne chez les jeunes au Sénégal." Working paper.

Diome, Modou. 2014. Between Representation Crisis, Social Movements Representivity Crisis and Media Propaganda: What Role for Senegalese Citizens? *In Liberalism and Its Discontents: Social Movements in West Africa*, ed. Ndongo Samba Sylla. Dakar: Rosa Luxemburg Foundation pp. 381–418.

Dionne, Kim Yi, Adam Banch and Zachariah Mampilly. 2015. "'Protest Is Always Hopeful': Examining the Third Wave of Popular Protest in Africa." *Washington Post*. June 12. www.washingtonpost.com/blogs/monkey-cage/wp/2015/06/12/protest-is-always-hopeful-examining-the-third-wave-of-popular-protest-in-africa/.

Diop, Alioune Badara. 2010. "Sénégal: les mouvements sociaux sous l'alternance." *Alternatives Sud* 17:139–145.

Diop, David. 1953. "Etudiant african devant le fait colonial." *Présence Africaine* 14:114–117.

Diop, Momar-Coumba and Mamadou Diouf. 1990. *Le Sénégal sous Abdou Diouf*. Paris: Karthala.

Diouf, Mamadou. 1996. "Urban Youth and Senegalese Politics: Dakar 1988–1994." *Public Culture* 8(2):225–249.

Diouf, Mamadou. 2005. "Wall Paintings and the Writing of History: Set/Setal in Dakar." *GEFAME Journal of African Studies* 2(1).

Diseko, Nozipho. 1992. "The Origins and Development of the South African Student's Movement (SASM): 1968–1976." *Journal of Southern African Studies* 18(1):40–62.

Dominguez-Torres, Carolina and Vivien Foster. 2011. "Niger's Infrastructure." World Bank Policy Research Working Paper 5698.

Dosh, Paul. 2009. "Tactical Innovation, Democratic Governance, and Mixed Motives: Popular Movement Resilience in Peru and Ecuador." *Latin American Politics and Society* 51(1):87–118.

Druker, Jeremy, Varvara Lokteva, Ioana Caloianu, and Joshua Boissevain. 2012. "Around the Bloc: Monkey Business in Slovakia, Romania's Stray Dogs Escape Death Row." *Transitions Online* 1(17).

Dubé, Lise and Serge Guimond. 1983. Relative Deprivation and Social Protest: The Personal-Group Issue. In *Relative Deprivation and Social Comparison: The Ontario Symposium*, Vol. 4, ed. Aldon Morris and Carol McClurg Mueller. Hillsdale, NJ: Lawrence Erlbaum Associates pp. 201–216.

Duflo, Esther. 2012. "Human Values and the Designation of the Fight against Poverty." *Tanner Lectures*.

Dulani, Boniface. 2009. Nurtured from the Pulpit: The Emergence and Growth of Malawi's Democracy Movement. In *Movers and Shakers: Social Movements in Africa*, ed. Stephen Ellis and Ineke van Kessel. Leiden: Brill pp. 138–156.

Dunlap, Al. 2004. Callous. In *Bad Leadership: What It Is, How It Happens, Why It Matters*, ed. Barbara Kellerman. Boston, MA: Harvard Business School Press pp. 119–146.

Dwyer, Peter and Leo Zeilig. 2012. *African Struggles Today: Social Movements since Independence.* Chicago, IL: Haymarket Press.

Easterly, William. 2005. "What Did Structural Adjustment Adjust? The Association of Policies and Growth with Repeated IMF and World Bank Adjustment Loans." *Journal of Development Economics* 76 (1):1–22.

Eifert, Benn, Edward Miguel and Daniel N. Posner. 2010. "Political Competition and Ethnic Identification in Africa." *American Journal of Political Science* 54(2):494–510.

Ekine, Sokari. 2010. *SMS Uprising: Mobile Phone Activism in Africa.* Capetown: Pambazuka Press.

el Hamalawy, Hossam. 2011. "Egypt's Revolution Has Been 10 Years in the Making." *The Guardian.* March 2. https://www.theguardian.com/commentisfree/2011/mar/02/egypt-revolution-mubarak-wall-of-fear.

Elischer, Sebastian. 2013. "Contingent Democrats in Action: Organized Labor and Regime Change in the Republic of Niger." GIGA Working Paper 231.

Ellis, Stephen. 2009. "Campus Cults" in Nigeria: The Development of an Anti-Social Movement. In *Movers and Shakers: Social Movements in Africa*, ed. Stephen Ellis and Ineke van Kessel. Leiden: Brill pp. 221–236.

Elnur, Ibrahim. 2009. *Contested Sudan: The Political Economy of War and Reconstruction.* New York, NY: Routledge.

Emerson, Robert M., Rachel I. Fretz, and Linda L. Shaw. 2011. *Writing Ethnographic Fieldnotes*. Chicago, IL: University of Chicago Press.

Engels, Bettina. 2015. "Social Movement Struggles against the High Cost of Living in Burkina Faso." *Canadian Journal of Development Studies* 36 (1):107–121.

Englebert, Pierre, ed. 2009. *Africa: Unity, Sovereignty and Sorrow*. Boulder, CO: Lynne Rienner.

Englebert, Pierre and Kevin C. Dunn, eds. 2013. *Inside African Politics*. Boulder, CO: Lynne Rienner.

Faiola, Anthony and Paula Moura. 2013. "Middle-Class Rage Sparks Protest Movements in Turkey, Brazil, Bulgaria and Beyond." *Washington Post*. June 28. www.washingtonpost.com/world/europe/middle-class-rage -sparks-protest-movements-in-turkey-brazil-bulgaria-and-beyond/2013/06 /28/9fb91df0-df61-11e2-8cf3-35c1113cfcc5story.html.

Fall, Madior. 2011. "Bul faale est mort – Vive 'Y'en a marre'!" April 3. www .ruepublique.net/index.php?option=comk 2&view = item&id = 589.

Fanon, Frantz. 1961/2005. *The Wretched of the Earth*. New York, NY: Grove Press.

Fanta, Fassil and Mukti P. Upadhyay. 2009. "Poverty Reduction, Economic Growth and Inequality in Africa." *Applied Economic Letters* 16 (18):1791–1794.

Fantasia, Rick. 1988. *Cultures of Solidarity: Consciousness, Action, and Contemporary American Workers*. Berkeley, CA: University of California Press.

Farmer, Paul. 1999. *Infections and Inequalities: The Modern Plagues*. Berkeley: University of California Press.

Fashoyin, Tayo and Ukandi Damachi. 1988. "Industrial Relations for African Economic Recovery." *Nigerian Journal of Industrial Relations* 2:47–59.

Fatton Jr., Robert. 1986. "Clientelism and Patronage in Senegal." *African Studies Review* 29(4):61–78.

Fauré, Yves-André and Jean-François Médard. 1995. L'Etat-*business* et les politiciens entrepreneurs. Néo-patrimonialisme et *big men*: économie et politique. In *Entreprises et entrepreneurs africains*, ed. A. Ellis and Yves-Andreé Fauré. Paris: Karthala pp. 289–309.

Faye, Cheikh Faty. 2013. "Porteur de pancartes: Me Mbaye Jacques Diop en rupture avec l'histoire." *Dakaractu*. https://www.dakaractu.com/Porteur -de-pancartes-Me-Mbaye-Jacques-DIOP-en-rupture-avec-l-histoire_a41558 .html.

Federici, Silvia, George Caffentzis and Ousseina Alidou. 2000. *A Thousand Flowers: Social Struggles against Structural Adjustment in African Universities*. Trenton, NJ: Africa World Press.

Fernandes, Leela, ed. 2006. *India's New Middle Class: Democratic Politics in an Era of Economic Reform*. Minneapolis, MN: University of Minnesota Press.

Fichtmüller, Anna. 2014. La Mobilisation Politique de la Classe Moyenne Ougandaise: Les Tactiques Hésitantes de la Pesanteur. In *L'Invention des Classes Moyennes Africaines: Enjeux Politiques d'une Catégorie Incertaine*, ed. Dominique Darbon and Comi Toulabor. Paris: Karthala pp. 215–235.

FIDH. 2012. "Niger: A Roadmap for the New Authorities Based on Respect for Fundamental Rights." International Federation for Human Rights Report N555a.

Fields, Gary S. 2000. "The Dynamics of Poverty, Inequality and Economic Well-Being: African Economic Growth in Comparative Perspective." *Journal of African Economies* 9:45–78.

Firebaugh, Glenn. 2003. *The New Geography of Global Income Inequality*. Cambridge, MA: Harvard University Press.

Fireman, Bruce and William H. Gamson. 1979. Utilitarian Logic in the Resource Mobilization Perspective. In *The Dynamics of Social Movements*, ed. Mayer N. Zald and John D. McCarthy. Cambridge, MA: Winthrop pp. 8–45.

Fletcher, Svenja. 2013. "40 Years after Hirschman's Tunnel Parable: Income Inequality, Economic Development and Aspirations Failures in Latin America." Paper Prepared for the IARIW-IBGE Conference on Income, Wealth and Well-Being in Latin America.

Foltz, William J. 1973. Political Opposition in Single-Party States of Tropical Africa. In *Regimes and Oppositions*, ed. Robert A. Dahl. New Haven, CT: Yale University Press pp. 143– 170.

Fortier, Amanda. 2016. "Lyrical Protest: Hip-Hop and Youth Activism in Senegal." January 19. www.worldpoliticsreview.com/articles/17702/lyrical-protest-hip-hop-and-youth-activism-in-senegal.

Fosu, Augustin Kwasi. 2008. "Inequality and the Growth-Poverty Nexus: Specification Empirics Using African Data." *Applied Economic Letters* 15 (7):563–566.

Foucher, Vincent. 2007. "Blue Marches": Public Performance and Political Turnover in Senegal. In *Staging Politics: Power and Performance in Asia and Africa*, ed. Julia C. Strauss and Donal B. Cruise O'Brien. New York, NY: Palgrave Macmillan pp. 111–132.

Francis, Dana J. 2007. *Explaining Democratic Differences in Mali, Burkina Faso and Niger*. Medford, MA: Tufts University. Doctoral dissertation.

Frankema, Eqout and Jutta Bolt. 2006. "Measuring and Analysing Educational Inequality: The Distribution of Grade Enrollment Rates in

Latin America and Sub-Saharan Africa." Groningen Growth and Development Centre Research Memorandum.

Fredericks, Rosalind. 2014. "'The Old Man Is Dead': Hip Hop and the Arts of Citizenship of Senegalese Youth." *Antipode* 46(1):130–148.

Frederiksen, Folke. 2011. "Print, Newspapers and Audiences in Colonial Kenya: African and Indian Improvement, Protest and Connections." *The Journal of the International African Institute* 81(1):155–172.

Freedom House. 2015. "Freedom in the World: Aggregate and Subcategory Scores." https://freedomhouse.org/report/freedom-world-aggregate-and -subcategory-scores.VZup7BPtmko.

Friedland, William. 1969. *Vuta Kamba: The Development of Trade Unions in Tanganyika*. Stanford, CA: Hoover Institution Press.

Friedman, Benjamin M. 2006. "The Moral Consequences of Economic Growth." *Society* 43(2):15–22.

Friedman, Thomas. 2013. "Takin' It to the Streets." *New York Times*. June 29. www.nytimes.com/2013/06/30/opinion/sunday/takin-it-to-the -streets.html.

Frohlich, Norman, Joe A. Oppenheimer and Oran R. Young. 1971. *Political Leadership and Collective Goods*. Princeton, NJ: Princeton University Press.

Galvan, Dennis Charles. 2001. "Political Turnover and Social Change in Senegal." *Journal of Democracy* 12(3):51–62.

Gambo. 2017. "La Halcia serait-elle en fin de mission?" August 10. www .nigerdiaspora.net/index.php/breves-niger/1713-la-halcia-serait-elle-en -fin-de-mission.

Gamson, William. 1990. *The Strategy of Social Protest*. Belmont, CA: Wadsworth Publishing Company.

Gandhi, Jennifer and Ellen Lust-Okar. 2009. "Elections under Authoritarianism." *Annual Review of Political Science* 12:403–422.

Gavin, Michelle. 2007. "Africa's Restless Youth." *Current History* 106 (700):220–226.

Gaye, Mandiaye. 2014. "Le machin des 'porteurs de pancartes,' un cheval de Troie pour arnaque." *Xalima.com*. http://xalimasn.com/le-machin-des -porteurs-de-pancartes-un-cheval-de-troie-pour-arnaque-par-mandiaye -gaye/.

Gazibo, Mamoudou. 2005. "Foreign Aid and Democratization: Benin and Niger Compared." *African Studies Review* 48(3):67–87.

Gazibo, Mamoudou. 2007. "Mobilisations Citoyennes et Emergence d'un Espace Public au Niger depuis 1990." *Sociologie et Sociétés* 39 (2):19–37.

Geertz, Clifford. 1973. *The Interpretation of Cultures*. New York, NY: Basic Books.

Gellar, Sheldon. 2013. The Rise of Citizen Movements and the Consolidation of Democracy under the Abdoulaye Wade Regime. In *Le Sénégal sous Abdoulaye Wade: Le Sopi à l'épreuve du pouvoir*, ed. Momar-Coumba Diop. Dakar: CRES-Karthala pp. 119–151.

Genova, James. 2012. "'Y'en a Marre!' (We're Fed Up!): Senegal in the Season of Discontent." *Origins: Current Events in Historical Perspective* 5(6).

Gerbaudo, Paolo. 2012. *Tweets and the Streets: Social Media and Contemporary Activism*. London: Pluto Press.

Gerber, Alan S. and Donald P. Green. 2000. "The Effects of Canvassing, Telephone Calls, and Direct Mail on Voter Turnout: A Field Experiment." *American Political Science Review* 94(3):653–663.

Gerhart, Gail M. and Clive L. Glaser. 2010. *From Protest to Challenge: A Documentary History of African Politics in South Africa, 1882–1990 (Volume 6)*. Bloomington, IN: Indiana University Press.

Gerlach, Christian. 2010. *Extremely Violent Societies: Mass Violence in the Twentieth-Century World*. Cambridge: Cambridge University Press.

Gervais, Myriam. 1995. "Structural Adjustment in Niger: Implementations, Effects and Determining Political Factors." *Review of African Political Economy* 63:27–42.

Gettleman, Jeffrey. 2016. "'Africa Rising'? 'Africa Reeling' May Be More Fitting Now." *New York Times*. October 17. https://www.nytimes.com/2016/10/18/world/africa/africa-rising-africa-reeling-may-be-more-fitting-now.html.

Giugni, Marco G., Doug McAdam and Charles Tilly, eds. 1998. *From Contention to Democracy*. New York, NY: Rowman and Littlefield.

Gladwell, Malcolm. 2010. "Small Change." *The New Yorker*. October 4.

Goldstone, Jack A. 1994. "Is Revolution Individually Rational? Groups and Individuals in Revolutionary Collective Action." *Rationality and Society* 6 (1):139–166.

Goldstone, Jack A. and Doug McAdam. 2002. Contention in Demographic Life-Course Context. In *Silence and Voice in the Study of Contentious Politics*, ed. Ronald R. Aminzade, Jack A. Goldstone, Doug McAdam, Elizabeth J. Perry, William H. Sewell, Sidney Tarrow, and Charles Tilley. Cambridge: Cambridge University Press pp. 195–221.

González-Bailón, Sandra, Javier Borge-Holthoefer, Alejandro Rivero, and Yamir Moreno. 2011. "The Dynamics of Protest Recruitment through an Online Network." *Scientific Reports* 1(197). DOI: 10.1038/srep00197.

Goodrich, S. 1992. "Political Instability as a Determinant of U.S. Foreign Direct Investment." Senior thesis, Harvard University.

Gopaldas, Ronak. 2015. "Ageing African Leaders Need to Bridge Generation Chasm." *BusinessDay*. February 4. www.bdlive.co.za/opinion/2015/02/04/ageing-african-leaders-need-to-bridge-generation-chasm.

Gosselain, Olivier P. 2008. Mother Bella Was Not a Bella: Inherited and Transformed Traditions in Southwestern Niger. In *Cultural Transmission and Material Culture: Breaking Down Boundaries*, ed. Miriam T. Stark, Brenda J. Bowser and Lee Horne. Tucson, AZ: University of Arizona Press pp. 150–177.

Gould, Deborah B. 2003. Passionate Political Processes: Bringing Emotions Back into the Study of Social Movements. In *Rethinking Social Movements: Structure, Meaning, and Emotion*, ed. Jeff Goodwin and James Jasper. Lanham, MD: Rowman and Littlefield pp. 155–175.

Graham, Carol and Stefano Pettinato. 2002. "Hardship and Happiness: Mobility and Public Perceptions during Market Reforms." *World Economics* 1(4):73–112.

Gramsci, Antonio. 1971. *Selections from the Prison Notebooks*. New York, NY: International Publishers.

Graybeal, N. Lynn and Louis A. Picard. 1991. "Internal Capacity and Overload in Guinea and Niger." *Journal of Modern African Studies* 29(2):275–300.

Greskovits, Béla. 1998. *The Political Economy of Protest and Patience: East European and Latin American Transformations Compared*. Budapest: Central European University Press.

Grier, Beverly. 1987. Contradiction, Crisis, and Class Conflict: The State and Capitalist Development in Ghana Prior to 1948. In *Studies in Power and Class in Africa*, ed. Irving Leonard Markovitz. New York, NY: Oxford University Press pp. 21–26.

Grillo, R.D. 1974. *Race, Class, and Militancy: An African Trade Union, 1939–65*. New York, NY: Chandler.

Gueye, Marame. 2013. "Urban Guerrilla Poetry: The Movement *Y'en a Marre* and the Socio-Political Influences of Hip Hop in Senegal." *The Journal of Pan African Studies* 6(3):22–42.

Guiso, Luigi, Paola Sapienza, and Luigi Zingales. 2013. "Time Varying Risk Aversion." NBER Working Paper 19284.

Gurr, Ted Robert. 1970. *Why Men Rebel*. Princeton, NJ: Princeton University Press.

Gusfield, Joseph R. 1966. "Functional Areas of Leadership in Social Movements." *The Sociological Quarterly* 7(2):137–156.

Gyimah-Brempong, Kwabena. 2002. "Corruption, Economic Growth, and Income Inequality in Africa." *Economics of Governance* 3:183–209.

Habyarimana, James, Macartan Humphreys, Daniel N. Posner, and Jeremy M. Weinstein. 2007. "Why Does Ethnic Diversity Undermine

Public Goods Provision?" *American Political Science Review* 101 (4):709–725.

Haeringer, Nicolas. 2012. "Y'en a marre, une lente sédimentation des frustrations." *Mouvements* 1(69):151–158.

Haggard, Stephan and Robert R. Kaufman. 2016. *Dictators and Democrats: Masses, Elites and Regime Change*. Princeton, NJ: Princeton University Press.

Haggard, Stephan and Robert R. Kaufman. 2012. "Inequality and Regime Change: Democratic Transitions and the Stability of Democratic Rule." *American Political Science Review* 3(106):495–516.

Handley, Antoinette. 2008. *Business and the State in Africa: Economic Policy-Making in the Neo-Liberal Era*. Cambridge: Cambridge University Press.

Hardt, Michael and Antonio Negri. 2017. *Assembly*. Oxford: Oxford University Press.

Harsch, Ernest. 2012. "An African Spring in the Making: Protest and Voice across the Continent." *The Whitehead Journal of Diplomacy and International Relations* 45:45–62.

Hartmann-Mahmud, Lori Lynn. 2004. "The Rural-Urban Dynamic and Implications for Development: Perspectives from Nigerien Women." *Journal of Contemporary African Studies* 22(2):227–252.

Hathie, Ibrahima. 2014. "Youth Unemployment: A Potential Destabilizing Force in Senegal?" 28 April. https://africaupclose.wilsoncenter.org/youth-unemployment-a-potential-destabilizing-force-in-senegal/.

Havard, Jean-François. 2001. "Ethos 'Bul Faale' et nouvelles figures de la réussite au Sénégal." *Politique Africaine* 2(82):63–77.

Havard, Jean-François. 2004. "De la victoire du 'sopi' à la tentation du 'nopi'?" *Politique Africaine* 4(96):22–38.

Heller, Nathan. 2016. "The Big Uneasy." *The New Yorker*. May 30.

Henderson, Ian. 1973. "Wage-Earners and Political Protest in Colonial Africa: The Case of the Copperbelt." *African Affairs* 72(288):288–299.

Hendrix, Cullen S. and Idean Salehyan. 2015. "Social Conflict in Africa Database (SCAD)." www.scaddata.org.

Herbst, Jeffrey. 1990. "War and the State in Africa." *International Security* 14 (4):117–139.

Herbst, Jeffrey. 2000. *States and Power in Africa*. Princeton, NJ: Princeton University Press.

Hertz, Thomas Nathaniel. 2001. *Education, Inequality and Economic Mobility in South Africa*. Doctoral dissertation, University of Massachusetts-Amherst.

Higgott, Richard and Finn Fuglestad. 1975. "The 1974 Coup d'Etat in Niger: Towards an Explanation." *Journal of Modern African Studies* 13(3):383–398.

Hipsher, Patricia L. 1998. Democratic Transitions as Protest Cycles: Social Movement Dynamics in Democratizing Latin America. In *The Social Movement Society*, ed. David S. Meyer and Sidney Tarrow. Thousand Oaks, CA: SAGE pp. 153–172.

Hirschman, Albert O. and Michael Rothschild. 1973. "The Changing Tolerance for Income Inequality in the Course of Economic Development." *Quarterly Journal of Economics* 87(4):544–566.

Hobson, John A. 1902/1965. *Imperialism: A Study*. Ann Arbor, MI: University of Michigan Press.

Hodgkin, Thomas. 1962. "Islam and National Movements in West Africa." *The Journal of African History* 3(2):3–7.

Holmquist, Frank and Michael Ford. 1994. "Kenya: State and Civil Society the First Year After the Election." *Africa Today* 41(4):5–26.

Honwana, Alcinda. 2015. "Enough Is Enough!" Youth Protests and Political Change in Africa. In *Collective Mobilisations in Africa: Enough Is Enough!*, ed. Kadya Tall, Marie-Emmanuelle Pommerolle and Michel Cahen. Leiden: Brill pp. 45–66.

Howard, Rhoda E. 1995. "Civil Conflict in Sub-Saharan Africa: Internally Generated Causes." *International Journal* 51(1):27–53.

Huntington, Samuel. 1991. *The Third Wave: Democratization in the Late Twentieth Century*. Norman, OK: University of Oklahoma Press.

Hymans, Jacques Louis. 1971. *Léopold Sédar Senghor: An Intellectual Biography*. Edinburgh: Edinburgh University Press.

Ibn-Oumar, Acheikh. 2013. "Learning the Hard Lessons of Arab Spring." *Al Jazeera*. December 18. https://www.aljazeera.com/indepth/opinion/2013/12/africa-learning-hard-lessons-arab-spring-2013121771840774707.html.

Ibrahim, Jibrin. 1994. "Political Exclusion, Democratization and Dynamics of Ethnicity in Niger." *Africa Today* 41(3):15–39.

Ibrahim, Jibrin. 1999a. "The Military and Democratisation in Niger." Report for the Nordic Africa Institute. www.nai.uu.se/publications/news/archives/993ibrahim/.

Ibrahim, Jibrin. 1999b. Transition et Successions Politiques au Niger. In *Les Figures du Politique en Afrique: Des Pouvoirs Hérités au Pouvoirs Elus*, ed. Momar-Coumba Diop and Mamadou Diouf. Paris: Editions Karthala et Codesria pp. 189–217.

Ibrahim, Jibrin and Abdoulaye Niandou Souley. 1998. The Rise to Power of an Opposition Party: The MNSD in Niger Republic. In *The Politics of Opposition in Contemporary Africa*, ed. Adebayo O. Olukoshi. Stockholm: Nordic Africa Institute pp. 144–170.

Inglehart, Ronald and Paul R. Abramson. 1999. "Measuring Postmaterialism." *American Political Science Review* 93(3):665–677.

International Labor Office. 1987. "The Role of the African Labour Force in Recessed Economies." Report of the ARLAC-JASPA Workshop, Harare, Zimbabwe, 15–27 June.

Isa, Muhammed Kabir. 2010. Militant Islamist Groups in Northern Nigeria. In *Militias, Rebels and Islamist Militants: Human Security and State Crises in Africa*, ed. Wafula Okumu and Augustine Ikelegbe. Pretoria: Institute of Security Studies pp. 313–340.

Isaacman, Allen. 1990. "Peasants and Rural Social Protest in Africa." *African Studies Review* 33(2):1–120.

Jackson, Robert H. 1973. "Political Stratification in Tropical Africa." *Canadian Journal of African Studies* 7(3):381–400.

Jackson, Robert H. and Carl G. Rosberg. 1982. *Personal Rule in Black Africa*. Berkeley, CA: University of California Press.

Jaime-Castillo, Antonio M. 2008. "Expectations of Social Mobility, Meritocracy and Demand for Redistribution in Spain." Paper Presented at the "Inequality beyond Globalzation" Conference, Neuchâtel, Switzerland, June 26-28.

James, C. L. R. 1969. *A History of Pan African Revolt*. Washington, D.C.: Drum and Spear Press.

Jansen, Stef. 2001. "The Streets of Beograd: Urban Space and Protest Identities in Serbia." *Political Geography* 20:35–55.

Jasper, James M. 1998. "The Emotions of Protest: Affective and Reactive Emotions In and Around Social Movements." *Sociological Forum* 13 (3):397–424.

Jean-Baptiste, Rachel. 2008. "'These Laws Should Be Made by Us': Customary Marriage Law, Codification and Political Authority in Twentieth-Century Colonial Gabon." *Journal of African History* 49 (2):217–240.

Jenkins, J. Craig. 1983. "Resource Mobilization Theory and the Study of Social Movements." *Annual Review of Sociology* 9:827–553.

Jeune Afrique. 2009. "Les pro-Tandja dénoncent 'un complot de la communauté internationale'." www.jeuneafrique.com/Article/DEPAF P20091215T125623Z/.

Johnston, Hank, Enrique Laraña and Joseph R. Gusfield. 2010. Identities, Grievances, and New Social Movements. In *New Social Movements: From Ideology to Identity*, ed. Enrique Laraña, Hank Johnston and Joseph R. Gusfield. Philadelphia, PA: Temple University Press pp. 3–35.

Jones, Philip. 1978. "The Appeal of the Political Entrepreneur." *British Journal of Political Science* 8(4):498–504.

Jones, William O. 1987. "Food-Crop Marketing Boards in Tropical Africa." *Journal of Modern African Studies* 25(3):375–402.

Kamau, Richard. 2015. "Kidero Inspects Westgate Mall Reconstruction Progress." *Nairobi Wire*. March 31. http://nairobiwire.com/2015/03/kid ero-inspects-westgate-mall-reconstruction-progress-photos.html.

Kang, Alice J. 2015. *Bargaining for Women's Rights: Activism in an Aspiring Muslim Democracy*. Minneapolis, MN: University of Minnesota Press.

Kapstein, Ethan B. and Nathan Converse. 2008. *The Fate of Young Democracies*. Cambridge: Cambridge University Press.

Karinge, Sarah. 2013. "The Elite Factor in Sub-Saharan Africa's Development: The Urgency in Bridging Disparity." *Journal of Developing Societies* 29(4):435–455.

Katzenstein, Mary Fainsod and Carol McClurg Mueller. 1987. *The Women's Movements of the United States and Western Europe*. Philadelphia, PA: Temple University Press.

Keck, Margaret E. and Kathryn Sikkink. 1998. *Activists Beyond Borders: Advocacy Networks in International Politics*. Ithaca, NY: Cornell University Press.

Keefer, Philip and Stephen Knack. 2002. "Polarization, Politics and Property Rights: Links between Inequality and Growth." *Public Choice* 111(1/2):127–154.

Keller, Bill. 2013. "The Revolt of the Rising Class." *New York Times*. June 30. http://www.nytimes.com/2013/07/01/opinion/keller-the-revolt -of-the-rising-class.html.

Keller, Edmond. 1991a. The State in Contemporary Africa: A Critical Assessment of Theory and Practice. In *Comparative Political Dynamics*, ed. Dankwart Rustow and Kenneth Erickson. New York, NY: Harper Collins pp. 134–159.

Keller, Suzanne. 1991b. *Ruling Class: Strategic Elites in Modern Society*. New Brunswick, NJ: Transaction.

Kelley, Sarah M. C. and Claire G. E. Kelley. 2009. Subjective Social Mobility: Data from Thirty Nations. In *The International Social Survey Programme 1984–2009*, ed. Max Haller, Roger Jowell and Tom W. Smith. New York: Routledge pp. 106–124.

Kelly, Catherine Lena. 2012. "Senegal: What Will Turnover Bring?" *Journal of Democracy* 23(3):121–131.

Kharas, Homi. 2011. "*The Emerging Middle Class in Developing Countries.*" Brookings Institution Report.

Kielbowicz, Richard B. and Clifford Scherer. 1998. The Role of the Press in the Dynamics of Social Movements. In *Research in Social Movements, Conflicts, and Change*, ed. Louis Kriesberg. Cambridge: Emerald Group Publishing pp. 114–116.

Kigwangalla, Hamisi. 2014. "Why Was There No 'African Spring'?" *Al Jazeera*. July 24. https://www.aljazeera.com/indepth/opinion/2014/07/why-was-there-no-african-sprin-2014724133730619939.html.

King, Gary, Robert O. Keohane and Sidney Verba. 1994. *Designing Social Inquiry*. Princeton, NJ: Princeton University Press.

Kirwin, Matthew F. and Wonbin Cho. 2009. "Weak States and Political Violence in Sub-Saharan Africa." Afrobarometer Working Paper 111.

Kivinen, Markku. 1989. "The New Middle Classes and the Labour Process." *Acta Sociologica* 32(1):53–73.

Klaas, Brian. 2008. "From Miracles to Nightmare: An Institutional Analysis of Development Failures in Côte d'Ivoire." *Africa Today* 55(1):109–126.

Klandermans, Bert. 1984. "Mobilization and Participation: Social-Psychological Expansions of Resource Mobilization Theory." *American Sociological Review* 49(5):583–600.

Klandermans, Bert. 1986. "New Social Movements and Resource Mobilization: The European and the American Approach." *International Journal of Mass Emergencies and Disasters* 4:13–38.

Klandermans, Bert. 2004. The Demand and Supply of Participation: Social-Psychological Correlates of Participation in Social Movements. In *The Blackwell Companion to Social Movements*, ed. David A. Snow, Sarah A. Soule and Hanspeter Kriesi. Malden, MA: Blackwell Publishing pp. 360–379.

Klandermans, Bert. 2015. Motivations to Action. In *The Oxford Handbook of Social Movements*, ed. Donatella della Porta and Mario Diani. Oxford: Oxford University Press pp. 219–230.

Klandermans, Bert, Jose Manual Sabucedo, Mauro Rodriguez and Marga De Weerd. 2002. "Identity Processes in Collective Action Participation: Farmers' Identity and Farmers' Protest in the Netherlands and Spain." *Political Psychology* 23(2):235–251.

Kllegman, Aaron. 2015. "Protests Continue in Burundi, Threaten to Destabilize East Africa." Center for Security Policy, May 7. www.centerforsecuritypolicy.org/2015/05/07/protests-continue-in-burundi-threaten-to-destabilize-east-africa/.

Klopp, Jacqueline M. and Janai R. Orina. 2002. "University Crisis, Student Activism, and the Contemporary Struggle for Democracy in Kenya." *African Studies Review* 45(1):43–76.

Knafo, Ariel, Carolyn Zahn-Waxler, Carol Van Hulle, JoAnn L. Robinson, and Soo Hyun Rhee. 2008. "The Developmental Origins of a Disposition toward Empathy: Genetic and Environmental Contributions." *Emotion* 8 (6):737–752.

Kohl, Herbert. 2005. *She Would Not Be Moved: How We Tell the Story of Rosa Parks and the Montgomery Bus Boycott*. New York, NY: The New Press.

Kolb, Felix. 2007. *Protest and Opportunities: The Political Outcomes of Social Movements*. Chicago, IL: University of Chicago Press.

Konings, Piet. 2011. *The Politics of Neoliberal Reforms in Africa: State and Civil Society in Cameroon*. Bamenda: Langaa Publishers.

Koopmans, Ruud. 2004. Protest in Time and Space: The Evolution of Waves of Contention. In *The Blackwell Companion to Social Movements*, ed. David A. Snow, Sarah A. Soule and Hanspeter Kriesi. Malden, MA: Blackwell Publishing pp. 19–46.

Kramon, Eric and Daniel N. Posner. 2011. "Kenya's New Constitution." *Journal of Democracy* 22(2):89–103.

Kriesi, Hanspeter. 1989. "New Social Movements and the New Class in the Netherlands." *The American Journal of Sociology* 94(5):1078–116.

Kriesi, Hanspeter. 1998. "The Transformation of Cleavage Politics: The 1997 Stein Rokkan Lecture." *European Journal of Political Research* 33(2).

Krishna, Anirudh. 2002. "Enhancing Political Participation in Democracies: What Is the Role of Social Capital?" *Comparative Political Studies* 35 (4):437–460.

Kron, Josh. 2011. "Protests in Uganda over Rising Prices Grow Violent." *New York Times*. April 21. www.nytimes.com/2011/04/22/world/africa/22uganda.html&r = 0.

Kurtulus, Gemici. 2003. "Spontaneity in Social Protest: April 2001 Shopkeeper Protests in Turkey." Working Paper for the "Theory and Research in Comparative Social Analysis" Series, UCLA.

Kurzman, Charles. 1998. "Waves of Democratization." *Studies in Comparative International Development* 33(1):42–64.

Laing, Aislinn. 2014. "South Africa Election: Jacob Zuma Promises More Opportunities for Non-Whites." *The Telegraph*. May 4. https://www.telegraph.co.uk/news/worldnews/africaandindianocean/southafrica/10807837/South-Africa-election-Jacob-Zuma-promises-more-opportunities-for-non-whites.html.

Lall, Sanjaya. 1995. "Structural Adjustment and African Industry." *World Development* 23(2):2019–2031.

Langer, Arnim and Kristien Smedts. 2013. "Seeing Is Not Believing: Perceptions of Horizontal Inequalities in Africa." CRPD Working Paper 16.

Laraña, Enrique, Hank Johnston, and Joseph R. Gusfield. 1994. *New Social Movements: From Ideology to Identity*. Philadelphia, PA: Temple University Press.

Larmer, Miles. 2011. *Rethinking African Politics: A History of Opposition in Zambia*. Burlington, VT: Ashgate.

Latumanga, Musambayi I. 2000. "Civil Society and the Politics of Constitutional Reforms in Kenya: A Case Study of the National

Convention Executive Council (NCEC)." Working paper, Series on Alternative Research in East Africa.

Lawrence, Adria K. 2013. *Imperial Rule and the Politics of Nationalism.* Cambridge: Cambridge University Press.

Le Gendre, Kevin. 2008. "Hip-hop with Harps." *The Guardian.* February 14. www.theguardian.com/music/2008/feb/15/worldmusic .urban.

LeBas, Adrienne. 2011. *From Protest to Parties: Party-Building and Democratization in Africa.* Oxford: Oxford University Press.

Lehman-Wilzig, Sam and Meir Unger. 1985. "The Economic and Political Determinants of Public Protest Frequency and Magnitude: The Israeli Experience." *International Review of Modern Sociology* 15(1/ 2):63–80.

Le Monde. 2011. "Face à la colère de la rue, le président sénégalais renonce à réformer la Constitution." *Le Monde.* June 23. www.lemonde.fr/afrique/ article/2011/06/23/face-a-la-colere-de-la-rue-le-president-senegalais-reno nce-a-sa-reforme-de-la-constitution15400073212.html.

Lenin, Vladimir. 1916/1999. *Imperialism: The Highest Stage of Capitalism.* Sydney: Resistance Books.

Lensik, Robert. 1996. *Structural Adjustment in Sub-Saharan Africa.* New York, NY: Longman.

Leonard, David K. and Scott Straus. 2003. *Africa's Stalled Development: International Causes and Cures.* Boulder, CO: Lynne Rienner.

Levi, Margaret and Gillian H. Murphy. 2006. "Coalitions of Contention: The Case of the WTO Protests in Seattle." *Political Studies* 54 (4):651–670.

Levine, Daniel H. 1992. *Popular Voices in Latin American Catholicism.* Princeton, NJ: Princeton University Press.

Levitsky, Steven and Lucan A. Way. 2010. "Why Democracy Needs a Level Playing Field." *Journal of Democracy* 21(1):57–68.

Lewis, Peter and Etannibi Alemika. 2005. "Seeking the Democratic Dividend: Public Attitudes and Attempted Reform in Nigeria." Afrobarometer Working Paper 52.

Licht, Amir N. and Jordan I. Siegel. 2004. "The Social Dimensions of Entrepreneurship." Working paper.

Lieberman, Matthew D., Darren Schreiber and Kevin N. Oschsner. 2001. "Is Political Cognition Like Riding a Bicycle? How Cognitive Neuroscience Can Inform Research on Political Thinking." *Political Psychology* 24(4):681–704.

Lin, Mingfeng, Henry C. Lucas Jr. and Galit Shmueli. 2013. "Too Big to Fail: Large Samples and the p-Value Problem." *Information Systems Research* 24(4):906–917.

Lindberg, Staffan I. 2006. *Democracy and Elections in Africa*. Baltimore, MD: Johns Hopkins University Press.

Lindberg, Staffan I. and Minion K.C. Morrison. 2008. "Area African Voters Really Ethnic or Clientelistic? Survey Evidence from Ghana." *Political Science Quarterly* 123(1):95–122.

Linz, Juan J. 1973. Opposition in and under an Authoritarian Regime: The Case of Spain. In *Regimes and Oppositions*, ed. Robert A. Dahl. New Haven, CT: Yale University Press pp. 171–260.

Lipset, Seymour Martin. 1959. "Some Social Requisites of Democracy: Economic Development and Political Legitimacy." *American Political Science Review* 53(1):69–105.

Little, Kenneth. 1974. *Urbanization as a Social Process: An Essay on Movement and Change in Contemporary Africa*. London: Routledge and Kegan Paul.

Lô, Magatte. 1987. *Sénégal: Syndicalisme et participation responsable*. Paris: L'Harmattan.

Lo, Sheba. 2014. Building Our Nation: Senegalese Hip Hop Artists as Agents of Social and Political Change. In *Hip Hop and Social Change in Africa*, ed. Msia Kibona Clark and Mickie Mwanzia Koster. New York, NY: Lexington pp. 27–48.

Lofchie, Michael. 2015. The Political Economy of the African Middle Class. In *The Emerging Middle Class in Africa*, ed. Mthuli Ncube and Charles Leyeka Lufumpa. New York, NY: Routledge pp. 34–59.

Lohmann, Suzanne. 1994. "Dynamics of Informational Cascades: The Monday Demonstrations in Leipzig, East Germany, 1989–1991." *World Politics* 47(1):42–101.

Loschky, Jay. 2014. "Arab Spring Largely Ignored in Sub-Saharan Africa." www.gallup.com/poll/172079/arab-spring-largely-ignored-sub-saharan-afr ica.aspx.

Luxemburg, Rosa. 1913/1963. *The Accumulation of Capital*. London: Routledge.

Macatory, Bénédicte, Makama Bawa Oumarou, and Marc Poncelet. 2010. "West African Social Movements 'against the High Cost of Living': From the Economic to the Political, from the Global to the National." *Review of African Political Economy* 37(125):345–359.

Machiavelli, Niccolo. 1532/2005. *The Prince*. Oxford: Oxford University Press.

Mahajan, Vijay. 2009. *Africa Rising: How 900 Million African Consumers Offer More than You Think*. Upper Saddle River, NJ: Pearson Prentice Hall.

Main, Alexander and Jake Johnston. 2009. "The Millennium Challenge Corporation and Economic Sanctions: A Comparison of Honduras with Other Countries." Center for Economic and Policy Research Issue Brief.

Major, Brenda. 1994. "From Social Inequality to Personal Entitlement: the Role of Social Comparisons, Legitimacy Appraisals, and Group Membership." *Advances in Experimental Social Psychology* 26:293–355.

Mamdani, Mahmood. 1990. "State and Civil Society in Contemporary Africa: Reconceptualizing the Birth of State Nationalism and the Defeat of Popular Movements." *Africa Development / Afrique et Développement* 15(3/4):47–70.

Mamdani, Mahmood. 2011. "Short Cuts." *London Review of Books* 33 (12).

Mampilly, Zachariah Cherian. 2011. *Rebel Rulers: Insurgent Governance and Civilian Life during War*. Ithaca, NY: Cornell University Press.

Manela, Erez. 2007. *The Wilsonian Moment: Self-Determination and the International Origins of Anticolonial Nationalism*. New York, NY: Oxford University Press.

Manning, Carrie. 2005. "Assessing African Party Systems after the Third Wave." *Party Politics* 11(6):707–727.

Marcus, Jon. 2017. "In One Country, Anger over Soaring College Costs Has Led to Violent Protest." *Hechinger Report*. March 8. http://hechingerre port.org/south-african-students-take-lead-protests-college-costs-equity/.

Markoff, John. 2009. The Global Wave of Democratization. In *Democratization*, ed. Christian W. Haerpfer, Patrick Bernhagen, Ronald F. Inglehart and Christian Welzel. Oxford: Oxford University Press pp. 55–73.

Markovitz, Irving Leonard. 1987. Introduction: Continuities in the Study of Power and Class in Africa. In *Studies in Power and Class in Africa*, ed. Irving Leonard Markovitz. New York, NY: Oxford University Press pp. 3–19.

Marshall, Monty G. 2013. "Polity IV Project: Political Regime Characteristics and Transitions, 1800–2013." www.systemicpeace.org/p olity/polity4.htm.

Martin, Joanne, Philip Brickman and Alan Murray. 1983. "Moral Outrage and Pragmatism: Explanations for Collective Action." *Journal of Experimental Social Psychology* (20):484–496.

Marx, David M. and Ray A. Friedman. 2009. "The 'Obama Effect': How a Salient Role Model Reduces Race-Based Performance Differences." *Journal of Experimental Psychology* 45(4):953–956.

Marx, Karl. 1846/1963. *Capital: A Critique of Political Economy*. New York, NY: International.

Mati, Jacob Mwathi. 2012a. *The Power and Limits of Social Movements in Promoting Political and Constitutional Change: The Case of the Ufungamano Initiative in Kenya (1999–2005)*. Doctoral dissertation, University of Witwatersrand.

Mati, Jacob Mwathi. 2012b. "Social Movements and Socio-Political Change in Africa: The Ufungamano Initiative and Kenyan Constitutional Reform Struggles (1999–2005)." *Voluntas: International Journal of Voluntary and Nonprofit Organizations* 23(1):63–84.

Mbaye, Jenny Fatou. 2011. *Reconsidering Cultural Entrepreneurship: Hip Hop Music Economy and Social Change in Senegal, Francophone West Africa.* Doctoral dissertation, London School of Economics and Political Science.

Mbeki, Thabo. 2004. "Questions that Demand Answers." *ANC Today* 4 (36).

Mbiba, Beacon. 2001. "The Political Economy of Urban and Peri-Urban Agriculture in Southern and Eastern Africa: Overview, Settings and Research Agenda." South Bank University London Working Paper 6.

McAdam, Doug. 1986. "Recruitment to High-Risk Activism: The Case of Freedom Summer." *American Journal of Sociology* 92(1):64–90.

McAdam, Doug and Ronnelle Paulsen. 1993. "Specifying the Relationship Between Social Ties and Activism." *American Journal of Sociology* 99 (3):640–667.

McCammon, Holly J. and Minyoung Moon. 2015. Social Movement Coalitions. In *The Oxford Handbook of Social Movements*, ed. Donatella della Porta and Mario Diani. Oxford: Oxford University Press pp. 326–339.

McCarthy, John D., Clark McPhail and Jackie Smith. 1996. "Images of Protest: Dimensions of Selection Bias in Media Coverage of Washington Demonstrations, 1982 and 1991." *American Sociological Review* 61 (3):478–499.

McCarthy, John D. and Mayer Zald. 1973. *The Trend of Social Movements in America: Professionalization and Resource Mobilization.* Morristown, NJ: General Learning Press.

McCarthy, John D. and Mayer Zald. 1977. "Resource Mobilization and Social Movements: A Partial Theory." *American Journal of Sociology* 82 (6):1212–1241.

McCarthy, John D. and Mayer Zald. 2002. The Enduring Vitality of the Resource Mobilization Theory of Social Movements. In *Handbook of Sociological Theory*, ed. Jonathan H. Turner. New York, NY: Kluwer Academic/Plenum Publishers pp. 533–565.

McCarthy, Michael. 2017. "What's Ahead for Venezuela? As the Protests Ramp Up, Here Are 5 Things to Watch." *Washington Post.* May 1. www .washingtonpost.com/news/monkey-cage/wp/2017/05/01/whats-ahead-for -venezuela-as-the-protests-ramp-up-here-are-5-things-to-watch/?utm term=.503341e0377f.

McClendon, Gwyneth. 2014. "Social Esteem and Participation in Contentious Politics: A Field Experiment at an LGBT Pride Rally." *American Journal of Political Science* 58(2):279–290.

McClendon, Gwyneth and Rachel Beatty Riedl. 2015. "Religion as a Stimulant of Political Participation: Experimental Evidence from Nairobi, Kenya." *Journal of Politics* 77(4):1045–1057.

McConnell, Tristan. 2014. "Occupy Kenya: Protesters March in Nairobi for an End to Violence." *Mint Press News*. November 26. www .mintpressnews.com/occupy-kenya-protesters-march-nairobi-end-vio lence/199334/

Mealer, Bryan. 2005. "Mass Protests against Togo's President Turn Violent." *Washington Post*. February 13. www.washingtonpost.com/wp -dyn/articles/A19794-2005Feb12.html.

Meier, Gerald M. and William Steel. 1989. *Industrial Adjustment in Sub-Saharan Africa*. New York, NY: Oxford University Press.

Meier, Patrick Philippe. 2007. "The Impact of the Information Revolution on Protest Frequency in Repressive Contexts." Paper presented at The Fiftieth International Studies Association (ISA) Convention, February 15th–18th, New York City.

Melber, Henning. 2016. *The Rise of Africa's Middle Class*. London: Zed Books.

Melucci, Alberto. 1996. *Challenging Codes: Collective Action in the Information Age*. New York, NY: Cambridge University Press.

Meredith, Martin, ed. 2011. *The Fate of Africa: A History of the Continent Since Independence*. New York, NY: PublicAffairs.

Meyer, David S. and Sidney Tarrow. 1998. A Movement Society: Contentious Politics for a New Century. In *The Social Movement Society*, ed. David S. Meyer and Sidney Tarrow. Thousand Oaks, CA: SAGE pp. 1–28.

Migdal, Joel S. 2001. *State in Society: Studying How States and Societies Transform and Constitute One Another*. Cambridge: Cambridge University Press.

Milanovic, Branko. 2016a. "All the Ginis Dataset." www.gc.cuny.edu/.

Milanovic, Branko. 2016b. *Global Inequality*. Cambridge, MA: Harvard University Press.

Milanovic, Branko, Peter H. Lindert and Jeffrey G. Williamson. 2007. "Measuring Ancient Inequality." NBER Working Paper 13550.

Miles, William F. S. and David A. Rochefort. 1991. "Nationalism Versus Ethnic Identity in Sub-Saharan Africa." *American Political Science Review* 85(2):393–403.

Miller, Andrew C. 2011. "Debunking the Myth of the 'Good' Coup d'Etat in Africa." *African Studies Quarterly* 12(2):45–70.

Mills, Greg. 1992. "Zambia and the Winds of Change." *The World Today* 48:16–18.

Mische, Ann. 2001. Juggling Multiple Futures: Personal and Collective Project-Formation among Brazilian Youth Leaders. In *Leadership and Social Movements*, ed. Colin Barker, Alan Johnson and Michael Lavalette. Manchester: Manchester University Press pp. 137–159.

Mische, Ann. 2011. *Relational Sociology, Culture, and Agency.* In *The Sage Handbook of Social Network Analysis*, ed. John Scott and Peter J. Carrington. Los Angeles: Sage pp. 80–97.

Mistry, Dina, Qian Zhang, Nicola Perra and Andrea Baronchelli. 2015. "Committed Activists and the Reshaping of Status-Quo Social Consensus." *Physical Review E* 92(4):042805.

Mitchell, Don and Lynn A. Staeheli. 2005. "Permitting Protest: Parsing the Fine Geography of Dissent in America." *International Journal of Urban and Regional Research* 29(4):796–813.

Mitra, Subrata K. 1992. *Power, Protest and Participation: Local Elites and the Politics of Development in India.* New York, NY: Routledge.

Mkandawire, Thandika and Charles C. Soludo. 1998. *Our Continent, Our Future: African Perspectives on Structural Adjustment.* Dakar: CODESRIA.

Moestrup, Sophia. 1999. "The Role of Actors and Institutions: The Difficulties of Democratic Survival in Mali and Niger." *Democratization* 6(2):171–186.

Mondlane, Eduardo. 1983. *The Struggle for Mozambique.* London: Zed Books.

Moore, Barrington. 1978. *Injustice: The Social Basis of Obedience and Revolt.* White Plains, NY: Sharpe.

Moore, Kelly. 1996. "Organizing Integrity: American Science and the Creation of Public Interest Organizations, 1955–1975." *American Journal of Sociology* 101(6):1592–1627.

Morgenthau, Ruth Schachter. 1964. *Political Parties in French-Speaking West Africa.* Oxford: Oxford University Press.

Morris, Aldon D. and Suzanne Staggenborg. 2005. Leadership in Social Movements. In *The Blackwell Companion to Social Movements*, ed. David A. Snow, Sarah A. Soule, and Hanspeter Kriesi. Malden, MA: Blackwell Publishing pp. 171–196.

Morris III, Charles E. and Stephen H. Browne. 2001. *Readings on the Rhetoric of Social Protest.* State College, PA: Strata Publishing.

Mueller, Carol. 1974. "Media Measurement Models of Protest Event Data." *Mobilization* 2(2):165–184.

Mueller, Lisa. 2013. "Democratic Revolutionaries or Pocketbook Protesters? The Roots of the 2009–2010 Uprisings in Niger." *African Affairs* 112(448):398–420.

Mueller, Lisa and Lukas Matthews. 2016. "The National Elections in Niger, February-March 2016." *Electoral Studies* 43:203–206.

Murphy, John P. 2011. "Protest or Riot? Interpreting Collective Action in Contemporary France." *Anthropological Quarterly* 84(4):977–1009.

Mutua, Makau. 2008. *Kenya's Quest for Democracy: Taming Leviathan.* Kampala: Fountain Publishers.

Mutunga, Willy. 1999. *Constitution-Making from the Middle: Civil Society and Transition Politics in Kenya, 1992–1997.* Nairobi: SAREAT.

Nam, Tachyun. 2006. "What You Use Matters: Coding Protest Data." *Political Science and Politics* 39(2):281–287.

Nasong'o, Shadrack W. 2007a. Negotiating the Rules for the Game: Social Movements, Civil Society and Kenya's Transition. In *Kenya: The Struggle for Democracy*, ed. Godwin R. Murunga and Shadrack W. Nasong'o. London: Zed Books pp. 19–57.

Nasong'o, Wanjala S. 2007b. Revisiting "The Two Faces of Civil Society" in Constitutional Reform in Kenya. In *Kenya: The Struggle for a New Constitutional Order*, ed. Godwin R. Murunga, Duncan Okello and Anders Sjögren. Dakar: CODESRIA pp. 97–115.

Ncube, Mthuli and Charles Leyeka Lufumpa, eds. 2015. *The Emerging Middle Class in Africa.* New York: Routledge.

Ncube, Mthuli, John Anyanwu and Kjell Hausken. 2013. "Inequality, Economic Growth, and Poverty in the Middle East and North Africa (MENA)." African Development Bank Working Paper 195.

Ndiaye, Aly Samba. 2013. "Nihilisme, admonestations et menaces contre le régime: Les dangereuses dérives de Y'En A Marre." *Le Témoin* 1112.

Ndiaye, Mamadou Sakhir. 2011. "Visite du mouvement M23 à Touba: Niasse, Tanor et Bathily manquent à l'appel." *Seneweb.* August 6. www.seneweb.com/news/Politique/visite-du-mouvement-m23-a-touba-niasse-tanor-et-bathily-manquent-a-l-rsquo-appeln49309.html.

Ndiaye, Sergine. 2000. "Student Activism and the Repressive State: Reflections on the Political History of Senegal since Independence." *Ufahamu: A Journal of African Studies* 28(1):125–138.

Nelson, Sarah. 2014. "The New Type of Senegalese under Construction: Fadel Barro and Aliou Sané on *Yenamarrisme* after Wade." *African Studies Quarterly* 14(3):13–32.

NewAfrican. 2012. "The Rise of the Middle Class in Africa." February 1. http://newafricanmagazine.com/the-rise-of-the-middle-class-in-africa/.

Ngayap, Pierre Flambeau. 1983. *Cameroun, Qui Gouverne?* Paris: L'Harmattan.

Ngugi, Wa Thiong'o. 1986. *Decolonising the Mind: The Politics of Language in African Literature*. Nairobi: East African Educational Publishers.

Ng'wanakilala, Fumbuka. 2014. "Tanzania Police Arrest Several People in Opposition Protests." *Reuters*. September 27. www.reuters.com/article/us -tanzania-politics-idUSKCN0HM0CM20140927.

Nicholls, Walter J. 2008. "The Urban Question Revisited: The Importance of Cities for Social Movements." *International Journal of Urban and Regional Research* 32(4):841–859.

Nissanke, Machiko and Erik Thorbecke. 2006. "Channels and Policy Debate in the Globalization-Inequality-Poverty Nexus." *World Development* 34 (8):1338–1360.

Nkinyangi, John A. 1991. "Student Protests in Sub-Saharan Africa." *Higher Education* 22:157–173.

Noble, Kenneth B. 1994. "French Devaluation of African Currency Brings Wide Unrest." *New York Times*. February 23. https://www.nytimes.com/ 1994/02/23/world/french-devaluation-of-african-currency-brings-wide-unr est.html.

Norval, Aletta J. 2001. The Politics of Ethnicity and Identity. In *The Blackwell Companion to Political Sociology*, ed. Kate Nash and Alan Scott. Malden, MA: Blackwell Publishing.

Nossiter, Adam. 2009. "Niger Senses a Threat to Its Scrap of Democracy." *New York Times*. July 13. www.nytimes.com/2009/07/14/world/africa/14 niger.html.

Ntarangwi, Mwenda. 2009. *East African Hip Hop*. Chicago, IL: University of Illinois Press.

Nugent, Paul. 2012. *Africa since Independence*. New York, NY: Palgrave Macmillan.

Odula, Tom. 2015. "700 Northern Kenya Teachers Protest Work over Terror Attacks." *World* Post. February 3. www.huffingtonpost.com/2015/ 02/03/kenya-teachers-protestn6606924.html.

Okojie, Christiana and Abebe Shimeles. 2006. "Inequality in Sub-Saharan Africa: A Synthesis of Recent Research on the Levels, Trends, Effects and Determinants of Inequality in its Different Dimensions." Overseas Development Institute Working Paper.

Olofsson, Gunnar. 2014. From the Working-Class Movement to the New Social Movements. In *Social Movements: Transformative Shifts and Turning Points*, ed. Savyasaachi and Ravi Kumar. New Delhi: Routledge pp. 33–59.

Olorunnisola, Anthony A. and Aziz Douai. 2013. *New Media Influence on Social and Political Change in Africa*. Hershey, PA: Information Science Reference.

Olson, James M. and Carolyn L. Hafer. 2001. Tolerance of Personal Deprivation. In *The Psychology of Legitimacy: Emerging Perspectives on Ideology, Justice, and Intergroup Relations*, ed. John T. Jost and Brenda Major. Cambridge: Cambridge University Press pp. 157–175.

Olson, James M. and Michael Ross. 1984. "Perceived Qualifications, Resource Abundance, and Resentment about Deprivation." *Journal of Experimental Social Psychology* 20(5):425–444.

Olson, James M., Neal J. Roesesc, Jennifer Meen and D. Joyce Robertson. 1995. "The Preconditions and Consequences of Relative Deprivation: Two Field Studies." *Journal of Applied Social Psychology* 25 (11):944–964.

Olson, Mancur. 1971. *The Logic of Collective Action: Public Goods and the Theory of Groups*. Cambridge, MA: Harvard University Press.

Olukoshi, Adebayo O. 1995. Bourgeois Social Movements and the Struggle for Democracy in Nigeria: An Inquiry into the "Kaduna Mafia". In *African Studies in Social Movements and Democracy*, ed. Mahmood Mamdani and Ernest Wamba-dia Wamba. Dakar: CODESRIA pp. 245–278.

Onuch, Olga and Iñaki Sagarzazu. 2017. "Don't Be Duped or Misled about the Venezuela Protests. These 5 Insights Will Help." *Washington Post.* May 25. www.washingtonpost.com/news/monkey-cage/wp/2017/05/25/dont-be-duped-or-misled-about-the-venezuela-protests-these-5-insights-will-help/?utmterm=.95d77cb1f6d5.

Opp, Karl-Dieter. 1988. "Grievances and Participation in Social Movements." *American Sociological Review* 53(6):853–864.

Opp, Karl-Dieter. 2009. *Theories of Political Protest and Social Movements: A Multidisciplinary Introduction, Critique, and Synthesis*. New York, NY: Routledge.

Orji, Nkwachukwu. 2016. Middle Class Activism in Nigeria. In *The Rise of Africa's Middle Class*, ed. Henning Melber. London: Zed Books pp. 129–146.

Osei, Anja. 2012. "Party System Institutionalization in Ghana and Senegal." *Journal of Asian and African Studies* 48(5):577–593.

Østby, Gudrun. 2007. "Horizontal Inequalities, Political Environment, and Civil Conflict: Evidence from 55 Developing Countries, 1986–2003." World Bank Working Paper.

Oxford Analytica. 2015. "Africa: 'Corrective Coups' Introduce Policy Dilemmas." Oxford Analytica report.

Page, John. 2012. "Can Africa Industrialise?" *Journal of African Economies* 21: ii86–ii125.

Parkin, Frank. 1968. *Middle Class Radicalism: The Social Base of the British Campaign for Nuclear Disarmament*. Manchester: Manchester University Press.

Penny, Joe and Mathieu Bonkoungou. 2014. "Thousands Protest in Burkina for Second Day, U.S. Joins Outcry." *Reuters.* October 29. www .reuters.com/article/2014/10/29/us-burkina-politics-idUSKBN 0II1JC20141029.

Perriello, Tom. 2017. "There Is Only One Side to the Story of Charlottesville." *Slate.* August 13. www.slate.com/articles/newsandpoli tics/politics/2017/08/tomperrielloonthecharlottesvill.

Perry, Alex. 2010. "A Coup in Niger Adds to West Africa's Instability." *Time.* February 19. http://content.time.com/time/world/article/0,8599,19 66681,00.html.

Phelan, Craig. 2014. "Trade Unions and 'Responsible Participation': Dahomey, 1958–1975." *Labor History* 55(3):346–364.

Pichardo, Nelson A. 1997. "New Social Movements: A Critical Review." *Annual Review of Sociology* 23:411–430.

Pickett, Kate and Richard Wilkinson. 2010. *The Spirit Level: Why Greater Equality Makes Societies Stronger.* New York, NY: Bloomsbury.

Pierskalla, Jan H. and Florian M. Hollenbach. 2013. "Technology and Collective Action: The Effect of Cell Phone Coverage on Political Violence in Africa." *American Political Science Review* 107 (2):207–224.

Piketty, Thomas. 1995. "Social Mobility and Redistributive Politics." *Quarterly Journal of Economics* 110(3):551–584.

Pilati, Katia. 2011. "Political Context, Organizational Engagement, and Protest in African Countries." *Mobilization: An International Journal* 16 (3):351–368.

Piven, Frances Fox and Richard A. Cloward. 1991. "Collective Protest: A Critique of Resource Mobilization Theory." *International Journal of Politics, Culture and Society* 4(4):435–458.

Piven, Frances Fox and Richard Cloward. 1977. *Poor People's Movements: Why They Succeed, How They Fail.* New York, NY: Pantheon.

Planète Afrique. 2009. "La Tazartche est un Désir de Péril." http://planetea frique.com/niger/Index.asp?affiche=NewsDisplay.asparticleid=4804rub= Politique.

Pommerolle, Marie-Emmanuelle. 2014. Mobilizing Resources in an International Activist Event: The Cases of the World Social Forum in Nairobi (2007) and Dakar (2011). In *From Silence to Protest: International Perspectives on Weakly Resourced Groups,* ed. Didier Chabanet and Frédéric Royall. Burlington, VT: Ashgate pp. 83–102.

Popkin, Samuel L. 1988. Political Entrepreneurs and Peasant Movements in Vietnam. In *Rationality and Revolution,* ed. Michael Taylor. Cambridge, MA: Cambridge University Press pp. 171–196.

Porter, Gina. 2002. "Living in a Walking World: Rural Mobility and Social Equity Issues in Sub-Saharan Africa." *World Development* 230 (2):285–300.

Portes, Alejandro and Kelly Hoffman. 2003. "Latin American Class Structures: Their Composition and Change during the Neoliberal Era." *Latin American Research Review* 38(1):41–82.

Posner, Daniel N. 1995. "Malawi's New Dawn." *Journal of Democracy* 6 (1):131–145.

Posner, Daniel N. 2005. *Institutions and Ethnic Politics in Africa.* Cambridge: Cambridge University Press.

Posner, Daniel N. and Daniel J. Young. 2007. "The Institutionalization of Political Power in Africa." *Journal of Democracy* 18(3):126–140.

Potts, Malcolm, Courtney Henderson, and Martha Campbell. 2013. "The Sahel: A Malthusian Challenge?" *Environmental and Resource Economics* 55(4):501–512.

Putnam, Robert. 1993. *Making Democracy Work: Civic Traditions in Modern Italy.* Princeton, NJ: Princeton University Press.

Quist-Arcton, Ofeibea. 2015. "Why the President of Ghana Said He Was Like a Dead Goat." *NPR.* September 21. www.npr.org/sections/goatsand soda/2015/09/21/442214549/why-the-president-of-ghana-said-he-was -like-a-dead-goat.

Rachleff, Peter. 2001. "The Current Crisis of the South African Labour Movement." *Labour/Le Travail* 47:151–169.

Radelet, Steven. 2010. *Emerging Africa: How 17 Countries Are Leading The Way.* Washington, D.C.: Center for Global Development.

Rajan, Raghuram G. and Arvind Subramanian. 2011. "Aid, Dutch Disease, and Manufacturing Growth." *Journal of Development Economics* 94 (1):106–118.

Raleigh, Clionadh, Andrew Linke, Hegre Håvard and Joakim Karlsen. 2010. "Introducing ACLED-Armed Conflict Location and Event Data." *Journal of Peace Research* 47(5):651–660.

Rallings, Colin. 1978. Political Behaviour and Attitudes among the Contemporary Lower Middle Class. In *The Middle Class in Politics*, ed. John Garrard, David Jary, Michael Goldsmith and Adrian Oldfield. Farnborough: Saxon House Books pp. 183–214.

Randall, Vicky and Lars Svåsand. 2002. "Political Parties and Democratic Consolidation in Africa." *Democratization* 9(3):30–52.

Ranger, Terence. 2010. The Invention of Tradition in Colonial Africa. In *Perspectives on Africa: A Reader in Culture, History, and Representation*, ed. Roy Richard Grinker, Stephen C. Lubkemann, and Christopher B. Steiner. West Sussex: Wiley-Blackwell pp. 450–461.

Ranger, Terence O. 1986. "Religious Movements and Politics in Sub-Saharan Africa." *African Studies Review* 29(2):1–69.

Rasmussen, Thomas. 1974. The Popular Basis of Anti-Colonial Protest. In *Politics in Zambia*, ed. William Tordoff. Berkeley, CA: University of California Press pp. 40–61.

Ravallion, Martin. 1997. "Can High-Inequality Developing Countries Escape Absolute Poverty?" World Bank Working Paper.

Ravallion, Martin and Michael Lokshin. 2000. "Who Wants to Redistribute? The Tunnel Effect in 1990s Russia." *Journal of Public Economics* 79:87–104.

Ray, Debraj. 2006. Aspirations, Poverty and Economic Change. In *Understanding Poverty*, ed. Abhijit V. Banerjee, Roland Bénabou, and Dilip Mookherjee. New York, NJ: Oxford University Press pp. 409–421.

Raynal, Jean-Jacques. 1993. *Les Institutions Politiques du Niger*. Saint-Maur, France: Sépia.

Reenock, Christopher, Michael Bernhard and David Sobek. 2007. "Regressive Socioeconomic Distribution and Democratic Survival." *International Studies Quarterly* 51:677–699.

Reicher, Steve, John Drury, Nick Hopkins and Clifford Stott. 2001. A Model of Crowd Prototypes and Crowd Leadership. In *Leadership and Social Movements*, ed. Colin Barker, Alan Johnson, and Michael Lavalette. Manchester: Manchester University Press pp. 178–195.

Resnick, Danielle. 2013. "Continuity and Change in Senegalese Party Politics: Lessons from the 2012 Elections." *African Affairs* 112 (449):623–645.

Resnick, Danielle and Daniela Casale. 2011. "The Political Participation of Africa's Youth: Turnout, Partisanship, and Protest." Working paper.

Reza, Avid, Basia Tomczyk, Victor M. Aguayo, Noel M. Zagré, Goumbi Kadadé, Curtis Blanton and Leisel Talley. 2008. "Retrospective Determination of Whether Famine Existed in Niger, 2005: Two Stage Cluster Survey." *BJM* 915:915–918.

RFI. 2010. "Ecowas to Meet over Niger as Protests Continue." *RFI*. February 15. http://www1.rfi.fr/actuen/articles/122/article_6867.asp.

Rice, Xan. 2011. "Swaziland Pro-Democracy Protests Met by Teargas and Water Cannon." *The Guardian*. April 12. www.theguardian.com/world/2011/apr/12/swaziland-riot-police-attack-democracy-protesters.

Rispens, Richard K.E. 2009. "Modern Economic Growth Theories and the 'Miracle' of the East Asian Tigers." Working paper, Erasmus University Rotterdam School of Economics.

Robinson, Mark and Gordon White. 1997. "The Role of Civic Organisations in the Provision of Social Services." Working paper, World Institute for Development Economics Research, Helsinki.

Robinson, Pearl T. 1994. "The National Conference Phenomenon in Francophone Africa." *Comparative Studies in Society and History* 36 (3):575–610.

Robnett, Belinda. 1996. "African-American Women in the Civil Rights Movement, 1954–1965: Gender, Leadership, and Micromobilization." *American Journal of Sociology* 101(6):1661–1693.

Roche, Christian. 2001. *Le Sénégal à la conquête de son indépendance (1939–1960): Chronique de la vie politique et syndicale, de l'empire française à l'indépendance.* Paris: Karthala.

Roessler, Philip. 2016. *Ethnic Politics and State Power in Africa: The Logic of the Coup-Civil War Trap.* Cambridge: Cambridge University Press.

Roger, Benjamin. 2015. "RDC: Ce que Kinshasa reproche à 'Y'en a marre,' 'Balai citoyen' et 'Filimbi'." *Jeune Afrique.* March 16. www.jeuneafrique.com/228294/politique/rdc-ce-que-kinshasa-reproche-y-en-a-marre-balai-citoyen-et-filimbi/.

Rohde, David. 2013. "The Revolt of the Global Middle Class." *The Atlantic.* June 23, 2013.

Rosenfeld, Bryn. 2017. "Reevaluating the Middle-Class Protest Paradigm: A Case-Control Study of Democratic Protest Coalitions in Russia." *American Political Science Review* 111(4):637–652.

Ross, Michael. 2008. "Oil, Islam, and Women." *American Political Science Review* 102(1):107–123.

Ross, Michael. 2012. *The Oil Curse: How Petroleum Wealth Shapes the Development of Nations.* Princeton, NJ: Princeton University Press.

Rotberg, Robert I. 2013. *Africa Emerges: Consummate Challenges, Abundant Opportunities.* Cambridge: Polity.

Rotberg, Robert I. and Ali A. Mazrui. 1970. *Protest and Power in Black Africa.* New York, NY: Oxford University Press.

Rowe, Martin. 2006. "Performance and Representation: Masculinity and Leadership at the Cairo Refugee Demonstration." Paper presented at the Fourth Annual Forced Migration Postgraduate Student Conference, University of East London, March 18–19.

Rueschemeyer, Dietrich, Evelyne Huber Stephens and John D. Stephens. 1992. *Capitalist Development and Democracy.* Chicago, IL: University of Chicago Press.

Rule, James B. 1988. *Theories of Civil Violence.* Berkeley, CA: University of California Press.

Runciman, W.G. 1966. *Relative Deprivation and Social Justice: A Study of Attitudes to Social Inequality in Twentieth-Century England.* Berkeley, CA: University of California Press.

Sacerdoti, Emilio and Philippe Callier. 2008. "Debt Relief Yields Results in Niger." IMF Survey Magazine: Countries and Regions.

Sachs, Jeffrey. 2014. "The Case for Aid." *Foreign Policy*. January 21.

Sandbrook, Richard. 1985. *The Politics of Africa's Economic Stagnation*. Cambridge: Cambridge University Press.

Sandgren, David P. 2012. *Mau Mau's Children: The Making of Kenya's Postcolonial Elite*. Madison, WI: University of Wisconsin Press.

Savané, Vieux and Baye Makébé Sarr. 2012. *Y'en a marre: Radioscopie d'une jeunesse insurgée au Sénégal*. Paris: L'Harmattan.

Sayles, Marnie L. 2007. "Relative Deprivation and Collective Protest: An Impoverished Theory?" *Sociological Inquiry* 54(4):449–465.

Scacco, Alexandra. 2008. "Who Riots? Explaining Individual Participation in Ethnic Violence." Working paper.

Scarritt, James R., Susan McMillan and Shaheen Mozaffar. 2001. "The Interaction between Democracy and Ethnopolitical Protest and Rebellion in Africa." *Comparative Political Studies* 34(7):800–827.

Scheve, Kenneth and David Stasavage. 2006. "Religion and Preferences for Social Insurance." *Quarterly Journal of Political Science* 1:255–286.

Schiavo-Campo, Salvatore, Giulio De Tommaso and Amit Mukherjee. 1999. "An International Statistical Survey of Government Employment and Wages." World Bank Policy Research Working Paper 1806.

Schmidt, Elizabeth. 2005. *Mobilizing the Masses: Gender, Ethnicity, and Class in the Nationalist Movement in Guinea, 1939–1958*. Portsmouth, NH: Heinemann.

Schmitter, Philippe C. and Terry Lynn Karl. 1991. "What Democracy Is ... and Is Not." *Journal of Democracy* 2(3):75–88.

Schumpeter, Joseph. 1934. *The Theory of Economic Development*. Cambridge, MA: Harvard University Press.

Schussman, Alan and Sarah A. Soule. 2005. "Process and Protest: Accounting for Individual Protest Participation." *Social Forces* 84 (2):1083–1108.

Schwandt, Thomas A. 1994. Constructivist, Interpretivist Approaches to Human Inquiry. In *Handbook of Qualitative Research*, ed. Norman K. Denzin and Yvonna S. Lincoln. Thousand Oaks, CA: Sage pp. 118–137.

Sears, David O. and John B. McConahay. 1970. "Racial Socialization, Comparison Levels, and the Watts Riots." *Journal of Social Issues* 26 (1):121–140.

Seawright, Jason and John Gerring. 2008. "Case Selection Techniques in Case Study Research: A Menu of Qualitative and Quantitative Options." *Political Research Quarterly* 61(2):294–308.

Seck, Assane. 2005. *Sénégal, émergence d'une démocratie moderne (1945–2005)*. Paros: Karthala.

Seddon, David and Leo Zeilig. 2005. "Class and Protest in Africa: New Waves." *Review of African Political Economy* 32(103):9–27.

Seissman, Steve, Adwoa Dunn-Mouton, Nancy Carman, and Mickey Harmon. 1989. "Structural Adjustment in Africa: Insights from the Experiences of Ghana and Senegal." Report to the United States House Committee on Foreign Affairs prepared by the Study Mission to Great Britain, Ghana, Senegal.

Senexbar. 2012. "Momar Samb: 'Moustapha Niasse n'a jamais quitté le M23'." January 24. www.senxibar.com/Moustapha-Niasse-n-a-pas-repondu-a-l-appel-du-M23a2735.html.

Shaffer, Martin B. 2000. "Coalition Work among Environmental Groups: Who Participates?" *Research in Social Movements, Conflicts, and Change* 22:111–126.

Shapiro, Ian. 2002. "Why the Poor Don't Soak the Rich." *Daedalus* 131 (1):118–128.

Sharma, K. L. 1984. "Caste and Class in India: Some Conceptual Problems." *Sociological Bulletin* 33(1–2):1–28.

Shorter, Edward and Charles Tilly. 1971. "The Shape of Strikes in France, 1830–1960." *Comparative Studies in Society and History* 13(1):60–86.

Shtulman, Andrew. 2017. *Scienceblind: Why Our Intuitive Theories about the World Are So Often Wrong*. New York, NY: Basic Books.

Sibeko, Sipiwe. 2016. "Police, Students Clash as South Africa's Wits University Reopens." *Reuters*. October 10. www.reuters.com/article/us-safrica-protests/police-students-clash-as-south-africas-wits-university-reopens-idUSKCN12A0M6?il=0.

Siegle, Joseph, Joel D. Barkan, William M. Bellamy, Christopher Fomunyoh, Marthurin C. Houngnikpo, Edward McMahon, Abdoulaye Niang, Davin O'Regan, Dave Peterson, and Oury Traoré. 2011. "Africa and the Arab Spring: A New Era of Democratic Expectations." Africa Center for Strategic Studies Special Report 1.

Simensen, Jarle. 1974. "Rural Mass Action in the Context of Anti-Colonial Protest: The Asafo Movement of Akim Abuakwa, Ghana." *Canadian Journal of African Studies* 8(1):25–41.

Sindic, Denis and Susan Condor. 2014. Social Identity Theory and Self-Categorisation Theory. In *Handbook of Global Political Psychology*, ed. Paul Nesbitt-Larking, Catarina Kinnvall, Tereza Capelos and Henk Dekker. New York, NY: Palgrave Macmillan pp. 35–55.

Singer, Matthew M. 2011. "Who Says 'It's the Economy?' Cross-National and Individual Variation in the Salience of Economic Performance." *Comparative Political Studies* 44(3):284–312.

Singh, Naunihal. 2014. *Seizing Power: The Strategic Logic of Military Coups*. Baltimore, MD: Johns Hopkins University Press.

Sklar, Richard L. 1979. "The Nature of Class Domination in Africa." *Journal of Modern African Studies* 17(4):531–552.

Skocpol, Theda. 1979. *States and Social Revolutions: A Comparative Analysis of France, Russia, and China*. Cambridge: Cambridge University Press.

Smith, Alex Duval. 2014. "'Africa's Che Guevara': Thomas Sankara's Legacy." *BBC*. 30 April. www.bbc.com/news/world-africa-27219307.

Smith, Linda Tuhiwai. 2012. *Decolonizing Methodologies*. New York: Zed Books.

Smith, Todd G. 2013. "Food Price Spikes and Social Unrest in Africa." Climate Change and African Political Stability Research Brief 11.

Smith, Zerik Kay. 1997. "'From Demons to Democrats': Mali's student movement 1991–1996." *Review of African Political Economy* 72:249–263.

Snidal, Duncan. 1985. "Coordination versus Prisoners' Dilemma: Implications for International Cooperation and Regimes." *American Political Science Review* 79(4):923–942.

Sokoloff, Kenneth L. and Stanley L. Engerman. 2000. "History Lessons: Institutions, Factor Endowments, and Paths of Development in the New World." *Journal of Economic Perspectives* 14(3):217–232.

Soko-lowska, Katarzyna. 2013. "Determinants and Perceptions of Social Mobility in Poland, 1992–2008." *Contemporary Economics* 8(1):89–102.

Sommers, Marc and Peter Uvin. 2011. "Youth in Rwanda and Burundi: Contrasting Visions." Report for the United States Institute of Peace.

Soule, Sarah A. 2004. Diffusion Processes within and across Movements. In *The Blackwell Companion to Social Movements*, ed. David A. Snow, Sarah A. Soule, and Hanspeter Kriesi. Malden, MA: Blackwell Publishing pp. 294–310.

Sounaye, Abdoulaye. 2009. Structuring Islam and the Culture of Democratization: The Case of Niger. In *Africa's Islamic Experience: History, Culture and Politics*, ed. Ali A. Mazrui. New Delhi: Sterling pp. 147–164.

Sowore, Omoyele. 2013. "Nigerians Still Waiting for Their 'African Spring'." *CNN*. January 14. https://www.cnn.com/2013/01/12/world/afr ica/nigeria-protests-african-spring/index.html.

Sparrow, Andrew. 2017. "WhatsApp Must Be Accessible to Authorities, Says Amber Rudd." *The Guardian*. March 26. www.theguardian.com/technology/2017/mar/26/intelligence-servicesaccess-whatsapp-amber-rudd-westminster-attack-encrypted-messaging.

Spitulnik, Debra. 2002. Alternative Small Media and Communicative Spaces. In *Media and Democracy in Africa*, ed. Hyden Goran, Leslie Michael and Folu Ogundimu. New Brunswick, NJ: Transaction pp. 177–205.

Srnicek, Nick and Alex Williams. 2015. *Inventing the Future: Postcapitalism and a World without Work*. London: Verso.

Staggenborg, Suzanne. 1988. "The Consequences of Professionalizatoin and Formalization in the Pro-Choice Movement." *American Sociological Review* 53(4):585–605.

Standing, Guy. 2011. *The Precariat: The Dangerous Class*. London: Bloomsbury Academic.

Statt, Nick. 2016. "WhatsApp Has Grown to 1 Billion Users." February 1. www.theverge.com/2016/2/1/10889534/whats-app-1-billion-users-face book-mark-zuckerberg.

Steinem, Gloria. 2015. *My Life on the Road*. New York, NY: Random House.

Stephan, Maria J. and Erica Chenoweth. 2008. "Why Civil Resistance Works." *International Security* 33(1):7–44.

Stewart, Catrina. 2015. "Kenya Garissa University Attack: President Faces Fury over 'Failure to Tackle Terror Threat'." *The Independent*. April 3. www.independent.co.uk/news/world/africa/kenya-garissa-university-at tack-president-faces-fury-over-failure-to-tackle-terror-threat-1015486 6.html.

Stewart, Frances. 2010. "Horizontal Inequalities as a Cause of Conflict." Background Paper, World Development Report.

Stichter, Sharon, ed. 1975. *Migrant Labour in Kenya: Capitalism and the African Response*. London: Longman.

Strode, Mary, Lee Crawfurd, Simone Dettling and Felix Schmieding. 2015. Jobs and the Labor Market. In *The Emerging Middle Class in Africa*, ed. Mthuli Ncube and Charles Leyeka Lufumpa. New York, NY: Routledge pp. 82–101.

Stürmer, Stefan and Bernd Simon. 2009. "Pathways to Collective Protest: Calculation, Identification, or Emotion? A Critical Analysis of the Role of Group-Based Anger in Social Movement Participation." *Journal of Social Issues* 65(4):681–705.

Stutje, Jan Willem. 2012. Introduction: Historiographical and Theoretical Aspects of Weber's Concept of Charismatic Leadership. In *Charismatic Leadership and Social Movements: The Revolutionary Power of Ordinary Men and Women*, ed. Jan Willem Stutje. New York, NY: Berghahn pp. 1–22.

Sumner, Andy. 2012. "The Buoyant Billions: How 'Middle Class' Are the New Middle Classes in Developing Countries? (And Why Does It Matter?)." Center for Global Development Working Paper 309.

Surowiecki, James. 2013. "Middle-Class Militants." *The New Yorker*. July 8, 2013.

Swainson, Nicola. 1977. "The Rise of a National Bourgeoisie in Kenya." *Review of African Political Economy* 4(8):39–55.

Sy, Alpha Amadou. 2012. *Le 23 Juin au Séégal (ou la souveraineté reconquise)*. Paris: L'Harmattan.

Sylla, Ndongo Samba. 2012. "Le Sénégal à trois jours des élections: la démagogie au service des oligarchies." February 23. www.rosalux.sn/wp-content/uploads/2012/02/d%C3%A9magogieSenegal.pdf.

Sylla, Ndongo Samba. 2014. *Les mouvements sociaux en Afrique de l'ouest*. Paris: L'Harmattan.

Tall, Arame. 2012. "Senegal: President Wade vs. the People." *Pambazuka News*. February 2. https://www.pambazuka.org/governance/president-wade-vs-people-senegal-danger.

Tarrow, Sidney. 1994. "Cycles of Collective Action: Between Moments of Madness and the Repertoire of Contention." *Social Science History* 17 (2):281–307.

Tarrow, Sidney. 1998. *Power in Movement: Social Movements and Contentious Politics*. Cambridge: Cambridge University Press.

Taylor, Charles Lewis and Jodice David A. 1983. *World Handbook of Political and Social Indicators*. New Haven, CT: Yale University Press.

Taylor, Scott D. 2012. *Globalization and the Cultures of Business in Africa*. Bloomington, IN: Indiana University Press.

Taylor, Zack and Jeffrey Zahka. 2004. "In Senegal, First an Implosion and Then a Transformation." *Frontlines*. March/April 2004. www.usaid.gov/news-information/frontlines/extreme-poverty/senegal-first-implosion-and-then-transformation.

Telzak, Samuel C. 2012. "The Tithes of Apartheid: Perceptions of Social Mobility among Black Individuals in Cape Town, South Africa." Centre for Social Science Research Working Paper 315.

Tettey, Wisdom J. 2001. "The Media and Democratization in Africa: Contributions, Constraints and Concerns of the Private Press." *Media Culture and Society* 23(1):5–31.

The Citizen. 2013. "Parliament Sinks to New Low As MPs Fight with Security Officers." September 5. http://www.thecitizen.co.tz/News/Parliament-sinks-to-new-low-as-MPs-fight-with-security-officers/1840340-1981690-132dm5dz/index.html.

The Economist. 2005. "The Worst Is Over." August 18.

The Economist. 2013. "Cry Freedom." January 29.

The Economist. 2013. "It Seems Popular, So Far." February 25.

The Economist. 2015. "Africa's Middle Class: Few and Far Between." October 24.

The Economist. 2016. "The March of Democracy Slows." August 20.

The World Bank. 2015. "Middle-Class Frustration Fueled the Arab Spring." World Bank feature story. www.worldbank.org/en/news/feature/2015/10/21/middle-class-frustration-that-fueled-the-arab-spring.

The World Bank. 2017. "World Development Indicators." http://data .worldbank.org/.

Thiat and Sidy Cissokho. 2011. "Y'en a Marre: Rap et contestation au Sénégal." *Multitudes* 3(46):26–34.

Thompson, E.P. 1963. *The Making of the English Working Class.* New York, NY: Vintage.

Tidjani, Bassirou. 1998. "African Unions under Structural Adjustment Programs." *Industrial Relations* 53(2).

Tilly, Charles. 1977. *Studying Social Movements/Studying Collective Action.* Ann Arbor, MI: University of Michigan Press.

Tilly, Charles. 2003. *The Politics of Collective Violence.* Cambridge: Cambridge University Press.

Tocqueville, Alexis de. 1835/1961. *De la Démocratie en Amérique.* Paris: Gallimard.

Transparency International. 2012. "Corruption Perceptions Index." www .transparency.org/cpi2012/results.

Tripp, Aili Mari, Isabel Casimiro, Joy Kwesiga and Alice Mungwa. 2009. *African Women's Movements: Changing Political Landscapes.* Cambridge: Cambridge University Press.

Tsai, Thomas C. 2010. "Food Emergency No Longer Taboo in Niger." *The Lancet* 375(9721):1151–1152.

Tumin, Melvin. 1967. *Social Stratification.* New York, NY: Prentice-Hall.

Turner, Frederick C. 1992. Social Mobility and Political Attitudes in Comparative Perspective. In *Social Mobility and Political Attitudes: Comparative Perspectives*, ed. Frederick C. Turner. New Brunswick, NJ: Transaction Publishers pp. 1–20.

Turshen, Meredith. 2010. The Political Economy of Women in Africa. In *African Women: A Political Economy*, ed. Meredith Turshen. New York, NY: Palgrave Macmillan pp. 1–22.

Umar, Muhammad S. 2006. *Islam and Colonialism: Intellectual Responses of Muslims of Northern Nigeria to British Colonial Rule.* Boston, MA: Brill.

UN News Centre. 2010. "Deploring Coup in Niger, Ban Calls for Peaceful Resolution." www.un.org/apps/news/story.asp/story.asp?NewsI D=33835&Cr=Niger&Cr1=.UxZxRldW.

van de Walle, Nicolas. 2001. *African Economies and the Politics of Permanent Crisis.* Cambridge: Cambridge University Press.

van de Walle, Nicolas. 2009. "The Institutional Origins of Inequality in Sub-Saharan Africa." *Annual Review of Political Science* 12:307–327.

van Stekelenburg, Jacquelien and Bert Klandermans. 2013. "The Social Psychology of Protest." *Current Sociology* 61(5–6):1–20.

van Walraven, Klaas. 2013. *The Yearning for Relief: A History of the Sawaba Movement in Niger.* Leiden: Brill.

Van Zomeren, Martijn, Russel Spears, Agneta H. Fischer and Colin Wayne Leach. 2009. "Put Your Money Where Your Mouth Is! Explaining Collective Action Tendencies through Group-Based Anger and Group Efficacy." *Journal of Personality and Social Psychology* 87(5):649–664.

Veltmeyer, Henry and James Petras. 2002. "The Social Dynamics of Brazil's Rural Landless Workers' Movement: Ten Hypotheses on Successful Leadership." *Canadian Review of Sociology and Anthropology* 39 (1):76–96.

Vircoulon, Thierry. 2016. "Burundi Turns to WhatsApp as Political Turmoil Brings Media Blackout." *The Guardian.* June 14. www.theguardian.com/ global-development/2016/jun/14/burundi-turns-to-whatsapp-as-political -turmoil-brings-media-blackout.

Walker, Iain and Leon Mann. 1987. "Unemployment, Relative Deprivation, and Social Protest." *Personality and Social Psychology Bulletin* 13 (2):275–283.

Wallerstein, Immanuel. 1961. *Africa: The Politics of Independence.* New York, NY: Vintage Books.

Walton, John and David Seddon. 1994. *Free Markets and Food Riots: The Politics of Global Adjustment.* Cambridge, MA: Blackwell Publishers.

Wang, Zhengxu, Long Sun, Liuqing Xu and Dragan Pavlićević. 2013. "Leadership in China's Urban Middle Class Protest: The Movement to Protect Homeowners' Rights in Beijing." *The China Quarterly* 214:411–431.

Wasserman, Herman. 2011. "Mobile Phones, Popular Media, and Everyday African Democracy: Transmissions and Transgressions." *Popular Communication* 9(2):146–158.

Weinstein, Jeremy M. 2007. *Inside Rebellion: The Politics of Insurgent Violence.* Cambridge: Cambridge University Press.

West, Michael O. 2002. *The Rise of an African Middle Class: Colonial Zimbabwe.* Bloomington, IN: Indiana University Press.

Weyland, Kurt. 2014. *Making Waves: Democratic Contention in Europe and Latin America since the Revolutions of 1848.* Cambridge: Cambridge University Press.

Wickham-Crowley, Timothy P. 1994. "Elites, Elite Settlements, and Revolutionary Movements in Latin America, 1950–1980." *Social Science History* 18(4):543–574.

Wilson, Timothy D. and Elizabeth W. Dunn. 2004. "Self-Knowledge: Its Limits, Value, and Potential for Improvement." *Annual Review of Psychology* 55:493–518.

Wiseman, John. 1986. "Urban Riots in West Africa." *Journal of Modern African Studies* 24(3):509–518.

Wood, Elisabeth Jean. 2000. *Forging Democracy from Below: Insurgent Transitions in South Africa and El Salvador*. Cambridge: Cambridge University Press.

Wood, Elisabeth Jean. 2001. "An Insurgent Path to Democracy: Popular Mobilization, Economic Interests, and Regime Transition in South Africa and El Salvador." *Comparative Political Studies* 34(8):862–888.

Wood, Elisabeth Jean. 2003. *Insurgent Collective Action and Civil War in El Salvador*. Cambridge: Cambridge University Press.

Woodis, Jack. 1961. *Africa: The Lion Awakes*. London: Lawrence and Wishart.

Woolard, Ingrid and Stephan Klasen. 2007. "Determinants of Income Mobility and Household Poverty Dynamics in South Africa." *Journal of Development Studies* 41(5):865–897.

World Bank. 2012. "*Niger: Country Profile*." World Bank Country Profile. http://web.worldbank.org/.

Wroe, Daniel. 2012. "Donors, Dependency, and Political Crisis in Malawi." *African Affairs* 111(442):135–144.

Yarwood, Janette. 2016. "The Power of Protest." *Journal of Democracy* 27 (3):51–60.

Yates, Douglas A. 1996. *The Rentier State in Africa: Oil Rent Dependency and Neocolonialism in the Republic of Gabon*. Trenton, NJ: Africa World Press.

Young, Crawford. 1986. Africa's Colonial Legacy. In *Strategies for African Development*, ed. Robert J. Berg and Jennifer Seymour Whitaker. Berkeley, CA: University of California Press pp. 25–51.

Young, Crawford. 2004. "Revisiting Nationalism and Ethnicity in Africa." James S. Coleman Memorial Lecture, UCLA, 7 December.

Young, Crawford. 2012. *The Postcolonial State in Africa: Fifty Years of Independence, 1960–2010*. Madison, WI: The University of Wisconsin Press.

Young, Crawford and Babacar Kante. 1992. Governance and Politics in Africa. In *Governance and Politics in Africa*, ed. Goran Hyden and Michael Bratton. Boulder, CO: Lynne Rienner pp. 57–74.

Young, Crawford, ed. 1994. *The African State in Comparative Perspective*. New Haven, CT: Yale University Press.

Young, Lauren E. 2016a. "Did Protests in Zimbabwe Really Go from 'Tweets to Streets'?" *Washington Post*. July 15. www.washingtonpost.com/news/monkey-cage/wp/2016/07/15/did-recent-protests-in-zimbabwe-really-go-from-tweets-to-streets/.

Young, Lauren E. 2016b. "The Psychology of Political Risk: The Effect of Fear on Participation in Collective Dissent." Paper presented at the Working Group in African Political Economy, January 6–9, NYU – Abu Dhabi.

Zaller, John R. 1992. "Political Awareness, Elite Opinion Leadership, and the Mass Survey Response." *Social Cognition* 8(1):125–153.

Zeilig, Leo. 2009. *Class Struggle and Resistance in Africa.* Chicago, IL: Haymarket Press.

Zeleza, Paul T. 2006. "Beyond Afropessimism: Historical Accounting of African Universities." *Pambazuka News.* August 30. https://www.pambazuka.org/governance/beyond-afropessimism-historical-accounting-african-universities.

Zelizer, Viviana. 2011. "How I Became a Relational Economic Sociologist and What Does That Mean?" Center for the Study of Social Organization Working Paper 5.

Zhao, Dingxin. 1996. "Ecologies of Social Movements: Student Mobilization During the 1989 Prodemocracy Movement in Beijing." *American Journal of Sociology* 103(6):1493–1529.

Zimbabwe Independent. 2003. "International Trade Unions Condemn ZCTU Attacks." *The Independent.* June 13. www.theindependent.co.zw/2003/06/13/international-trade-unions-condemn-zctu-attacks/.

Zolberg, Aristide R. 1972. "Moments of Madness." *Politics and Society* 2:183–207.

Index